SUPER MARIO ADVANCE®
D1258521
1

PRIMA'S OFFICIAL STRATEGY GUIDE

Bryan Stratton

Prima Games
A Division of Prima Communications, Inc.

3000 Lava Ridge Court
Roseville, CA 95661
(916) 787-7000
www.primagames.com

Acknowledgements

Bryan Stratton would like to thank: Jill Hinckley, Sara Wilson, and Michelle Pritchard of Prima for keeping me honest and sane; Cammy Budd, Miho Hattori, and Ralph Zerr of Nintendo, as well as Luke and the other crack commandos of Nintendo Security; Holly, the true princess of the Mushroom Kingdom; little brother Steve for doing his best to help out with this book; the offices of Berry, Appleman, and Lydon for being so flexible; David Hodgson for the amazing combustible laptop; and Mom and Dad Stratton, who broke down after a month of harassment in 1988 and bought us the original NES Super Mario Bros. 2...who said that playing video games wouldn't get you anywhere?

Extra special thanks to Shigeru Miyamoto and Nintendo for the creation and high-profile re-release of Super Mario Bros. 2, my personal favorite Mario game of all time.

Project Editor: Jill Hinckley
Editorial Assistant: Michelle Pritchard
Product Manager: Sara E. Wilson

ISBN: 7615-3633-7
Library of Congress Catalog Card Number: 001089884
Printed in the United States of America

01 02 03 04 GG 10 9 8 7 6 5 4 3 2 1

Table of Contents

Welcome to Super

Thanks for purchasing *Super Mario Advance: Prima's Official Strategy Guide.* This guide has everything you need to complete *Super Mario Bros. 2* while discovering all of the secret items and challenges along the way. It also features an in-depth look at the original *Mario Bros.*, with extensive strategies that will help you conquer the updated version of Mario's very first starring role!

The Story of Super Mario Bros. 2

Unlike most Mario games, which are usually set in Peach's Mushroom Kingdom, *Super Mario Bros. 2* takes place in Subcon, the land of dreams. The story begins in one of Mario's dreams. He is climbing a huge set of stairs that don't seem to end. Finally, he reaches the end of the stairs and comes to a door. When Mario opens it, he sees a whole new world, filled with new creatures and challenges.

As Mario looks out over the new world, he hears a voice say, "This is Subcon, the land of dreams. The evil toad, Wart, has used his magic to lay a curse upon the land. Please defeat Wart and free us from his spell. Oh—and remember that Wart hates vegetables. Hurry! We need your help!" As soon as the voice finishes, a lightning bolt crashes overhead. Mario falls off of the huge staircase...and wakes up on the floor, next to his bed.

A short time later, Mario, his younger brother Luigi, the princess Peach, and her faithful retainer Toad are hiking in the mountains, looking for a good spot to have a picnic. They wind up finding more than just a place to eat lunch; they came across a cave that holds a magic doorway to Subcon. The four friends waste little time in entering the doorway and setting out to save Subcon from Wart's evil schemes.

The story continues in World 1-1 of *Super Mario Bros. 2....*

Mario Advance!

Menus and Play Modes

Choosing a Game

Super Mario Advance features two updated Mario classics on one Game Pak: *Super Mario Bros. 2* and *Mario Bros. Super Mario Bros. 2* is a single-player adventure game, while *Mario Bros.* has cooperative ("Classic") and head-to-head ("Battle") modes for up to four players.

For more information on Mario Bros., including how to link multiple Game Boy Advance systems and/or begin a single- or multiplayer game, please refer to Chapter 10.

To start *Super Mario Bros. 2*, pop in the Game Pak and hit the power switch. From the title screen, select "Single Player" by pressing Ⓐ, then "*Super Mario Bros. 2*" from the next screen.

After choosing to play *Super Mario Bros. 2*, select the file you want to save to by using ↑ or ↓, then Ⓐ. Three save game slots are available. A "New" button next to the slot indicates that no saved game is present; otherwise, the slot will display the last level saved. To erase a saved game, choose "Erase" from the bottom of the menu, press Ⓐ, then choose the game you wish to erase and press Ⓐ again. To erase all files, turn the power off, then press and hold SELECT, START, L, R, Ⓐ, and Ⓑ while turning the power on. Keep the buttons pressed for five seconds after turning the power on.

Once you've chosen a file, choose which character to use. Use ← and → to cycle through the characters and press Ⓐ to make your choice. For details on the characters and their abilities, see the "Characters" section below.

After selecting your character, a screen showing your progress through the game will appear. All of the 20 *Super Mario Bros. 2* levels are displayed in a grid, and any level in which you collected all five Ace Coins is marked with a star. Press Ⓐ to go to the title screen of the level you are about to play; press Ⓐ again to begin.

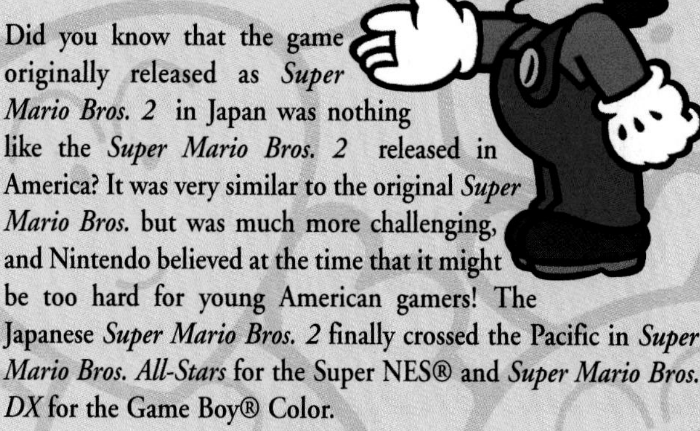

Did You Know?

Did you know that the game originally released as *Super Mario Bros. 2* in Japan was nothing like the *Super Mario Bros. 2* released in America? It was very similar to the original *Super Mario Bros.* but was much more challenging, and Nintendo believed at the time that it might be too hard for young American gamers! The Japanese *Super Mario Bros. 2* finally crossed the Pacific in *Super Mario Bros. All-Stars* for the Super NES® and *Super Mario Bros. DX* for the Game Boy® Color.

Pause Menu

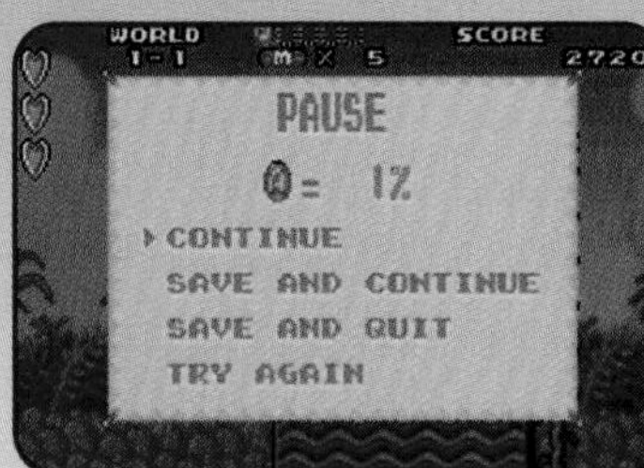

At any time during *Super Mario Bros. 2*, except when in a pipe with a ferris wheel or in Subspace, you can press START to pause the game and bring up the Pause Menu. The Pause Menu offers four choices for how to continue your game. When you are ready to resume, select your choice by using ↑ or ↓, then Ⓐ:

- **Continue:** This option unpauses the game and lets you continue from the same place you paused, with all Hearts and Ace Coins intact.
- **Save and Continue:** This option is the same as Continue, but it also records your progress in your save game slot and keeps track of how many Ace Coins you have collected since you last saved.
- **Save and Quit:** This option also records your game progress in your save game slot, but it then quits the game, returning you to the *Super Mario Advance* title screen.
- **Try Again:** This option restarts the current level. You lose all Ace Coins and Mushrooms collected in the level.

The Pause Menu also appears if your life meter is reduced to zero and you have no more chances. It functions in the exact same way as when you bring it up by pressing START.

The Cast of Characters

Mario and Friends

Each character in *Super Mario Bros. 2* has unique abilities that help him or her get through Wart's challenges. Some obstacles can only be overcome with certain characters. Each character has three statistics: Power (how quickly they can pick things up), Speed (how fast they can move), and Jump (how high and far they can jump).

Mario

A plumber by profession and a hero by nature, Mario is the most well-rounded character with high values in Power, Speed, and Jump. When you are exploring a new world for the first time, Mario is the guy to go with.

Power: ★★★★☆
Speed: ★★★★☆
Jump: ★★★★☆

Luigi

The lanky guy in green loves his big brother, Mario, but he's not about to be outdone by him. Although he's not quite as strong or fast as Mario, he has an impressive jump that allows him to avoid many obstacles altogether.

Power: ★★★☆☆
Speed: ★★★☆☆
Jump: ★★★★★

Peach

Apparently, being raised as a princess doesn't prepare one for the adventuring life as well as does the manly art of plumbing, because Peach's stats are very low compared to Mario and Luigi's. However, she has a unique hovering jump that helps make up for her shortcomings; if you hold down Ⓐ after jumping, Peach floats for one-and-a-half seconds.

Power: ★★☆☆☆
Speed: ★★☆☆☆
Jump: ★★★☆☆

Toad

In the original *Super Mario Bros.*, Toad was just a guy who hung around at the end of every level and told you that Peach was in another castle. This time, however, the spunky little 'shroom is taking a more active role. He's not much for jumping, but his power and speed are unmatched.

Power: ★★★★★
Speed: ★★★★★
Jump: ★★☆☆☆

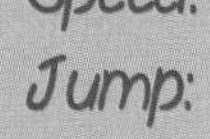

Did You Know?

Did you know that the *Super Mario Bros. 2* game you're now playing was originally a Japanese game called *Doki Doki Panic*? When Nintendo made the decision not to release the Japanese version of *Super Mario Bros. 2* in America, they retouched *Doki Doki Panic*'s graphics and released it as *Super Mario Bros. 2* in the States instead.

The Bad Guys

As Mario and company move through Subcon, they encounter strange and dangerous enemies, each with its own attacks and defenses. Learning to recognize enemies and anticipate their moves quickly is a must for getting through *Super Mario Bros. 2*.

Shy Guy

Shy Guys are the most common enemies in Subcon. Red Shy Guys will walk off the edge of platforms, and Blue Shy Guys will turn around and go the other way. Giant Shy Guys produce Hearts if you throw them.

Snifit

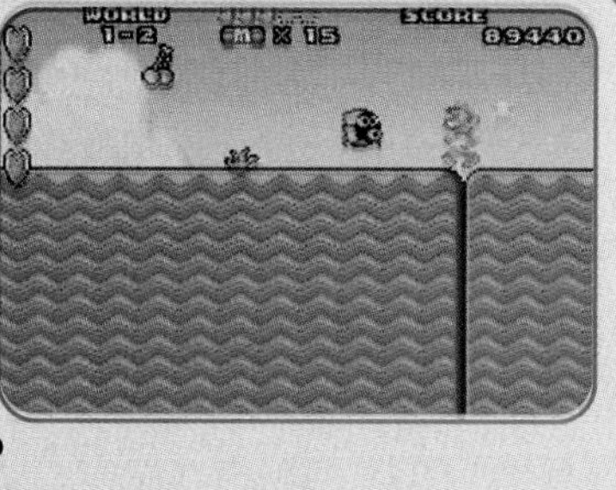

Snifits look a lot like Shy Guys, but they also fire nightmare bullets from their mouths. Red and Blue Snifits behave like Red and Blue Shy Guys, and Gray Snifits just jump up and down while shooting.

Beezo

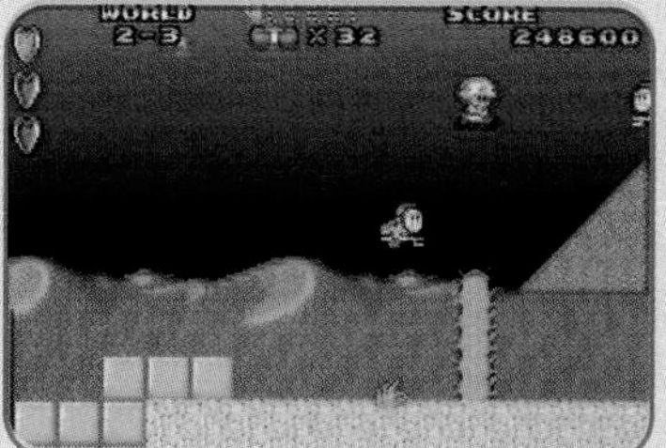

Beezos buzz through the air toward you, doing their best to poke you with their sharp little forks. They often attack in packs, so watch their flight patterns to avoid them. You can ride a Beezo's back by jumping onto it and pressing ← or → to move in the same direction it's flying.

Ninji

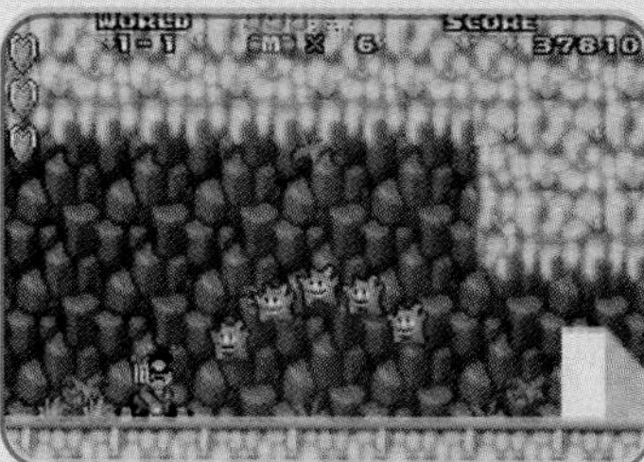

Ninjis are little star-like creatures that seem to enjoy the simple pleasure of bouncing up and down. Some of them move left and right as they jump, but many of them stay in the same place. Watch their jumping patterns to avoid being hit.

Flurry

You'll only find Flurrys in the icy lands of World 4. They are extremely fast and often attack in packs, but their traction is no better than yours, and you can easily lure them off the edge of a slippery platform.

Pidgit

Pidgits are flightless crows that need flying carpets to soar through the sky. If you jump on a Pidgit's head as he swoops down to attack you, you can pick him up and take control of his carpet.

Spark

You'll find Sparks in caverns and vases. They attach themselves to platforms, which they race around furiously. You can't touch a Spark without losing a Heart, but they are vulnerable to thrown objects and POW Blocks.

Phanto

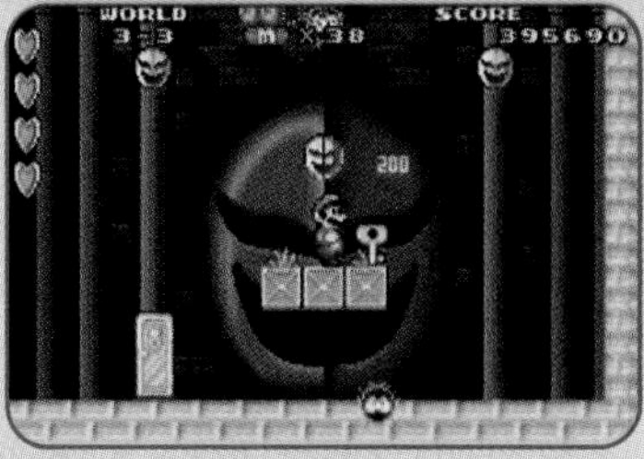

The sinister Phanto only comes after you when you take a Key from his lair. He chases you relentlessly from screen to screen, no matter where you go, and the only way to get rid of him is to put the Key down.

Panser

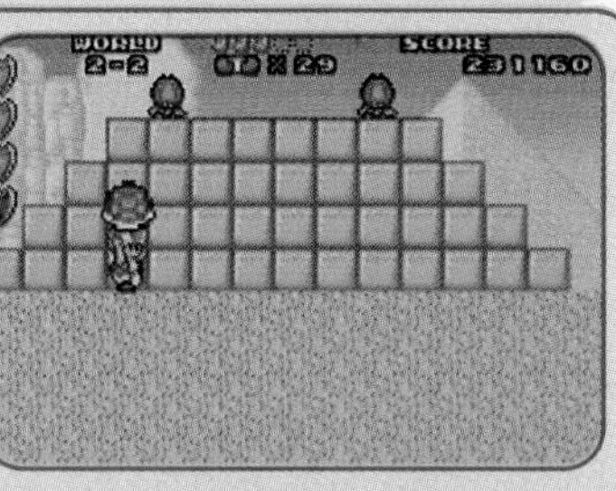

Pansers are fireball-spitting flowers that come in three colors. Red Pansers stay in one spot and shoot fireballs in arcs to the right and left. Green Pansers are also rooted to the ground, but they only shoot straight up. Blue Pansers move along platforms and fire to the right and left, making them the most dangerous.

Hoopster

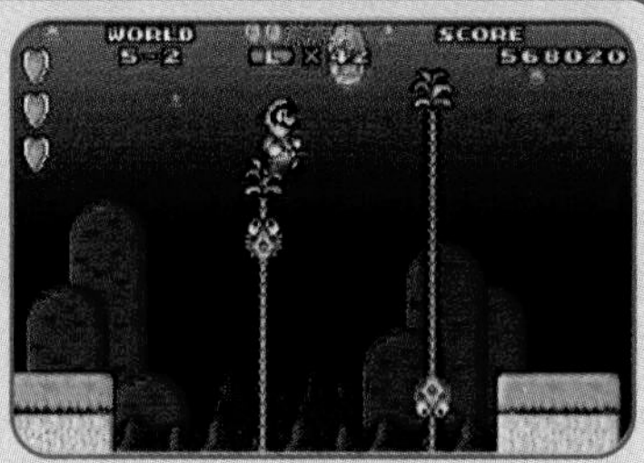

Round as basketballs and almost as bright, Hoopsters spend their time going up and down ladders and vines. They move faster going down than they do climbing up, and if they see you climbing above or below them, they'll charge at you to protect their turf. You can jump on a Hoopster and ride it along a vine if you don't feel like climbing.

Trouter

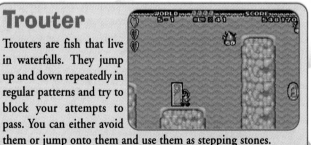

Trouters are fish that live in waterfalls. They jump up and down repeatedly in regular patterns and try to block your attempts to pass. You can either avoid them or jump onto them and use them as stepping stones.

Porcupo

Subcon doesn't have many Porcupos, which is a good thing. Their spiny backs make them impossible to jump on without suffering damage, and you can't pick them up either. You'll have to use a thrown object or a POW Block to defeat them.

Albatoss

No, that's not a typo; these birds are, in fact, called Alba*tosses*. They earned the name after Wart drafted them into his air force and ordered them to carry—and toss—Bob-Ombs at his enemies. You can jump on an Albatoss's back to hitch a ride, and, unlike Beezos, you don't have to hold down a directional button when you do.

Bob-Omb

Little round guys with short fuses and explosive tempers, Bob-Ombs will chase you until their fuses burn low and they start to flash. Three seconds later, they explode, so don't be caught near one. They're not too bright and can be lured into blowing up walls, sand pits, and each other.

Tweeter

Tweeters are sort of a slower version of Ninjis. They're white birds that jump around aimlessly and often travel in packs. You can sometimes find them near Bosses, which is handy because you can also pick them up and throw them at Bosses.

Cobrat

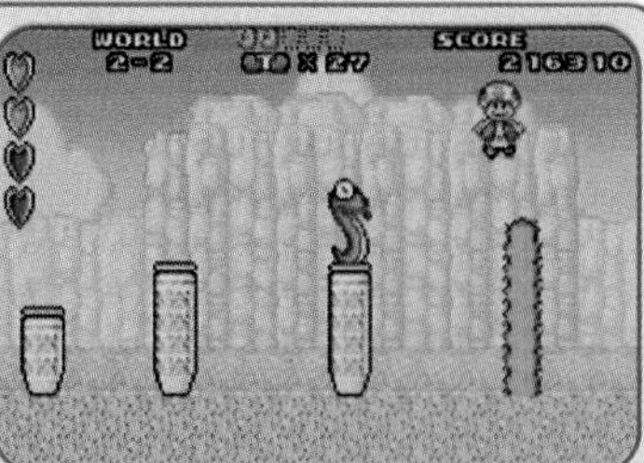

Elite stealth units in Wart's army, Cobrats lurk under the surface of sandy plains and pipes and leap out as you approach, firing bullets at you as they do. Fortunately, you only find them in desert areas and can take them out with a thrown object while they're lying in wait.

Pokey

Pokeys are actually four enemies in one. They consist of four cactus balls; when you pluck the top one off, the one below it becomes the new head! Fortunately, they move slowly, and you can take them out quickly by throwing an object at their bottom segments.

Autobomb

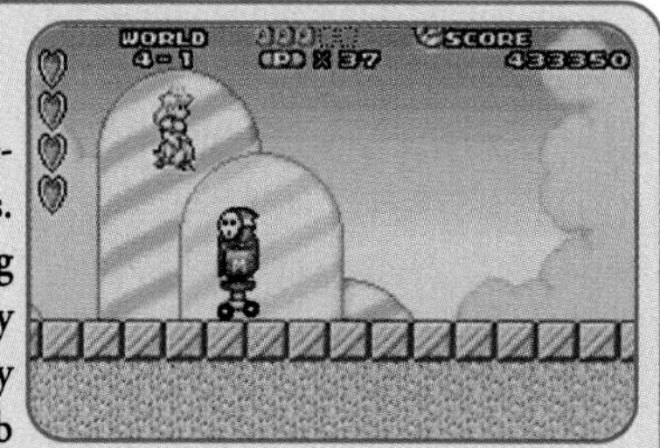

Autobombs are not enemies in and of themselves. They are fireball-spewing cannons that Red Shy Guys ride. Pluck the Shy Guy off of the Autobomb and it stops firing. You can safely ride Autobombs across spiky areas after removing their pilots.

Ostro

Another vehicle of sorts for Shy Guys, Ostros give Shy Guys more speed and height. You can remove the Shy Guys from Ostros and ride them, just as you can with the Autobombs. Ostros always give Hearts when they are knocked out.

Did You Know?

Mario didn't have a name when he first came to America in the arcade classic, *Donkey Kong*. He was referred to only as "Jumpman," and he was a carpenter, not a plumber. He got his name from Nintendo of America's earliest landlord, who interrupted one of the first meetings of the fledgling company to demand overdue rent. Mario the landlord not only got his back rent, he also got video game immortality. Sometimes, it pays to hassle people!

The Bosses

Birdo

Birdo is the hardest working Boss in the business. She appears more than a dozen times in the game as the Boss of Worlds 1-1, 1-2, 2-1, 2-2, 3-1, 3-2, 4-2, 5-1, 5-2, 6-1, 6-2, and 7-1 and makes two appearances in World 7-2 and one in 6-3. Birdo comes in three colors: Pink Birdo shoots eggs from her snout, Red Birdo shoots eggs and fireballs, and Green Birdo shoots fireballs. Throw her eggs or any other object at her to defeat her. Fun Fact: You can jump on Red or Green Birdo's head and press Ⓑ to remove her hair bow, but if you throw it at her, it won't hurt her...it'll just pop back onto her head. Unfortunately this does not work for Pink Birdo.

Mouser

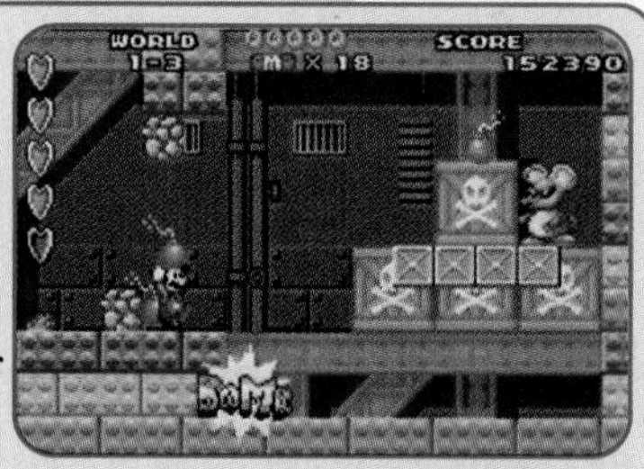

Mouser is a shades-wearing punk rodent with an endless supply of Bombs to throw at you. He appears as the Boss of Worlds 1-3 and 6-3. Luckily, for all of his attitude, he's not very tough. Catch the Bombs he throws and throw them right back at him to defeat him.

Tryclyde

A three-headed snake, Tryclyde is the fire-spitting Boss of World 2-3. Each of his mouths fires independently of the others, making it very tough to get close to him. He's very vulnerable to thrown objects, such as Mushroom Blocks.

SUPER MARIO ADVANCE

Items

As you move through Subcon, you can pick up several items that will come in handy on your quest. You can pluck many of these from the ground by pressing Ⓑ while standing over a plant. Others are hidden under Mushroom Blocks or in Subspace.

Robirdo

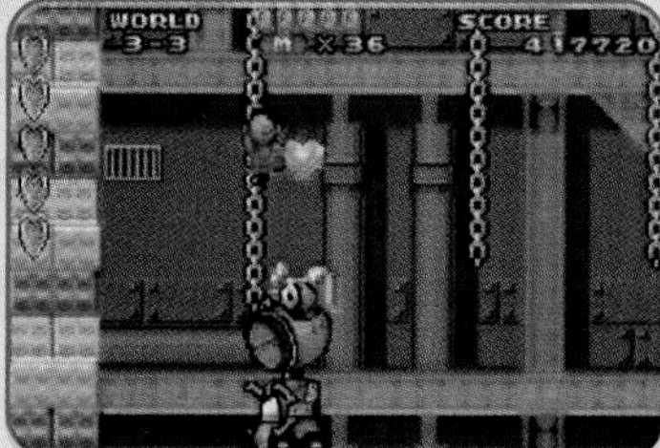

Robirdo is a clanking, mechanized version of your old pal Birdo and is the Boss of World 3-3. Like the regular Birdo, Robirdo spits eggs at you, but they're much larger than normal. It also has a jump attack that sends a paralyzing shockwave along the ground, and a charging attack. Throw the eggs back at it to defeat it, but don't get in its way unless you're tired of living.

Fry Guy

A big ball of fire with a red-hot temper, Fry Guy swoops around the end of World 4-3 as the Boss of the ice world (rather ironically). You don't want to get near him; keep your distance and throw Mushroom Blocks instead. Once you hit him three times, he splits into four smaller Fry Guys, each of which you need to hit with a Mushroom Block to finally win the fight.

Clawgrip

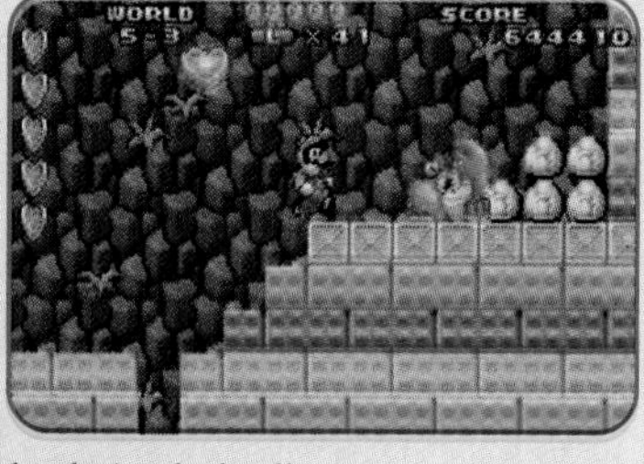

Clawgrip was your average everyday crab until Wart's Dream Machine transformed him into the hard-shelled, rock-throwing Boss of World 5-3. Jump over the boulders he hurls (with deadly accuracy) and pick them up to use them against him.

Wart

The ruthless conqueror of Subcon, the evil toad Wart imprisoned all of Subcon's residents in a magic pipe and proceeded to use his Dream Machine to create a nightmarish horde of monsters to keep anyone from rescuing them. Wart, like many wicked despots, hates Vegetables. He spends his time in his lair firing magic bubbles at the Vegetables that pop out of the Dream Machine. If you can grab the Vegetables and force-feed them to Wart before he can destroy them, he will suffer a terminal overdose of vitamins and minerals, and his slimy reign of terror will come to an end.

1UP Mushroom

1UP Mushrooms give you an extra chance when you pick them up. Sometimes they are encased in bubbles that you can only break by hitting them three times with thrown objects.

Ace Coin

One hundred Ace Coins are scattered throughout the twenty levels of *Super Mario Bros. 2*, five in each level. Collect them all for a 100-percent-clear rating.

Bomb

Pluck these out of the ground and place them in front of walls or enemies to blow them up. You have about five seconds after plucking them before they blow up (they start flashing just before they're about to go off).

Cherry

You'll find Cherries scattered around most of Subcon, floating in midair. Run into them to collect them. Once you collect five Cherries in the same level without losing a life, a Starman appears from the bottom of the screen. You can also grab Cherries in Subspace and grab the same ones again once you leave Subspace.

Coin

In Subspace, every plant visible on the screen produces a Coin when plucked, and each Coin gives you a shot at the Bonus Chance minigame at the end of each level. The actual plants are untouched outside of Subspace. Note that you can only pluck Coins twice in Subspace. After you pluck Coins twice, the plants produce Vegetables.

Heart

You'll often find Hearts floating above the ground; run into them to collect them. Each Heart you get replenishes your life meter by one.

Heart Radish

Like other Vegetables, these grow in the ground throughout Subcon. Pluck them to get a Heart.

Key

Keys, which Phantos guard, open locked doors. Pick up each Key and run with it; Phanto will chase you. Drop it to throw Phanto off the trail. To open a locked door, press ↑ while holding the Key and standing in the doorway. Keys are the only items that do not slow you down or shorten your jumps while you're carrying them. Also, you can throw them to knock out enemies and they won't disappear after you do so.

Magic Potion

You can pluck Magic Potions from the ground and drop them on any solid surface to create a doorway into Subspace. If you create the door in the right place and enter it, you might find hidden Mushrooms with which to power up. You can only remain in Subspace for about ten seconds per Potion, so don't be lazy once you enter the door.

Mushroom

If you enter Subspace in the correct places, you can find Mushrooms. Pick up the Mushrooms to add a Heart to your life meter and completely refill it at the same time. Most levels have three Mushrooms hidden in them.

Mushroom Block

You'll find these stacked in the strangest places. You can throw them as weapons, stack them as stepstools, or hide behind them as fireproof barriers. Sometimes you will find Roulettes hidden under them, so be sure to check every one you find!

POW Block

You can pluck POW Blocks from the ground or find them just lying around Subcon. Pick them up and drop them to knock out every enemy on the screen. Giant POW Blocks bounce several times, doing even more damage to your foes.

Rocket Ship

You won't find many of these in Subcon, but if you reach an area where there's nowhere else to go, and there's an unplucked plant nearby, it's probably a Rocket Ship that will take you up to the next area, drop you off, and explode harmlessly overhead.

Roulette

Roulettes are always hidden, either under a Mushroom Block or in a stone wall. Pick up the Roulette to start it spinning between a Heart, a Starman, and a Bomb. Press Ⓑ when the item you want is displayed to smash the Roulette and get that item.

Shell

Often found inside of pipes, you can pluck Shells from the ground and throw them at enemies. Shells will slide along the ground and knock out everything in their path, including you if you're not careful. They will also bounce off of solid objects, so watch out. Every enemy you knock out with a Shell produces a Heart.

Spark Chaser

Only found at the bottom of certain pipes, Spark Chasers are meant to be thrown at the Sparks racing around the room the Spark Chaser is found in. The Spark Chaser destroys every Spark it hits, and if it hits more than five Sparks before disappearing, you get a 1UP mushroom.

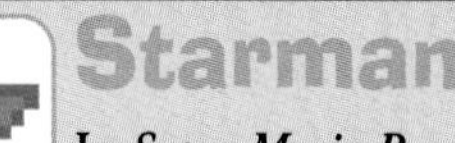

Starman

In *Super Mario Bros. 2*, Starmen are only found in Roulettes. They also appear after collecting five cherries in the same level with the same life. Starmen make characters temporarily invincible when they get one. While invincible, run after enemies and rival players to defeat them.

Time Stop

When you pick your fifth Large Vegetable of a level, you get a Time Stop instead of a Vegetable. All of the enemies in the level freeze for about ten seconds, giving you a chance to run by them or knock them out. Be careful though; they will still hurt you if you hit them.

Vegetable (Small, Large, and Giant)

Much to Wart's chagrin, Vegetables grow all over Subcon. Stand on top of a Vegetable's leaves and press Ⓑ to pluck it, before throwing it at your enemies. There are many types of Vegetables, from Carrots to Turnips to Pumpkins, and they come in three sizes: Small, Large, and Giant.

Did You Know?

Did you know that *Super Mario Advance* marks the third time *Super Mario Bros. 2* has been released in America? It was originally released for the Nintendo Entertainment System in 1988, and then again with updated graphics as part of *Super Mario All-Stars* for the Super Nintendo in 1993. *Super Mario Advance* is not only the smallest version to date, it's also the best-looking, and it sports several gameplay options not found in either of the other two versions, such as the Ace Coin hunt and Yoshi's Egg Challenge and the addition of Robirdo as World 3's Boss.

Controls

Mario and friends have various actions to help them get through their quest and defeat Wart. Mastering each is vital to making it through Subcon's 20 levels.

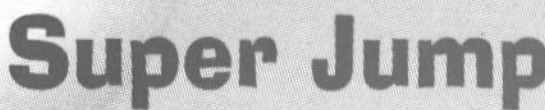

Standing Jump

Pressing Ⓐ while standing still makes your character jump straight up. This jump gives you the least height and no distance, but you can press ← and → while in the air to steer your character.

Super Jump

Press and hold ↓ to make your character duck. Wait until your character starts flashing, then press Ⓐ to perform a Super Jump and leap one-and-a-half times higher than normal.

Running Jump

Press Ⓐ while moving left or right to execute a running jump. Not only do you jump slightly higher than you would if you were making a standing jump, you also jump much farther, especially if you are dashing when you jump.

Lifting

Press Ⓑ while standing on a plant, enemy, or item to lift it in the air and carry it. Larger objects take longer to lift. You can move and jump while carrying an object, but it will slow you down slightly.

Throwing

To throw an object that you're carrying, press Ⓑ again. If the object is a Mushroom Block, Potion, or Bomb, and you are standing still, you will drop it at your feet in the direction you are facing. Any other object will be tossed at a 45-degree angle. You can also press Ⓑ while running to throw the object farther. Throw objects at most enemies to defeat them—you can even throw enemies at other enemies.

Digging

Press Ⓑ when standing on sand to dig a hole in the sand and drop down into it. Continue pressing Ⓑ to dig farther down. You can jump out of the hole you've dug by walking to the right or left and jumping.

Dashing

Press and hold Ⓑ or Ⓡ while pressing ← or → to dash and run faster than normal. Ⓡ is the best way to dash when you're carrying an object or standing on sand, as pressing Ⓑ will make you drop the object or dig into the sand.

Climbing

Press ↑ or ↓ when standing on (or falling or jumping past) chains, ladders, and vines. Watch out for enemies such as Hoopsters who might be above or below you.

Entering Doors and Pipes

To enter a door, stand in the doorway and press ↑. If the door is locked, you need to be holding a Key to open it. To enter a pipe, stand on top of the pipe and press ↓. Leave the pipe by jumping out of the top of it. You cannot carry items into doors or pipes, but you can carry items out of pipes.

Level Goals

Obviously, the main objective of every level is just to make it to the end in one piece, but there are a couple of other things to consider along the way. Three Mushrooms are hidden in Subspace in most of the levels (4-1 and 6-2 are the exceptions with less Mushrooms), and the more Hearts you have in your life meter, the better your chances of finishing the level.

As mentioned above, there are also five Ace Coins scattered throughout each level. Collecting all five Ace Coins in a level gives you a "perfect" rating for the level and marks the level with a star on the grid that is shown before each level. To find out what happens when you collect all 100 Ace Coins, check out Chapter 9.

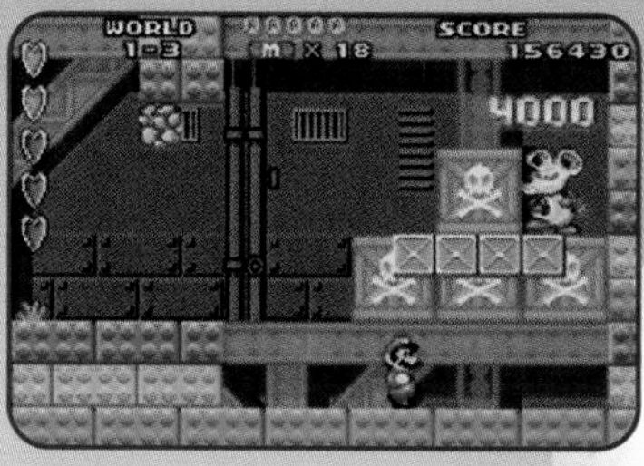

Finally, you need to beat each level's end Boss to clear that level. Usually, that involves throwing some sort of object at the Boss—often its own weapon or a Mushroom Block—until you defeat it. The level is not cleared and will not be marked as such on the grid shown before each level until you defeat a level's end Boss. You will also not have the opportunity to play the Bonus Chance minigame at the end of the level.

Bonus Chance

After you clear a level, you get to play the Bonus Chance slot machine minigame and win 1UP Mushrooms. The number of times you get to pull the handle depends upon how many Coins you collected in Subspace. Ace Coins do not count toward your Coin total.

When the game begins, all three pictures on the slot machine are spinning, and your default wager is one Coin. You can increase your wager by pressing ➔ and decrease it by pressing 🡐, but you cannot wager less than one Coin.

Once you have your wager set, press Ⓐ to stop the first picture on the slot machine. Press it again to stop the second picture, and press it a third time to stop the third picture. The number of Coins you wagered and the pictures you stopped on determine your payoff (see table). Skill is not involved; it's all luck!

Bonus Chance Payoff

Pictures Shown	Payoff
1 Cherry in the first picture	*1UP x your wager*
2 Cherries in the first two pictures	*2UP x your wager*
3 Cherries	*3UP x your wager*
3 Sevens	*5UP x your wager*
3 of any other picture	*2UP x your wager*

World 1-1

Starting Out

Mario and friends begin their Game Boy Advance adventure atop a fluffy white cloud. Either descend the cloud steps below and to the left of the starting point, or walk off the right edge of the first cloud. Either way, you'll come across a Giant Blue Shy Guy who will leave you with a Heart if you knock him out.

The Giant Blue Shy Guy is the only enemy in this little intro world. Next to the Shy Guy is a Large Vegetable—use it to put him to sleep. There are only two other plants; both are at the bottom of the screen, and both are Hearts.

To exit the intro level, jump on top of the Elevator Platform at the bottom of the screen. It will propel you up to the exit doorway. Hop off of the Elevator Platform, run over to the door, and press ↑ to begin Mario's quest.

The Adventure Begins

Head right and you'll encounter two Red Shy Guys, one Giant Red Shy Guy, and a Tweeter before seeing the first Ace Coin suspended in midair above your head. The four plants between the entrance to the level and the Coin are (from left to right) one Large Vegetable, two Small Vegetables, and another Large Vegetable.

Jump up to get the Ace Coin, then climb the vine to the right. On the platform next to the top of the vine are a Blue Shy Guy and four plants. From left to right, the plants are three Small Vegetables and a Magic Potion. Pluck the Magic Potion first and drop it anywhere on the platform.

Go through the doorway created by the Magic Potion to enter Subspace and find your first Mushroom. While in Subspace, don't forget to pluck the three remaining plants to receive three Coins to use in the Bonus Chance minigame at the end of the level.

Descend the vine and move to the right until you reach a POW Block on a short pole surrounded by Red Shy Guys and a Tweeter. Jump on top of the POW Block and pick it up using Ⓑ.

Wait until at least five enemies are onscreen, then drop the POW Block for lots of extra points and a 1UP.

Using the POW Block will only give you a 1UP if there are more than four enemies onscreen at once. If there aren't, consider backtracking slightly to pick up a few enemies and carrying them closer to the POW Block before using it.

To the right of the POW Block are several platforms and a log bridge. Watch out for the Shy Guys and Tweeters. All of the plants on the platforms and bridge are Small Vegetables—good for throwing at enemies.

A waterfall with two log platforms comes after the log bridge. Cross the waterfall by jumping onto the logs while they are at the top of the waterfall. If you do it right, you'll also get the second Ace Coin, which hovers above the two log platforms. The two plants on the platforms to the right of the waterfall are both Giant Vegetables; don't use them yet.

Several Blue Shy Guys patrol the platforms to the right of the Giant Vegetables. A POW Block sits atop the Shy Guys' platforms. Grab the POW Block and head to the right until you see Red Shy Guys and a Tweeter, then lure them back to the left until they're on the same screen as the Blue Shy Guys. As soon as more than four enemies are onscreen, drop the POW Block and collect your 1UP.

Continue moving right until you cross another log bridge. Enter the door to the right of the bridge, and you'll find yourself in a cavern with a jumping Ninji and two plants. Hop on top of the Ninji and jump when he's at the top of his own leap to snag the third Ace Coin.

You will also see a 1UP Mushroom encased in a bubble sitting on a platform in the waterfall to the left of the Ace Coin. Pick up the Ninji, stand at the bottom of the vine, and throw the Ninji at the bubble. The bubble ripples but doesn't break. Pick up each of the Large Vegetable plants near the entrance and throw them at the Mushroom bubble as well. The bubble bursts on the third hit, and you can hop onto the Mushroom and pick it up for an extra chance.

If you've been plucking all of the Large Vegetables along the way, you might get a Time Stop instead of the crucial second Vegetable, which will leave you one projectile short of being able to burst the Mushroom's bubble. To keep that from happening, pluck both Vegetables and then leave the cavern. Return to the cavern and repeat until you get the Time Stop (which you may or may not want to use), then leave the cavern once more and return to get the Mushroom.

Climb the vine to reach the upper level of the cavern. To the right of the top of the vine are three plants (two Small Vegetables and one Giant Vegetable) and five Ninjis jumping in a "wave" formation. Pluck the Giant Vegetable and throw it just as the first Ninji begins his jump. The Vegetable will hit all five Ninjis, giving you not only a bunch of points and a Heart, but a 1UP as well. Exit the cavern via the doorway to the right of the Ninjis.

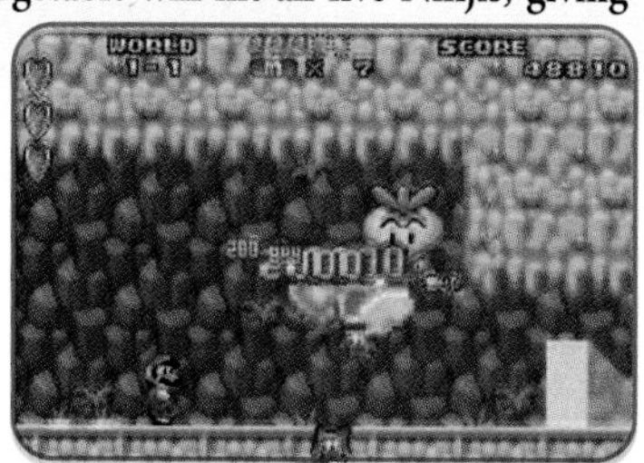

Whenever you leave an area through a door and return to it by going back through the same door, all of the enemies and plants reappear. So, if you're in the mood to pick up a lot of extra chances, return to the cavern and repeat the Giant Vegetable vs. Ninjis maneuver until your thumb gets tired or you have 99 1UPs, whichever comes first.

(Short)Cut to the Chase

If you're just trying to get through World 1-1 as quickly as possible and don't care for collecting all the Ace Coins and Mushrooms, there is a shortcut in the cavern that takes you directly to World 1-1's Boss, Birdo. Starting at the cavern exit doorway, run to the left (by holding down Ⓑ and ←) and jump across the waterfall. Mario and Toad might have trouble making the jump, but it's no problem for Peach or Luigi.

On the left side of the waterfall are a Blue Shy Guy, three plants (all Bombs), and a ladder leading down to a doorway that is blocked by a stone wall. Jump up to the Blue Shy Guy, pick him up, and throw him out of your way. Next, pluck a Bomb and stand facing the ladder. Wait for the Bomb to start flashing, then throw it down the ladder.

If your timing is good, it will detonate next to the stone wall and shatter two or more blocks, leaving enough space to squeeze through and get to the door. The door

(Short)Cut to the Chase continued

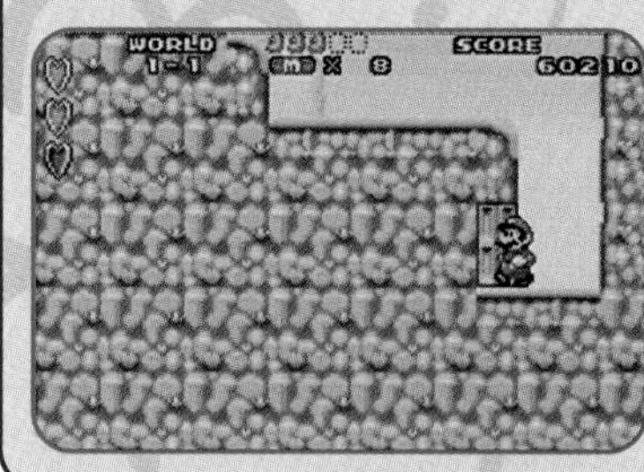

leads to a stair-shaped cliff. Jump (or Super Jump, if necessary) up the steps of the cliff, then continue heading up and left until you reach Birdo.

After exiting the cavern, jump up onto the platform above the cavern doorway and move left, jumping over the waterfall. On the other side of the waterfall are three plants and a Blue Shy Guy. The leftmost plant is a 1UP Mushroom; the other two are Small Vegetables.

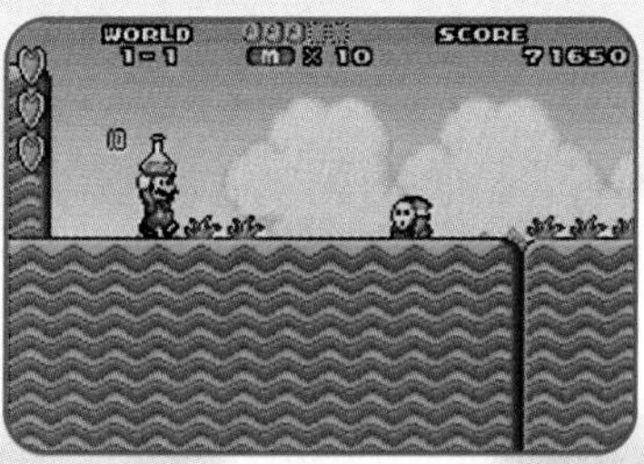

After getting the 1UP Mushroom, return to the cavern door. Between the cavern door and the vine on the right edge of the screen are eight plants. From left to right, they are a Magic Potion, a Large Vegetable, a Giant Vegetable, four Small Vegetables, and a Shell. Pluck the Magic Potion and drop it so that you can see the seven other plants on the same screen as the Magic Potion door.

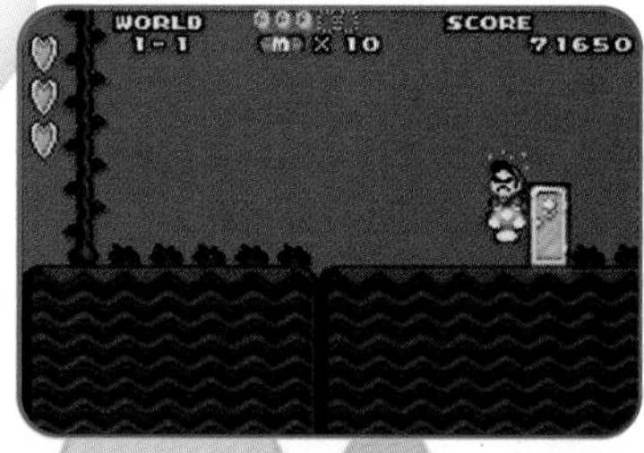

Enter the Magic Potion door to pick up your second Mushroom and as many Coins as you can grab in the time limit. If you make good use of your Ⓑ or Ⓡ dash, you should be able to get all seven before time expires. Once you're done, climb the vine and head up.

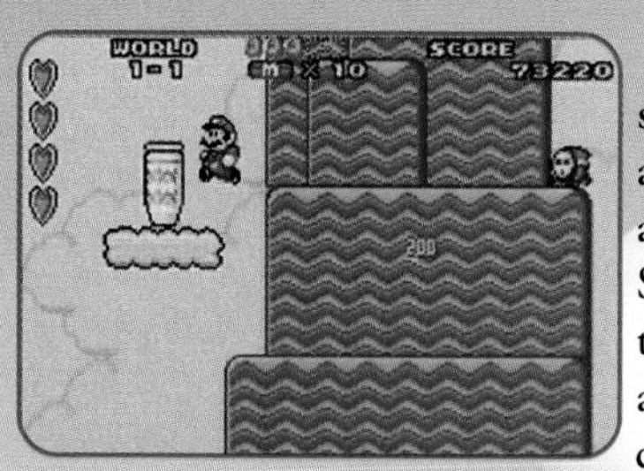

At the top of the vine are a series of ascending platforms, a few Ninjis and Shy Guys, and a couple of plants (all Small Vegetables). Jump up the platforms until you come across a pipe sitting on a cloud. Jump on top of the pipe and press ↓ to enter it. There are two plants in the pipe; the one on the right is a Small Vegetable and the one on the left is a Magic Potion.

Pluck the Magic Potion and ride the rotating platforms to the top of the room, then jump to leave the pipe while still holding the Magic Potion. Jump up onto the cloud above the pipe and drop the Magic Potion on the cloud. Enter the doorway to find the last Mushroom of the level.

After picking up the Mushroom, continue jumping up the platforms. To the right of the top platform is the fourth Ace Coin. Grab it, then jump onto the cloud platform above. Climb the vine leading up from the cloud platform and continue up until you come to three vines and the fifth Ace Coin.

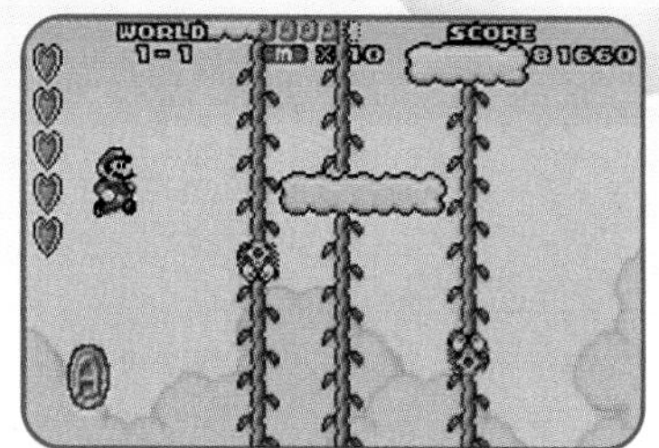

Wait until the Hoopster on the left vine is all the way at the bottom of the vine, then jump on top of it and ride it up the vine until you're next to the Ace Coin. Jump off the Hoopster, grab the Ace Coin, and keep climbing the vines and jumping across the clouds until you reach the last vine, which leads to World 1-1's Boss, Birdo.

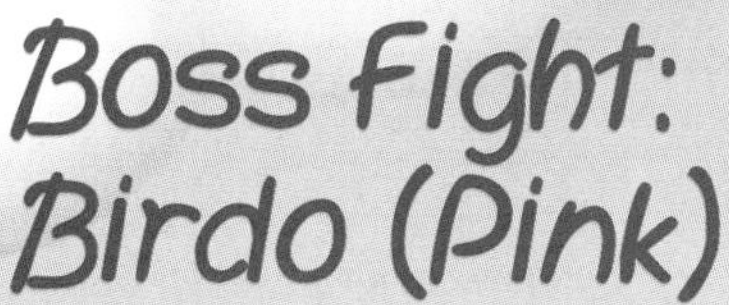

Boss Fight: Birdo (Pink)

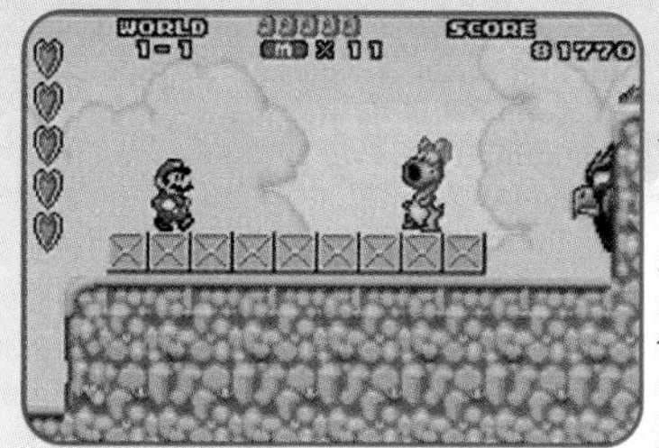

Beating Birdo should present very little challenge. From the top of the vine, move right along the cloud floor, then jump the gap, landing on Birdo's pedestal. Approach Birdo until she says, "That's as far as you go!" Now, the battle begins.

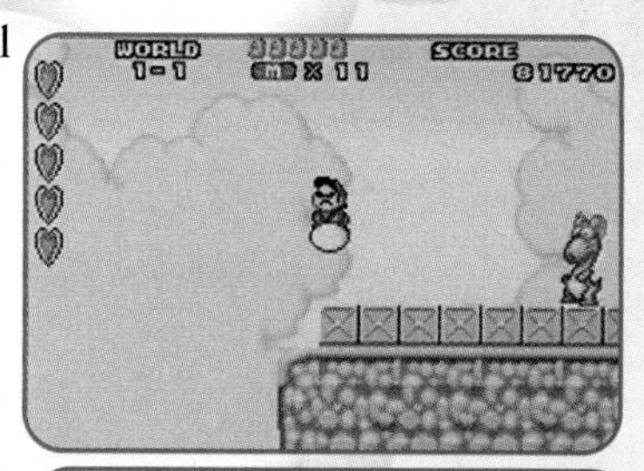

To defeat Birdo, wait until she fires an egg from her mouth, then jump up onto the egg and press Ⓑ to pick it up. Run at Birdo and throw the egg at her. Once you hit Birdo with three eggs, she will be knocked off the screen, leaving behind a Crystal Ball.

If the battle is going poorly and you need more Hearts, a Heart plant is to the right of Birdo, above the bird mouth gate. You can also hop on top of an egg and ride it all the way to the left of the screen. You'll pick up two Hearts along the way.

Hop on top of the Crystal Ball and press Ⓑ to pick it up. The Crystal Ball will vanish and the bird mouth gate to the right will open. Walk through the gate to complete the level and play the Bonus Chance minigame before moving on to World 1-2.

World 1-2

World 1-2 starts you off on a low platform with several other higher platforms to the right and a Pidgit floating around them on a magic carpet. Past the platforms is a gaping chasm, too wide for even Luigi or Peach to jump. You have to jump on the Pidgit and pick him up as he swoops down toward you.

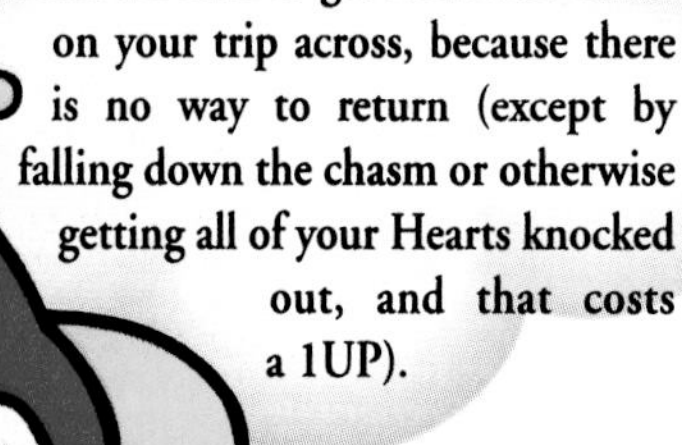

Once you do, you have control over his carpet and can ride it across the chasm. Start by flying along the bottom of the screen to pick up an Ace Coin, then move up and to the right to find a second Ace Coin. It's a little tricky to get both Ace Coins and dodge the swarm of Beezos that attack in midair, but it can be done. Be sure to get both Ace Coins on your trip across, because there is no way to return (except by falling down the chasm or otherwise getting all of your Hearts knocked out, and that costs a 1UP).

Once you safely reach the canyon's right edge, duck down the first pipe to find a Tweeter and a 1UP Mushroom. Leave the pipe and pluck the plant to the left of it. You get a Magic Potion, which you must drop between the two pipes in order to get a Mushroom in Subspace.

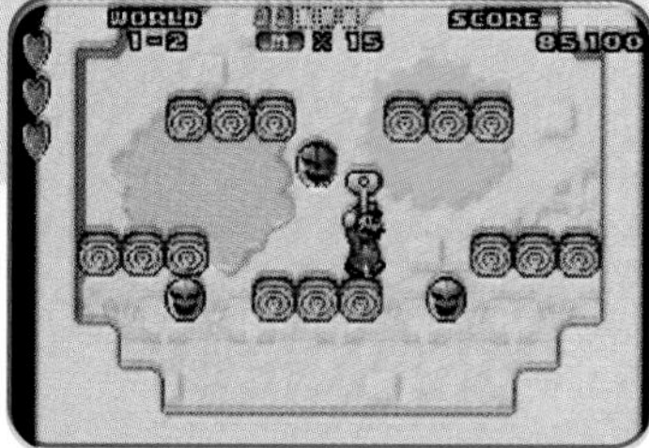

Enter the second pipe once you've gotten the Mushroom. A Key sits on a platform, surrounded by three immobile Phantos. Jump onto the Key and pick it up with Ⓑ; a Phanto will come alive and start chasing you. As quickly as you can, jump out of the pipe.

The Phanto will chase you anywhere you go as long as you have the Key, and you can't stop him. If he's getting too close for comfort, throw the Key and wait for him to disappear before picking it back up. Carry the Key to the locked door to the right of the second pipe and enter.

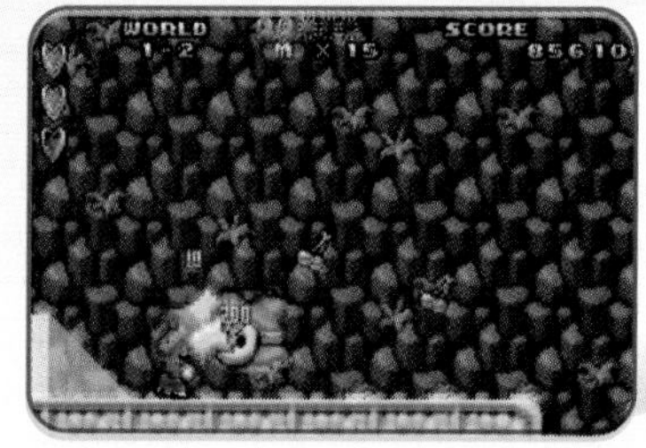

The Key vanishes as you enter the door, and you find yourself in a cavern with a Giant Red Shy Guy heading toward you. Jump on top of the Shy Guy, pick it up, and hurl it at the Snifit to the right. Between the entrance and the Snifit's perch are four plants (a Large Vegetable, a Bomb, and two more Large Vegetables).

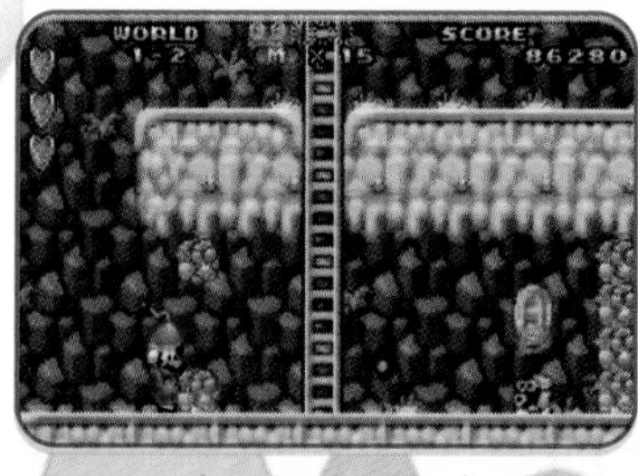

On the Snifit's tiny platform are two Bomb plants, followed by two more past the gap to the right. A little farther to the right is a stone wall with another Snifit, a ladder, an Ace Coin, and another stone wall on the opposite side. Use the Bombs to blow open the stone wall, get rid of the Snifit, and jump up to grab the Ace Coin. You don't need to worry about the second stone wall next to the Ace Coin.

Climb the ladder to the next platform. Surrounding the ladder are four plants; from left to right, they are a Bomb, a Magic Potion, and two more Bombs. To the right of the ladder and plants is a third stone wall that keeps you from moving any farther to the right. Use the Bombs to destroy the third stone wall, then drop a Magic Potion on the ground where the wall used to be to get a Mushroom.

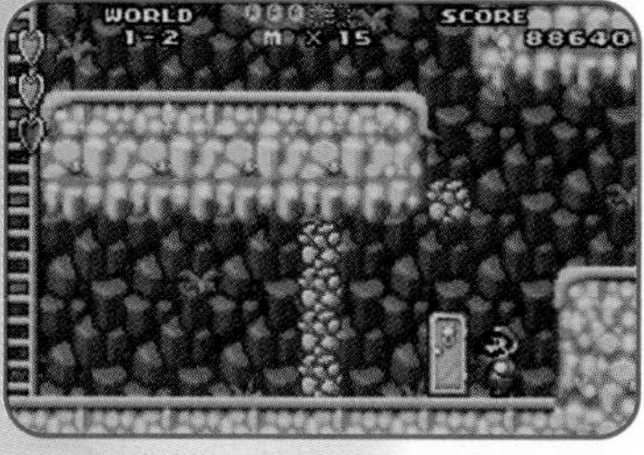

Once you're finished playing with Potions and Bombs, head right to find the cavern exit. Jump up to the platform directly above the door and move left, watching out for the Snifit along the way. At the leftmost edge of the platform is an Ace Coin and a Magic Potion plant.

Pluck the plant and drop the Magic Potion on the ground below the Ace Coin to find another Mushroom in Subspace. Upon returning from Subspace, jump up to grab the Ace Coin, then head back to the cavern door and take a running jump off of the right edge of the platform to grab the final Ace Coin.

Instead of using the Magic Potion to get the Mushroom right away, you might want to bring it back to the entrance of the cavern. There are several plants to the right of the door, and each is worth a Coin if you pluck it in Subspace. You can then duck back into the cavern and come back out to pick up the Magic Potion again, this time using it for the Mushroom.

Boss Fight: Birdo

After you grab the Ace Coin, proceed through the door to the right to fight Birdo again. The method for beating her is exactly the same as it was at the end of World 1-1: hop on an egg, pick it up, and throw it at Birdo. Three hits and Birdo's down for the count.

If you need Hearts, you can pluck one near the entrance to Birdo's room, or you can Super Jump while on Birdo's pedestal to find another. Once Birdo is defeated, grab the Crystal Ball she leaves behind to open the bird mouth gate and exit World 1-2.

World 1-3

At the beginning of World 1-3, you start on a platform with two plants. The left one is a Giant Vegetable and the right one is a Heart. Pluck the Heart if you need it, then pluck the Giant Vegetable, carry it to the right, and use it to take out the two Snifits.

Jump onto the Snifits' platform and jump across the top of the platforms to the left. At the left end of the platforms is the first Ace Coin. There are also five Cherries along the way, and if you get all five, you'll get a Starman as well.

After getting the Ace Coin, move right along the platforms. Immediately to the left of the log bridge are two plants. The left one is a Small Vegetable and the right one is a Magic Potion. Pluck the Magic Potion and drop it in the middle of the log bridge to enter Subspace and get a Mushroom.

Cross the bridge and the log platforms following it. At the waterfall to the right of the log platforms, time your jumps carefully and leap from log to log while the logs are near the top of the waterfall. Following the waterfall logs is a platform with five plants on it, but don't grab any of the plants just yet.

Keep heading right, crossing a smaller waterfall with two floating logs, and you'll come to a log platform with three plants on it and two under it. The leftmost plant under the log platform is a Magic Potion. Pluck the Magic Potion and carry it while backtracking left across the small waterfall. It's not as easy going left across the logs, so time your jumps very carefully.

You need to drop the Magic Potion on top of the platform between the two waterfalls (the one with the five plants). To do this, Super Jump onto the waterfall log to the left of the platform just as it's starting to fall, then jump to the right quickly. If your skills are sharp, you'll be standing on top of the platform, holding the Magic Potion. Drop the Magic Potion on top of the platform, grab your Mushroom and Coins, and head back across the small waterfall to the right.

Continue heading right until you come to a door. Just past the door is a pipe and an Elevator Platform (which looks just like a regular green platform until you stand on it). You can't go down the pipe, but you can jump on top of the Elevator Platform, which will propel you up and within jumping distance of the third Ace Coin.

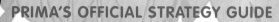

So What's Up With That Pipe?

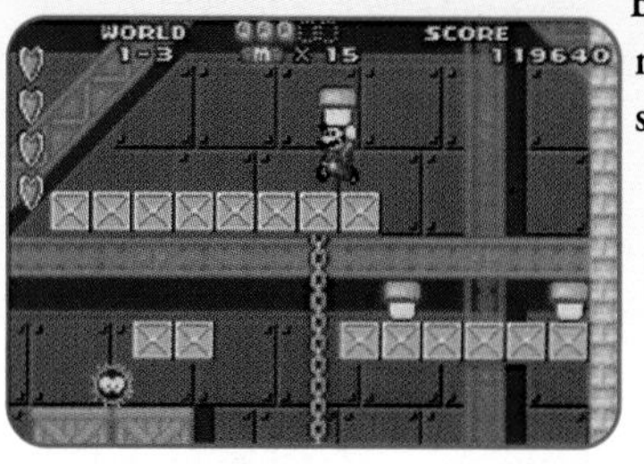

The pipe near the third Ace Coin doesn't seem to serve a purpose...at least not normally. If you drop a Magic Potion near it and enter Subspace, the pipe becomes a Warp Pipe that will instantly scoot you to World 4-1. Of course, you'll miss out on all of the Ace Coins, 1UPs, etc. in Worlds 2 and 3, but it's a good shortcut for those who just want to get to the end of the game quickly.

After getting the Ace Coin, go through the door to the left to enter the cavern. The cavern is a tall stretch of horizontal platforms and vertical chains, and your first task is to get to the top. If the jump between the two platforms above the stack of Mushroom Blocks is too high even for your character's Super Jump, grab a Mushroom Block, throw it up on to the next platform, and use it as a stepping stone to move up.

Underneath the bottom left Mushroom Block is a Roulette. Picking up the Roulette sets it spinning between Bombs, Stars, and Hearts. When the image of the item you want is displayed, press Ⓑ to break open the Roulette and get your item.

Near the top of the Cavern is a pipe. Go down into the pipe to find two plants. The left one is a Magic Potion and the right is a Small Vegetable. Pluck the Magic Potion and leave the pipe, then drop the Magic Potion on the platform between the pipe and the plant on the left side of the screen (it's a Heart Radish, by the way). Enter Subspace and pick up the Mushroom, which appears right on top of the plant, making powering up and Coin collecting easy.

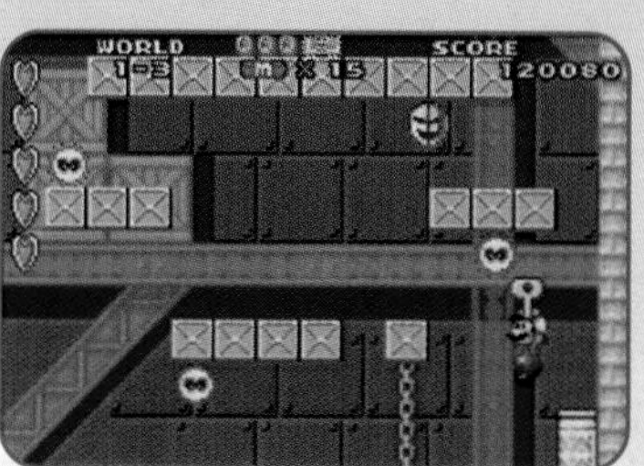

Jump up the last few platforms until you reach the door in the center of the top platform. Inside the door is a Key surrounded by Phantos and a Spark. Grab the Key, exit the room, and get down to the bottom of the cavern as fast as you possibly can, keeping to the right whenever possible. Drop the Key if Phanto starts buzzing you a little too closely.

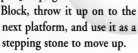

At the very bottom of the cavern is a small platform and a locked door to the right and a row of nasty spikes with a Giant Blue Shy Guy walking across them to the left. Leave the Giant Blue Shy Guy alone; if you make a mistake, you might land on his head rather than the unforgiving spikes.

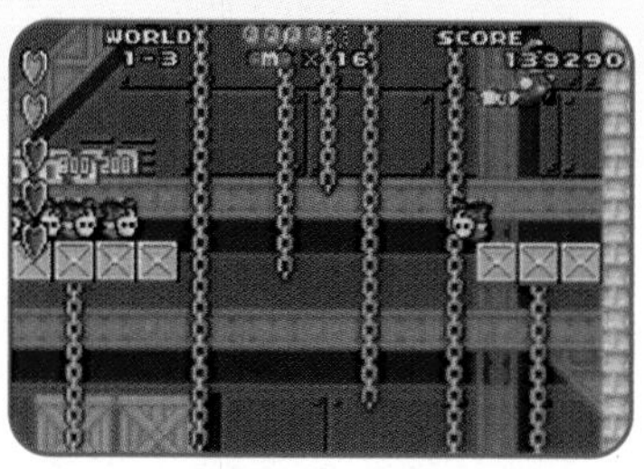

Unlock the door with the Key and enter it, but head right back out again. On the left side of the screen, above the spikes, is the fourth Ace Coin. Above the locked door is a Blue Shy Guy patrolling a small platform with a plant on it. The plant is a POW Block, and because the Blue Shy Guy on the right and his four friends on the left are all onscreen at once, you can drop the POW Block for a 1UP.

World 1 Walkthrough

If you drop the Key (or leave it somewhere) offscreen, Phanto recovers it and takes it all the way back up to the top of the cavern again. Unlock the door first, then go about your business.

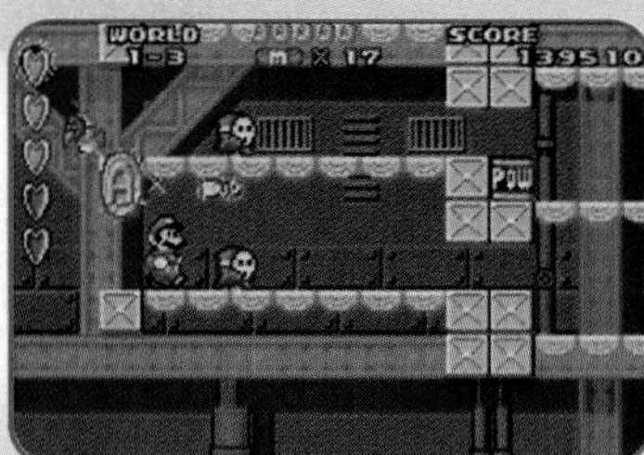

This next area is a horizontal cavern. Jump to the right across the platforms. The first plant you come across is a Small Vegetable, followed by a Heart. Throw the Small Vegetable to take out the fast-moving Spark on the platform to the right, then run off the edge of the Spark's platform to reach the second of three horizontal platforms with Snifits on them, and the fifth Ace Coin.

Use the POW Block to eliminate the Snifits, timing it so that there are at least five enemies onscreen at once. This way you get a 1UP out of it. Continue jumping and running to the right until you come to a Crystal Ball and a gate like the one you saw after defeating Birdo.

Boss Fight: Mouser

Jump on top of the Crystal Ball and pick it up to open the gate. Enter the gate, and you'll find yourself in Mouser's lair. Mouser is at the right edge of the room, behind a stone wall. The three plants next to the wall are Bombs. Use the Bombs to blow open the wall.

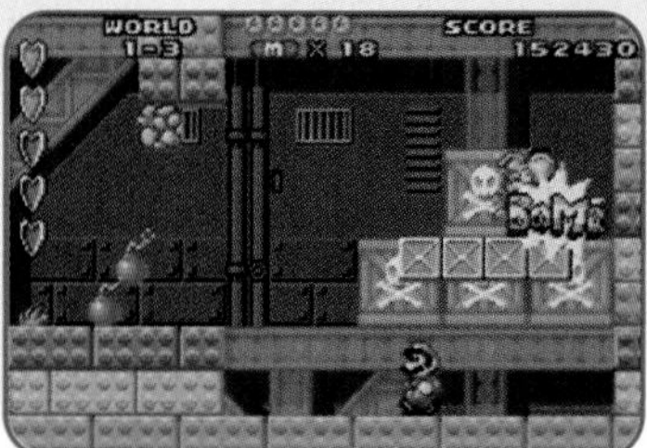

Once the wall is open, you can approach Mouser, who hurls Bombs in volleys of three. Once he invites you to "have some Bombs," the fight begins. Pick up the Bombs as soon as they land (or just run into them in midair to automatically grab them), then jump and throw them onto Mouser's platform.

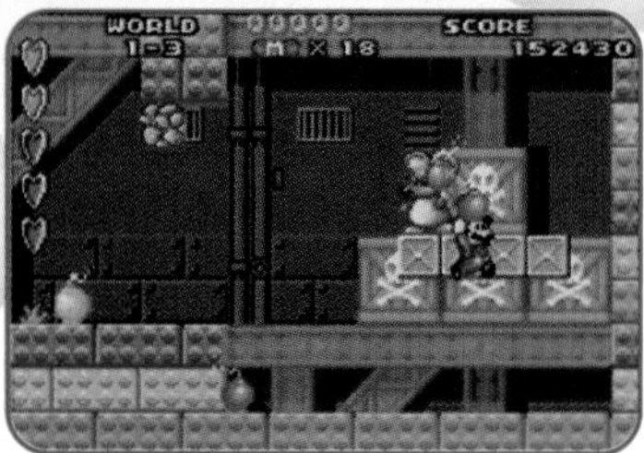

The easiest Bombs to catch are the ones that land in the corner below and to the left of Mouser's platform. Mouser cannot hit you if you are standing directly underneath him. If your Hearts are running low, you can pluck three from the platform with the circling Spark and another one right near the entrance to the room.

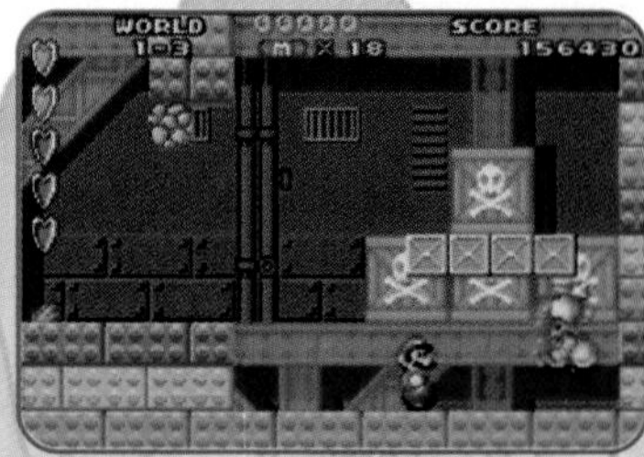

Once Mouser is hit by three Bomb explosions, he's blown offscreen, and a doorway appears. Enter the doorway to complete the level and put World 1 behind you.

World 2-1

Desert Nights

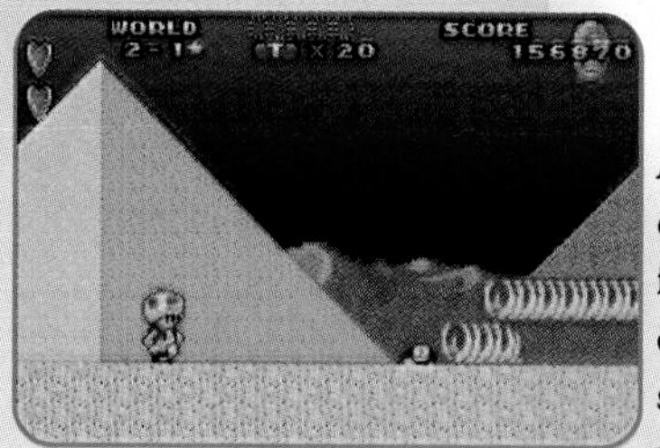

After defeating Mouser at the end of World 1-3, Mario and friends appear in a sandy desert underneath a starry sky. Toad and Mario are both good choices for this level.

To the left of your starting position is a Heart Radish, which you should pluck if you're not at full health.

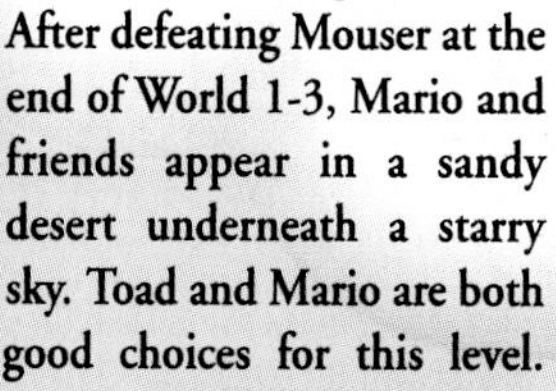

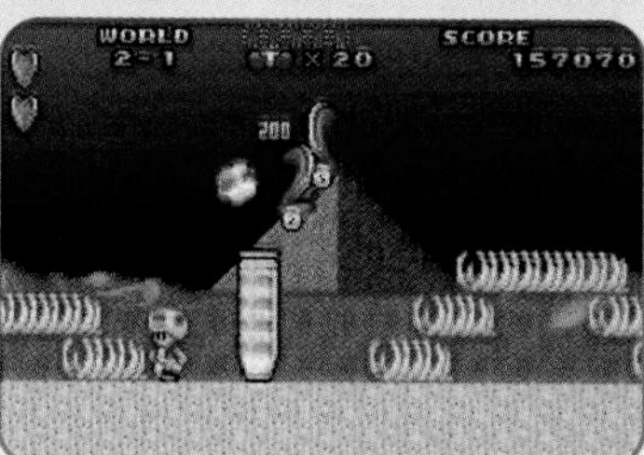

Move right until you come to a small platform made of bones, and watch out for the Cobrat in front of it; it'll leap out of the ground, chase you, and fire bullets at you once you get close to it. Above the bone platform is the level's first Ace Coin. Collect it and continue to the right.

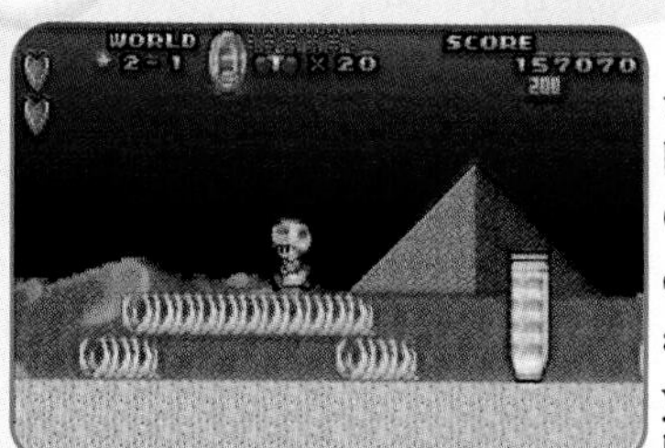

If you go down the first pipe you encounter, you'll find a Shell and a Snifit. Grab the Shell, take it out of the pipe, and use it to knock out the two Shy Guys between the next two bone platforms. Hop across the platforms to the right, making sure to avoid the bouncing Shell and the Cobrat in the pipe just after the second platform.

If you want another Shell, get rid of the Cobrat in the pipe, then enter the pipe, which is identical to the first one. To the right of the pipe is a platform with four plants on it. The first is a Magic Potion, and the other three are Small Vegetables. Drop the Magic Potion on the platform to find a Mushroom.

Just past the platform with the Magic Potion is a short stretch of quicksand. Keep jumping as you run across it to avoid being sucked under. If you need a Heart, get rid of the Blue Shy Guy on the small bone platform past the cacti, and Super Jump to snag the Heart floating above.

Hovering above the cactus to the bone platform's right is the level's second Ace Coin. Super Jump off the top of the cactus to grab it, then continue to the right toward the Panser and Shy Guys on the upcoming stepped platform. There's a Magic Potion under the Panser, and a Mushroom is located on top of the stepped platform in Subspace.

Between the right edge of the Panser platform and the cactus just after it is a Shell. Pluck the Shell and use it to knock out the Cobrat lying in wait in the quicksand, to the right. The Shell doesn't sink in the quicksand but bounces back and forth between the cacti on either side. Also, an Ace Coin is floating above the quicksand.

To get the Ace Coin, time your jump carefully so that you land atop the bouncing Shell, then duck down and get ready to Super Jump. Jump just as you pass underneath the Ace Coin to get it, and be careful to avoid the Shell when you land.

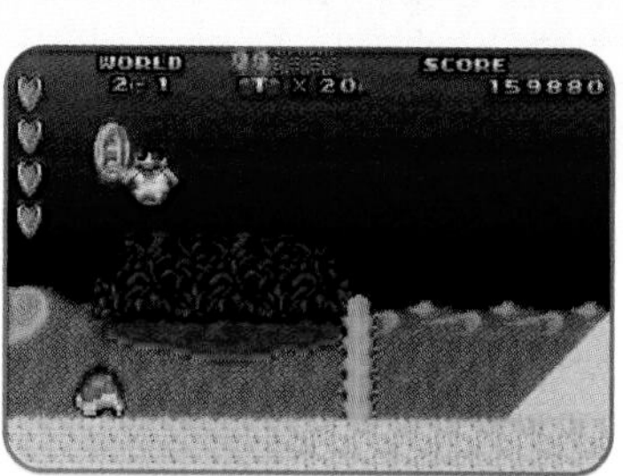

To the quicksand patch's right is a pyramid with a door, and just past that is a plant that gives you a Magic Potion if you pluck it. Get the Magic Potion, then backtrack slightly to the left and drop it near the first cactus you see. The Mushroom will appear on top of the cactus in Subspace.

Secrets of the Pyramids

Once you get the Mushroom, return to the pyramid door and enter it. You appear on a stone platform above a huge sand floor with a Shy Guy and a Giant Ninji on either side of you. Use the Shy Guy to knock out the Ninji (or vice versa), then walk off of the platform and stand on the sand.

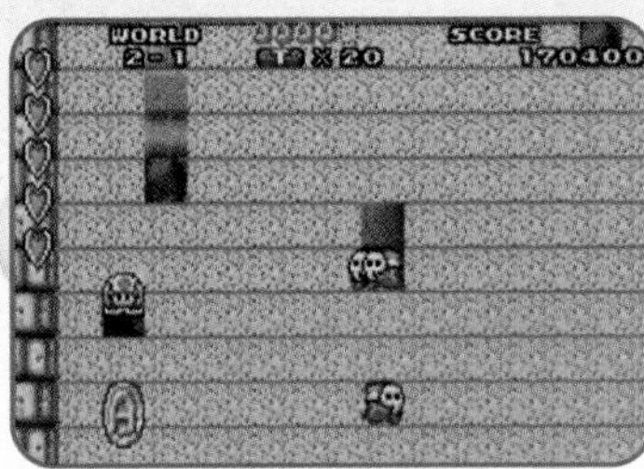

Press Ⓑ to dig out a block of sand, and continue digging until you reach the bottom. Pay attention to the Red Shy Guys in the sand. They'll follow you down the hole, so stay way in front of them. Grab the last two Ace Coins, both of which will be visible in the sand as you make your way down.

At the bottom of the sand floor is a ladder leading down to a small room with a pipe and a door. Drop down the pipe to pluck a 1UP Mushroom, then leave the pipe and enter the door to begin the end-of-level Boss fight with your old pal Birdo.

Boss Fight: Birdo (Pink)

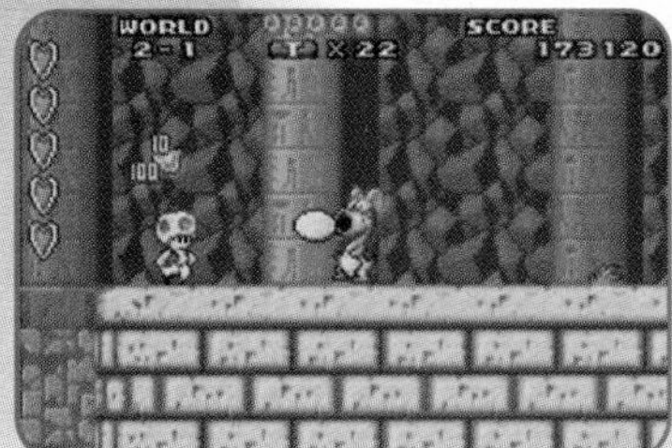

Birdo hasn't learned any new tricks since you fought her last, so follow the same plan of attack: jump on her eggs, pick them up, and throw them at her. As usual, three hits gets rid of Birdo, and picking up the Crystal Ball she leaves behind opens the gate to the end of World 2-1, located at the room's far right.

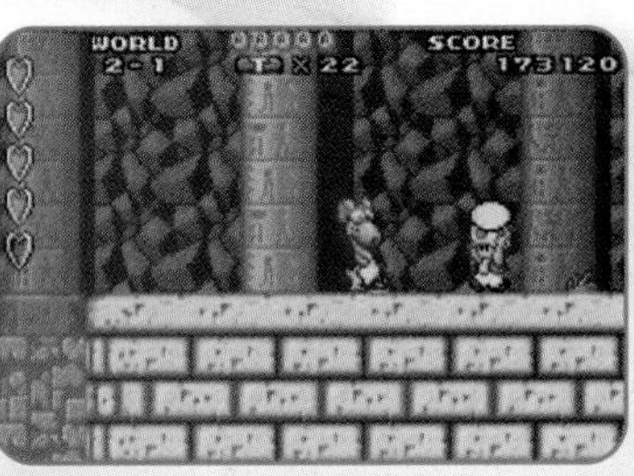

If you had no trouble with Birdo the last two times, you'll have no trouble this time either. The only new wrinkles are the small chasms on either side of Birdo's platform. Don't pick up an egg if you're riding over a chasm, or you'll plummet off the bottom of the screen, lose a chance, and have to start the fight over with only one Heart. If you need Hearts, pluck the plant on either side of Birdo.

World 2-2

Back to the Desert

World 2-2 starts you off in a small cavern. Jump up and right along the platforms to find a doorway leading out on the cavern's right side. Enter the doorway to exit the cavern and return to the desert world outside.

As you exit, pluck the Shell plant to the right of the entrance and hurl it at the Red Shy Guys marching toward you. You'll eliminate the enemies, and you'll also get a few Hearts from doing so.

Just past the Shy Guys is a bone platform with an Ace Coin hovering above it. Super Jump off of the platform to get the Ace Coin, then jump on top of the Cobrat waiting for you in the quicksand to the bone platform's right. Pick up the Cobrat and carry it to the right, jumping along the three cacti. Hurl the Cobrat at the Beezo that buzzes you as you cross the cacti.

To the cacti's right is a pipe containing a Cobrat. Pluck the Cobrat out of the pipe to enter it; you'll find a Shell inside. Carry the Shell out of the pipe and use it to take out the Shy Guy to the pipe's right.

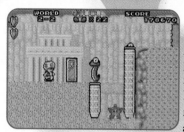

To get a Magic Potion, pluck the first plant to the pipe's right. Toss the Magic Potion on the ground near where you plucked it and enter the doorway to get a Mushroom. The other two plants to the Magic Potion's right are Large Vegetables—good for eliminating the two Cobrats in the next two pipes to the right.

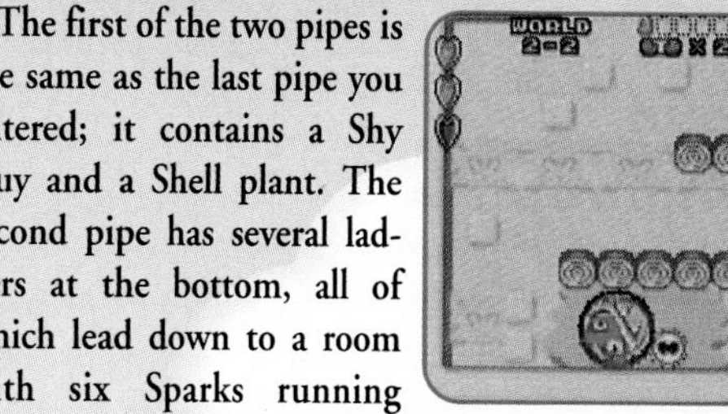

The first of the two pipes is the same as the last pipe you entered; it contains a Shy Guy and a Shell plant. The second pipe has several ladders at the bottom, all of which lead down to a room with six Sparks running along the walls and a Spark Chaser on a platform. Pick up the Spark Chaser and throw it at the outside wall to get Hearts and a 1UP if it hits every Spark. Leave the pipe by jumping up to the ladders and climbing up.

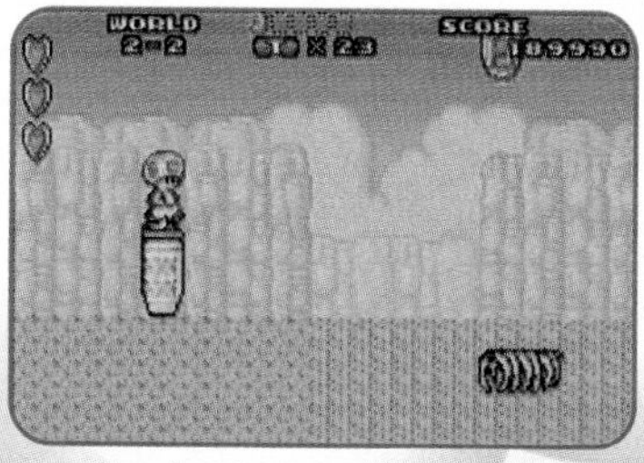

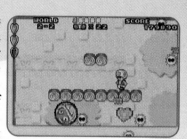

Keep moving right, past the cacti, into the quicksand, and past the next pipe with a Cobrat in it. Although you should dispatch the Cobrat, you don't need to go down into the pipe, because it only contains another Shell. Just past the pipe is an area of stronger quicksand, with a bone platform that starts at the top of the quicksand and descends, returning to the top after it falls off the screen.

The level's second Ace Coin floats high above the "falling" bone platform. If you're playing as Luigi, he can reach it simply by jumping off of the bone platform when it's near the top of the quicksand. For any other character, you have to jump onto the bone platform as soon as it starts poking over the top of the quicksand, then squat down and Super Jump up to get the Ace Coin. Several Cobrats in pipes on either side of the Ace Coin fire bullets at you, so either be very careful or prepare to take a Heart or two of damage.

Shy Guy Cavern

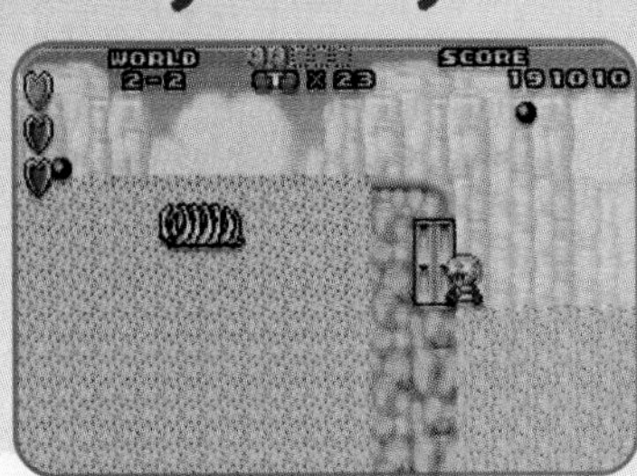

Immediately to the right of the strong quicksand is a small drop-off with a door to the left. Enter the door to reach a small cavern. To the left of the door is a stone wall, and to the right are stepped platforms and a few plants. The three plants on the second step to the right are Bombs. The two plants on the third step are Heart Radishes.

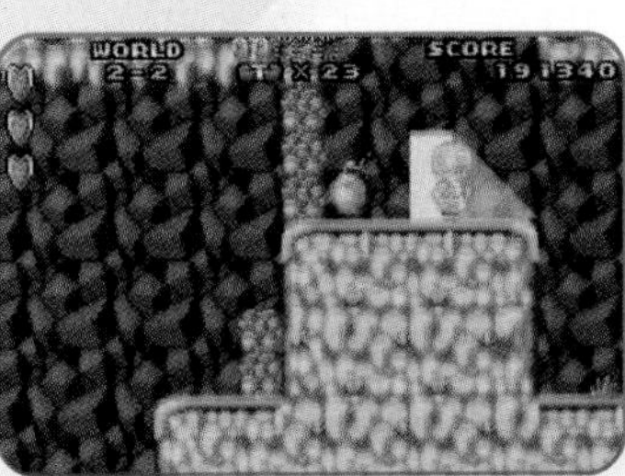

To get past the stone wall to the door's left, drop to the second platform on the right, pluck a Bomb, jump (or Super Jump) back to the doorway, and place the Bomb by the wall. If you do it correctly, the Bomb will blast away enough of the wall for you to pass through. If you do it incorrectly, the Bomb will explode too far away from the wall to damage it; also, if you're too close, you'll suffer a Heart's worth of damage.

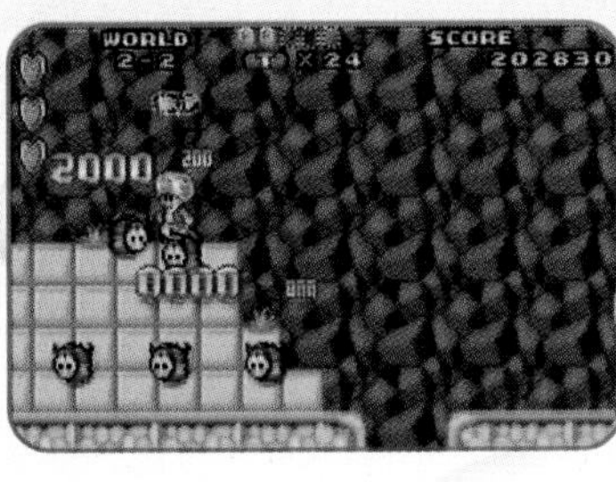

Once you blow up the wall, head left to find a stepped platform containing five Blue Shy Guys and five plants. The leftmost plant on the platform's upper level is a POW Block. For a 1UP, pluck it and drop it while all five Shy Guys are visible onscreen.

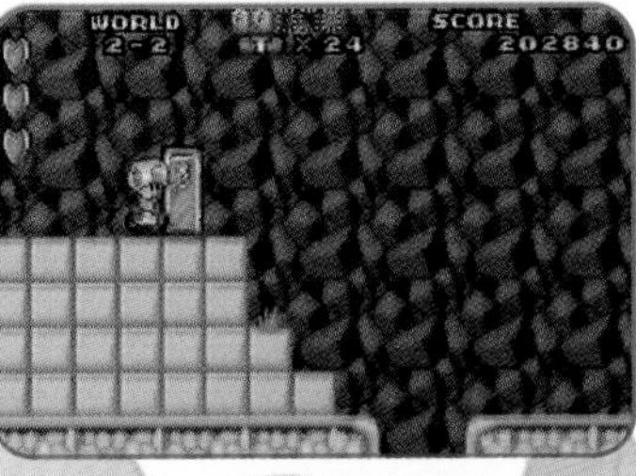

The plant just to the right of the POW Block is a Magic Potion. Pluck it and drop it right where you found it to get a Mushroom. The other three plants are only Vegetables, which come in handy for eliminating the two Blue Shy Guys that reappear after you return from Subspace.

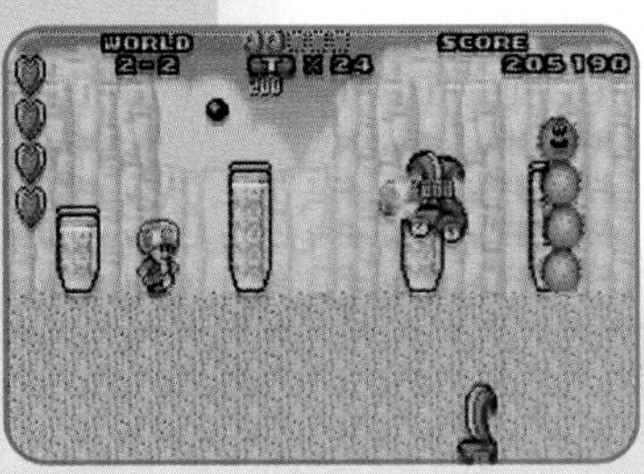

Once you have your Mushroom, head out the door through which you entered to return to the desert. To the right of the door are six pipes, each of which (with one exception) has a Cobrat in it. Each Cobrat pipe contains only a Shell. Every time you exit a pipe, all of the Cobrats you defeated return to hassle you again, so you might want to avoid ducking down most of the pipes.

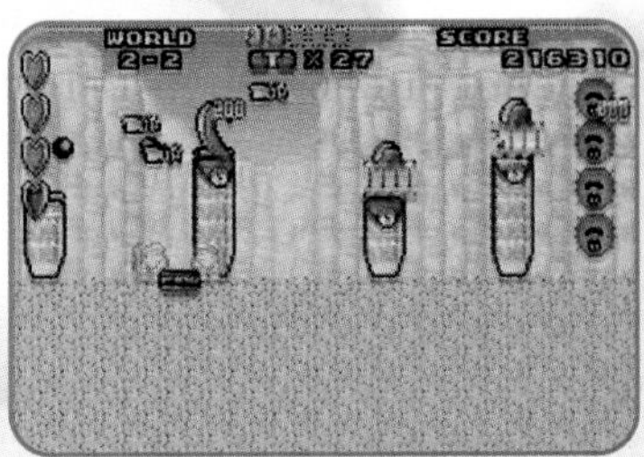

The one pipe you do want to enter, however, is the second pipe—the one without a Cobrat. At the bottom right is a Heart Radish, and to the left is a POW Block plant. Grab the POW Block and exit the pipe. Use the POW Block to get rid of as many Cobrats as you can fit onscreen at once.

Once you pass Pokey and Cobrats, duck down the last pipe to grab a Shell, then exit the pipe and continue past the cactus to the pipe's right. (Remember: defeated enemies return after you leave a pipe, so watch out for the Cobrats' shots.) Use the Shell to eliminate the two Pansers on the stepped platform to the cactus's right, and jump off of the platform to pick up the level's third Ace Coin.

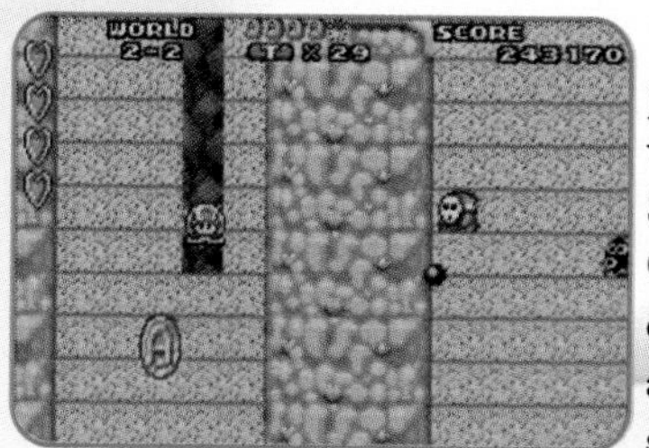

Climb down the vine to the stepped platform's right to reach another pit with a deep sandy floor, a Red Shy Guy, and a Giant Ninji at the bottom of the vine. Dig out a block of sand, then pick up the Shy Guy when it passes through the block you dug out. Throw the Shy Guy at the Ninji to eliminate both and get a Heart.

Start digging again. If you pick up five Cherries on the way down, you can get a Starman and eliminate the Shy Guys following you. **Do not** dig under the cleared-out area around the fifth Cherry (you'll see why in a moment). About halfway down, grab the Ace Coin. When you're near the bottom and the sand floor divides into two paths separated by a rock wall, take the left path and continue digging down.

The left sand path takes you to the fifth Ace Coin and leads to a pipe and two plants at the bottom. The left plant is a Magic Potion. Grab it, jump back to the cleared-out area of sand around the fifth Cherry, and drop it. The Mushroom will appear in the cleared-out area in Subspace. If you dug under the cleared-out area on the way down, the Mushroom might fall down the hole you dug, never to be seen again. If you go in the pipe first, the sand will restore itself and you won't ever lose the Subspace Mushroom.

Once you get the Mushroom, return to the left sand path's bottom and enter the pipe (the other plant is only a Small Vegetable, by the way). At the bottom of the pipe is a 1UP Mushroom plant. Pluck it and then leave the pipe.

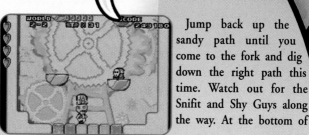

Jump back up the sandy path until you come to the fork and dig down the right path this time. Watch out for the Snifit and Shy Guys along the way. At the bottom of the path is the door to Birdo's lair. Enter it and prepare for battle.

Boss Fight: Birdo (Red)

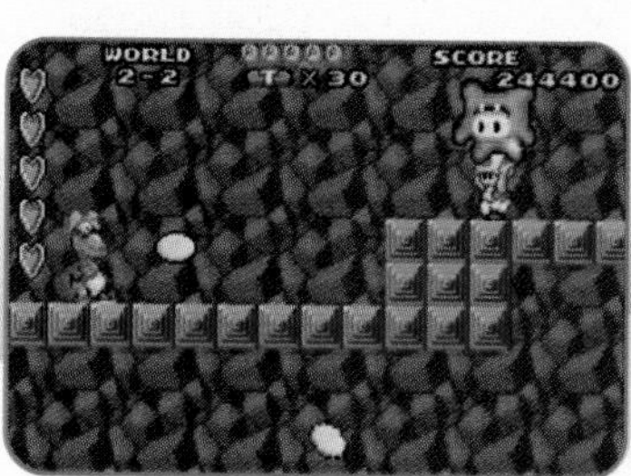

Birdo's lair has a plant and a Giant Ninji near the entrance. Pluck the plant for a Heart, then grab the Giant Ninji, carry him to the right, and chuck him down the gap to the Mushroom Blocks' right. As you do, you'll see Birdo overhead, pacing along a blue platform.

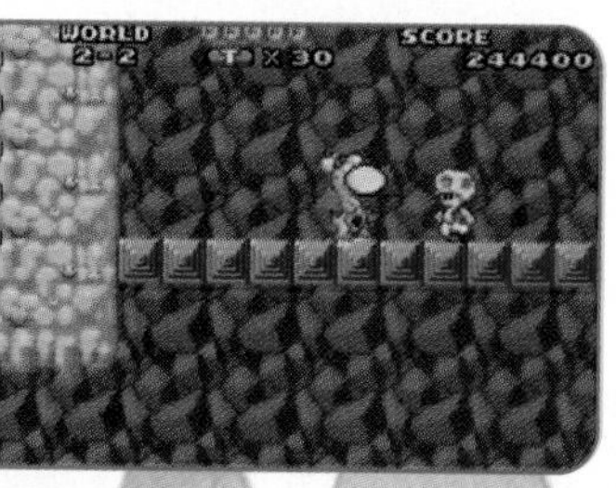

To reach Birdo, jump the gap into which you threw the Giant Ninji. You might need to use a Super Jump or stack Mushroom Blocks at the edge of the gap and jump off of them to clear it.

From the other side of the gap, jump (or Super Jump) up to the next level on the right, and jump onto the blue platform from there.

TIP

You can hit Birdo with Mushroom Blocks and Giant Ninji as well, if you carry them up there.

Once you reach the blue platform, move left to fight Birdo. This time, instead of merely firing eggs, Birdo also shoots fireballs. If a fireball hits you, you lose one Heart, so be careful not to leap onto a fireball by mistake. Aside from that, this is the same deal as before: grab the eggs as they sail by, and hit Birdo with three of them. Then, grab the Crystal Ball to open the gate to the blue platform's right and exit World 2-2.

World 2-3

The End of the Desert

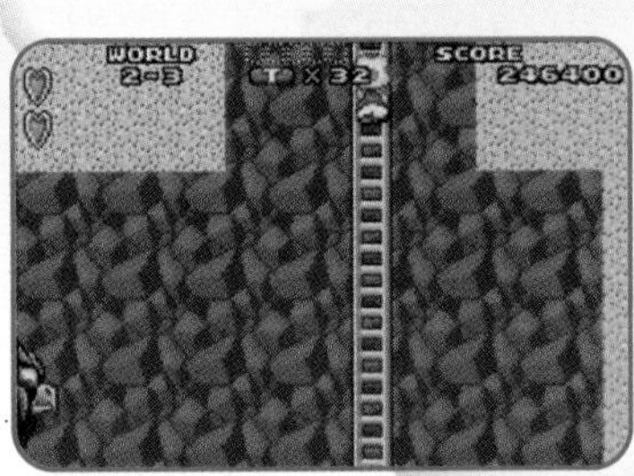

From the start point in World 2-3, climb the ladder out of the cavern to return to the desert world outside. Pluck the first plant to the ladder's top right to get a Magic Potion, being careful to avoid the Beezos. Bring the Potion over to the platforms to the ladder's left and drop it. A Mushroom appears on top of the platforms in Subspace.

The two plants around the platforms are both Hearts, which are handy if you're restarting the level but aren't necessary if you just grabbed the Mushroom. Move right past the ladder and jump on top of the cactus (the four plants between the cactus and the ladder are all Large Vegetables, none of which you need).

When a Beezo buzzes by from left to right, jump from the top of the cactus onto the Beezo and hold ➔ to avoid falling from its back. The Beezo takes you right to the level's first Ace Coin. Just past the Ace Coin is a tall platform with a door. Jump off of the Beezo onto the platform and enter the door. Luigi can reach this area by doing a Super Jump.

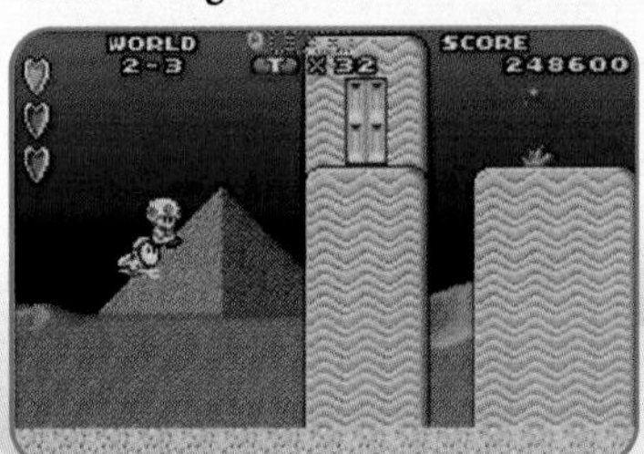

Inside is a small room with nine plants, four to the door's right and five to the left. Pluck the plant immediately to the right to get a Magic Potion, and drop the Magic Potion anywhere among the five plants to the left to get a Mushroom and all of the Coins you're able to grab before the Subspace time limit expires.

The other plants are all Small Vegetables, except for one Large Vegetable, and none of them are necessary. Exit the room through the door and hop across the tops of the platforms to the right. The first two hold Small Vegetable plants; the third (separated from the other two by a small gap) is a 1UP Mushroom. Pluck the 1UP Mushroom, then jump off of the platform to the ground below.

The first plant to the last platform's bottom right is a Heart. Pluck it if you need it, then continue to the right. Once again, jump on top of any of the cacti to the Heart Radish's right and hop on top of a Beezo headed right. Hold ➔ to stay on the Beezo's back and collect the level's second Ace Coin. This Ace Coin can also be collected by performing a Super Jump with any character.

Jump up to the stone platform and pluck the left plant to get a Magic Potion. While carrying the Magic Potion, walk off the stone platform, then off the log platform. You'll land on a sand floor with a Giant Shy Guy and a Tweeter patrolling a locked door. Drop the Magic Potion on the sand floor and enter the door to get the level's third Mushroom. When you return from Subspace, both enemies should be gone.

Jump off the Beezo and continue right. Aside from the perpetually annoying Beezos, only three more enemies are between you and the screen's right end: two Pokeys and a Cobrat in the sand. The easiest way to deal with the Pokeys is to grab an enemy and throw it at their base.

At the screen's right edge is a pyramid with a door. Enter, and you appear on a platform in a long vertical cavern with two pits on either side. On a small platform on the left pit is a pipe with a POW Block plant inside. Take the POW Block out of the pipe, and drop off of the platform's right edge, keeping just left of center on the way down to grab the Ace Coin below.

If you miss the Ace Coin on the way down, there is no way to go back and try to get it without starting the level over or losing a 1UP.

After grabbing the Ace Coin, you either land on a platform made of logs or a smaller stone platform directly above it. You also have company: five Shy Guys pace the log platform. Drop the POW Block to eliminate them and pick up a 1UP.

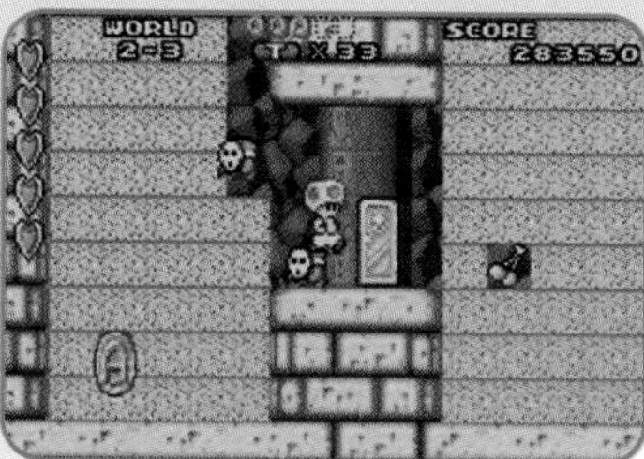

Once you've gotten the Mushroom, start digging through the sand, keeping to the left and avoiding the Red Shy Guys scattered throughout. At the bottom is an Ace Coin and a small plateau with a door and a Heart Radish next to it. Pluck the heart if you need it, then enter the door.

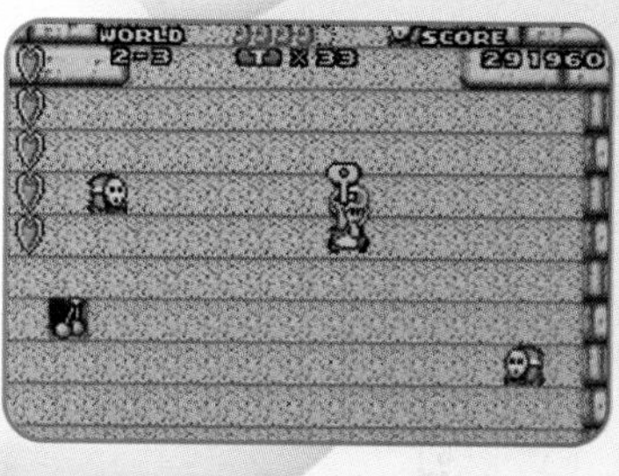

Inside the door is a Key on a platform with a Spark running around it. Dodge the Spark, grab the Key, then hightail it out. Jump up through the sand until you reach the locked door, then open the door with the Key and enter.

Dropping the Key in the sand makes it difficult to pick up again. You have to position yourself over the Key and dig it out before you can lift it. If you keep jumping, you should outrun Phanto with no problem.

The locked door leads into the room just before the Boss room. To the door's right is an expanse of sand with four Cherries buried in it and a fifth one floating at the right end. Grab enough Cherries to get a Starman, then run to the right and take out the Panser sitting atop a sandy platform. Hovering above the Panser is the level's last Ace Coin. Grab it, then continue to the right.

After the Panser, there are only a few cacti and pipes with Cobrats before the Boss room. Each pipe contains a POW Block plant. Grab the POW Block and use it when more than four enemies are onscreen to get a 1UP. To proceed to the Boss room, pick up the Crystal Ball between the last two pipes and enter the gate to the right.

Boss Fight: Tryclyde

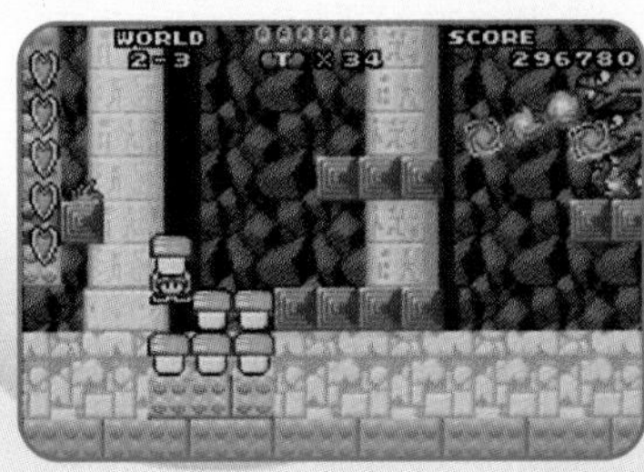

Both plants in Tryclyde's lair are to his left, and they're both Hearts. Use them if you need them. Tryclyde sits on a platform on the room's right side and spits fireballs. Each fireball takes away a Heart, so don't step in front of them.

Tryclyde has a Tweeter friend hanging out below his platform. If you run out of Mushroom Blocks, you can launch the Tweeter at Tryclyde.

To Tryclyde's left are two platforms and six Mushroom Blocks. To defend yourself against Tryclyde's attacks, stack two or three Mushroom Blocks between the platforms; Tryclyde's fireballs can't penetrate the Mushroom Blocks. Pick up the remaining blocks and toss them at Tryclyde. Hit him with three Mushroom Blocks to defeat him and open a doorway. Enter it to complete World 2.

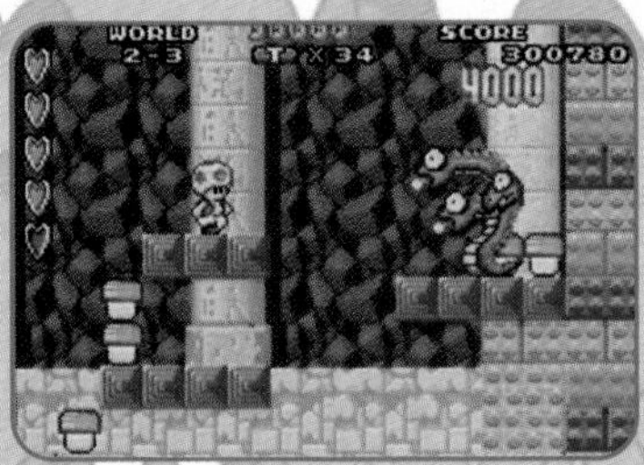

World 3-1

Back on the Home Turf

World 3-1's grassy platforms and waterfalls resemble World 1. Any character will do here. The first two plants to the right of the start point are Small Vegetables, perfect for bonking the two Red Shy Guys marching toward you. If you hit both with one shot, you'll get a Heart.

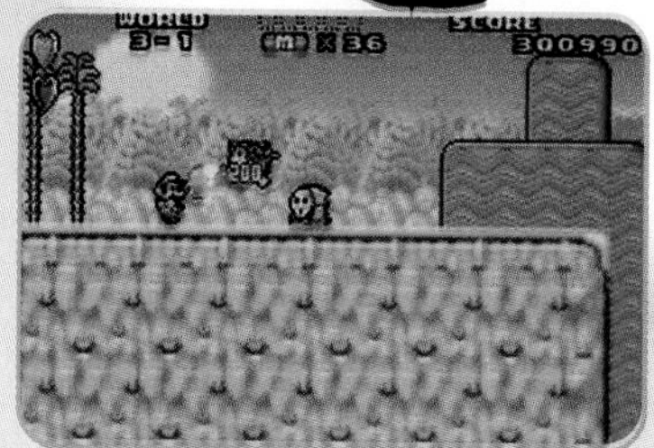

After taking out the two Shy Guys, continue right until you see a door. Above the door is a Heart Radish. When you enter, you appear on a grassy stepped platform next to a huge waterfall. Jump (or Super Jump) up the platform's three levels and grab the Ace Coin floating above it, then drop back down to the door.

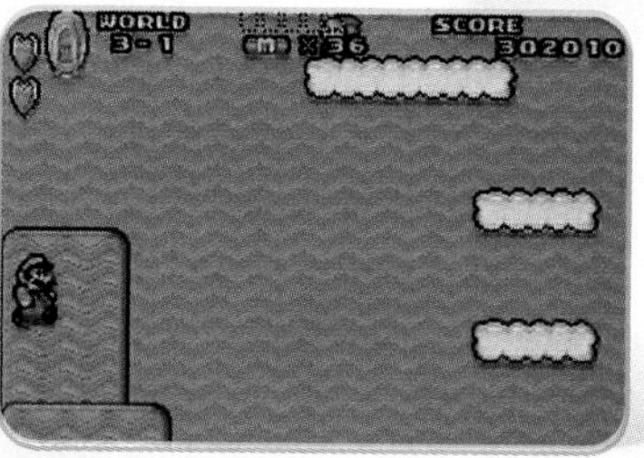

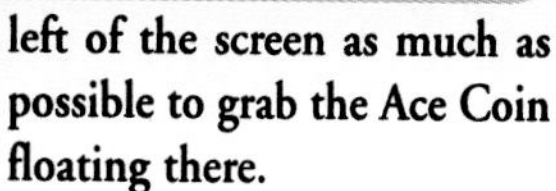

Walk off the platform's right edge—it seems as if you'll plummet off of the screen and lose a chance, but the waterfall extends down quite a distance. Stick to the left of the screen as much as possible to grab the Ace Coin floating there.

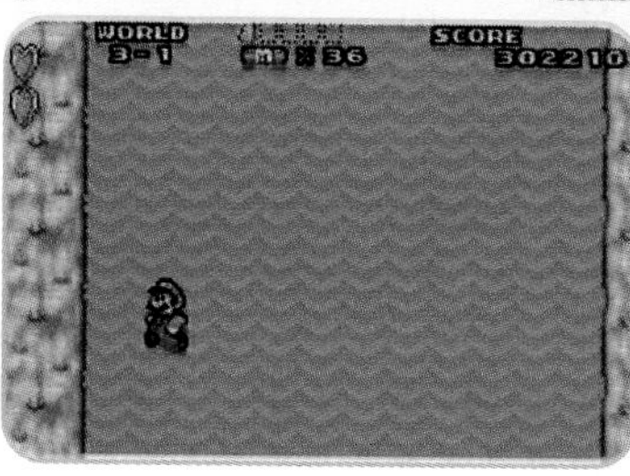

As soon as you get the Ace Coin, veer sharply toward the center to land on a small platform at the bottom. If you miss it, you'll fall off the screen and lose a chance. Once you're safely on the platform, enter the door at the bottom of it.

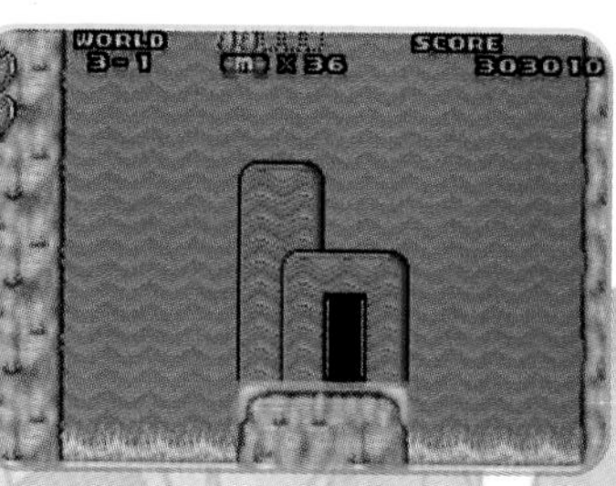

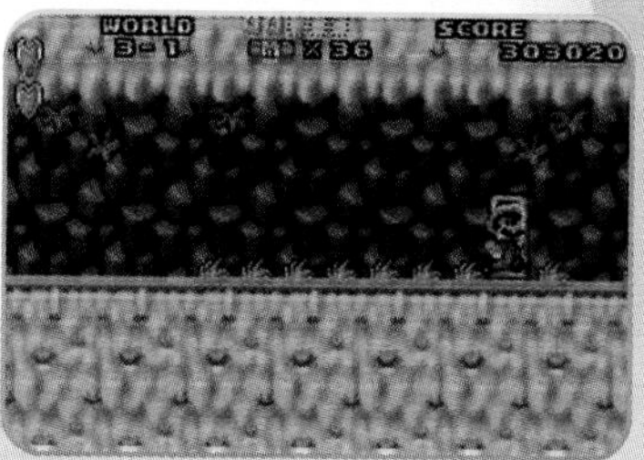

The door leads into a narrow horizontal cavern with 15 plants in a row on the floor. Pluck the sixth plant from the right to get a Magic Potion. Do not pluck any others, because each intact plant is worth a Coin in Subspace. Drop the Magic Potion right where you found it and enter the door for a Mushroom and a bunch of Coins, then enter the door at the cavern's far right to return to the top of the waterfall.

Warp to World 5

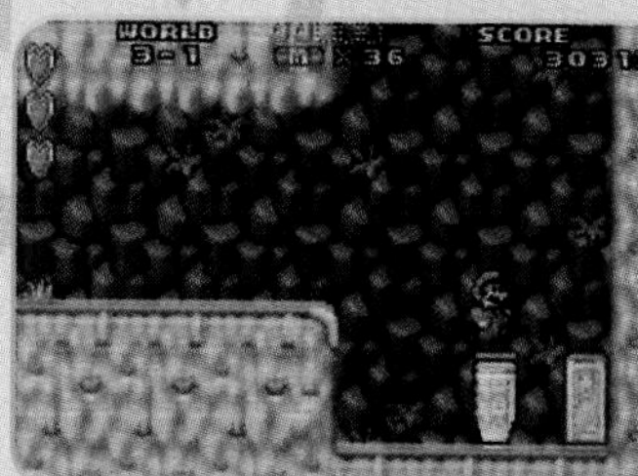

In the cavern with the plants and Magic Potion is a pipe that you can't enter. Like the seemingly useless pipe from World 1-3, this is a Warp Pipe. Drop the Magic Potion next to it, enter the door to Subspace, and enter the pipe from there. The screen will dissolve and you instantly warp to World 5-1. You forfeit all of the goodies for Worlds 3 and 4, but it's a great way to skip ahead and get through the game quicker.

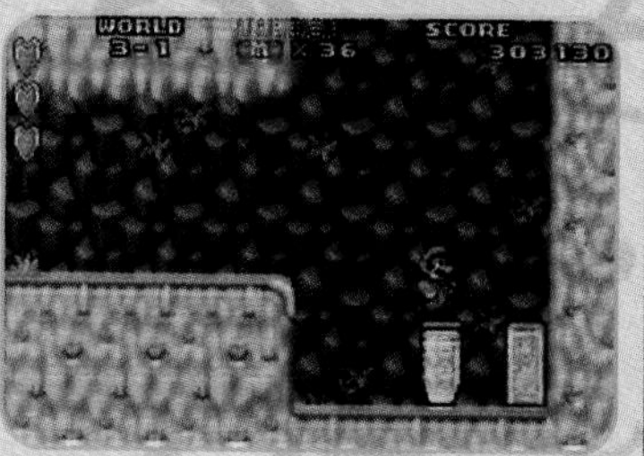

Jump onto the cloud platform hovering above the waterfall, then ascend the cloud steps, watching out for the Blue Shy Guys. Once you get to the last cloud platform, you'll see your old friend Pidgit and his magic carpet. As before, wait until Pidgit swoops toward you, then jump on his head and pick him up to gain control of the magic carpet.

Once you have the magic carpet, press ↑ to float above the waterfall, and watch out for the Beezos. Stay to the center of the screen initially; doing so will put you in a good position to grab the third Ace Coin. Continue floating up, and stay to the left to grab the fourth Ace Coin.

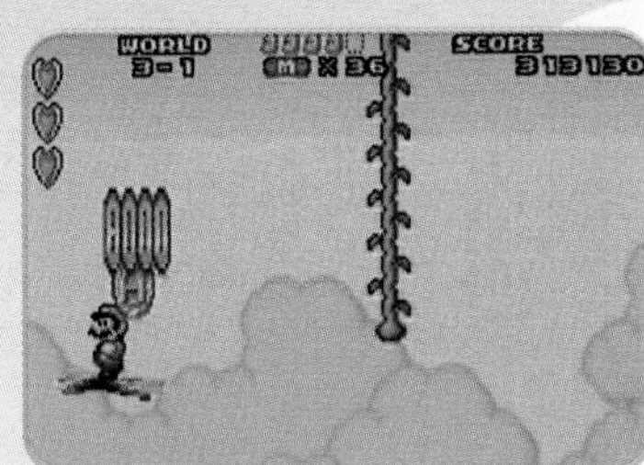

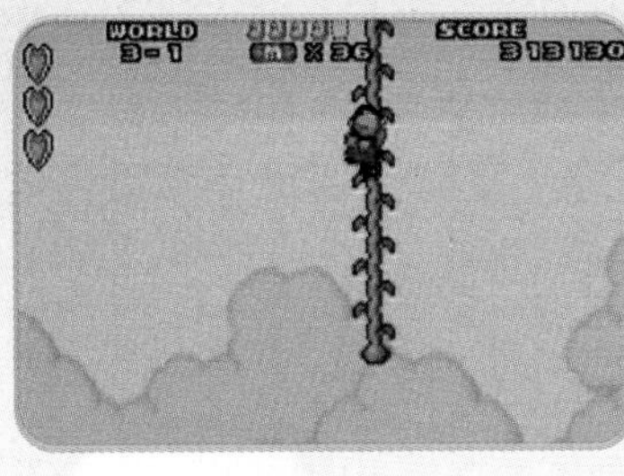

To the right of the fourth Ace Coin is a vine leading up. Float over to it to grab it and climb up past the top of the screen. The magic carpet might disappear before you can get to the vine. If that happens, steer onto a cloud and repeat the process.

At the top of the vine is a horizontal cloud platform with a Giant Blue Shy Guy. Pick up the Shy Guy and use him to dispatch the Panser to the right, above the top of the vine. Jump along the cloud platforms to the right, passing over a very thin grassy platform with two plants, until you come to a Mushroom Block and another Panser.

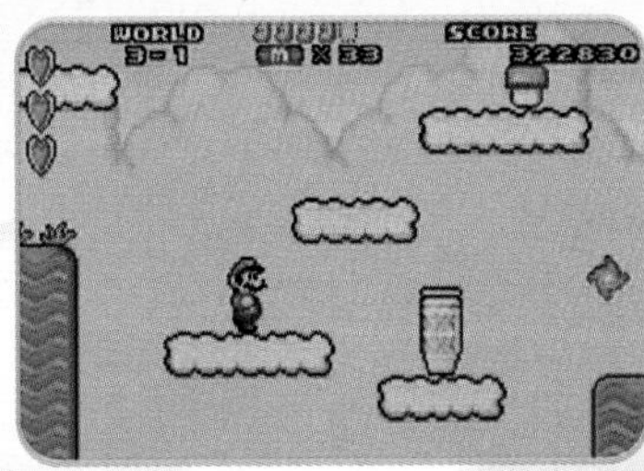

Use the Mushroom Block to take out the Panser, then backtrack to the left along the lower cloud platforms. Duck down the first pipe you come across to find six Sparks and a Spark Chaser at the bottom. If you take out at least five Sparks with the Spark Chaser, you'll get a 1UP.

Leave the pipe and continue left until you reach the narrow grassy platform with two plants. Pluck the left plant for a Magic Potion, and drop the Magic Potion near the three Mushroom Blocks on the cloud to the left. The Mushroom will appear in Subspace at the cloud platform's edge, just past the Mushroom Blocks.

After acquiring the Mushroom, continue backtracking to the left until you reach the vine you climbed. Off of the screen to the left is a hidden cloud platform with a door to the fifth Ace Coin. Peach and Luigi are the only characters that can make the Running Jump to the platform; if you're playing as Mario or Toad, you'll either have to skip the last Ace Coin for now, sacrifice your current character to return as Peach or Luigi and get the Coin, or wait until you defeat Birdo at the end of the level.

If the Giant Blue Shy Guy returned, get rid of him again and take a Running Jump off the platform's left side. The cloud platform on which you land has a door that opens into a small cavern. Pluck a plant near the stone wall to get a Bomb, and use the Bomb to blow open the wall and get the last Ace Coin.

From this cavern, you can also go directly to the Boss fight with Birdo. Super Jump off of the stone wall on the room's left side and run to the left along the top of the screen to face Birdo (and skip to this section's "Boss Fight: Birdo" section). If you'd rather face her after getting the third Mushroom, exit the cavern via the same door you came in and backtrack to the right, defeating the same enemies like you did the first time.

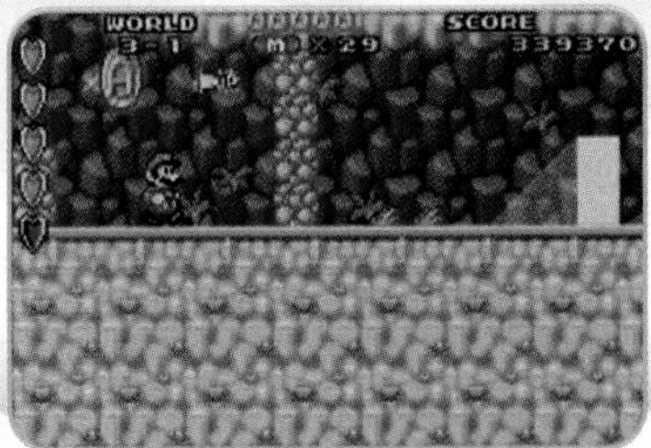

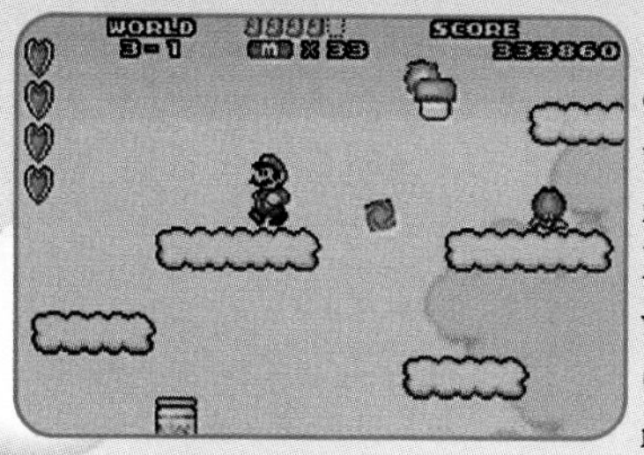

To get the third Mushroom, continue to the right along the cloud platforms until you reach the second Panser. Eliminate the Panser with whatever is handy (Mushroom Blocks work nicely), and jump onto the grassy platforms to the right of the Panser's former location.

Be careful! There's a Panser and a Blue Shy Guy on top of the grassy platform. Get rid of them by plucking a Vegetable from the ground, then descending the ladder in the middle of the platform.

The first plant to the ladder's bottom right is a Magic Potion. Position yourself so that you can see the grassy platform's entire left edge, then drop the Magic Potion.

CAUTION

Do not drop the Magic Potion at the ladder's base! Because you use ↑ to climb ladders and enter doors, you will start climbing the ladder instead of entering the door to Subspace!

When you enter Subspace, the Mushroom drops onto the platform's right edge. Climb the ladder and run over to the Mushroom before time expires—a little tricky but not impossible. Once you get the Mushroom and return from Subspace, climb the ladder and jump off of the grassy platform's right end to reach the door to Birdo's lair.

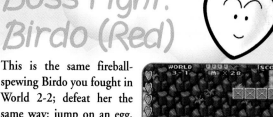

Boss Fight: Birdo (Red)

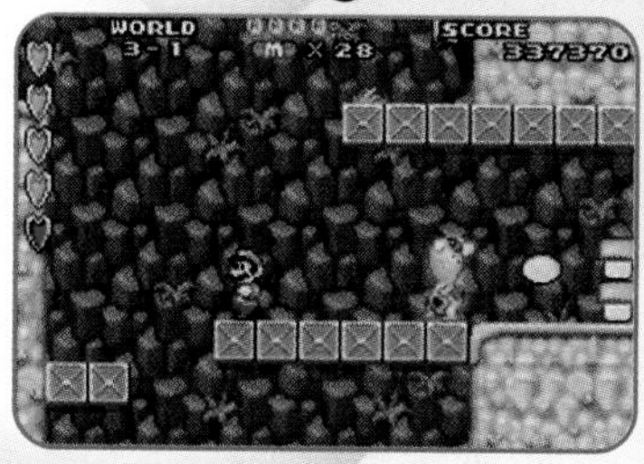

This is the same fireball-spewing Birdo you fought in World 2-2; defeat her the same way: jump on an egg, lift it up, and throw it at her. You can also throw the Mushroom Blocks to her right, if you wish. Once you defeat Birdo, grab the Crystal Ball and exit World 3-1 through the gate above.

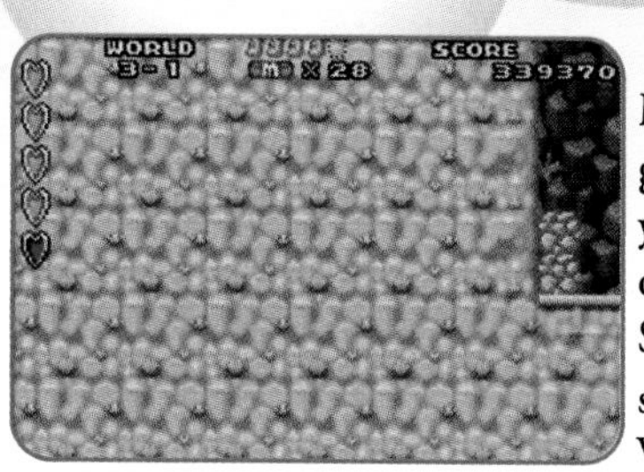

If you've been playing as Mario or Toad and couldn't get the fifth Ace Coin, now is your chance. Once the gate opens, jump on top of it and Super Jump off the top of the screen, holding → as you do. Walk right along the top of the screen until you drop down into the cavern with the Ace Coin. Super Jump back out and to the left to return to the gate and continue on your way.

World 3-2

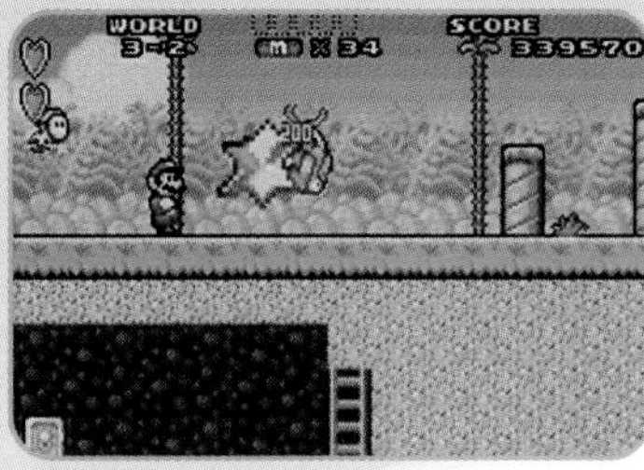

World 3-2 throws many enemies at you; expect this level to test your skills more than any previous level. As you move right from the World 3-2 start point, a Red Shy Guy on an Ostro charges as Beezos swoop by. Jump on the Red Shy Guy, pick him up, and throw him at his Ostro to defeat both and pick up a Heart.

If you need another Heart, pluck the Heart Radish to the first pillar's right, just past the Ostro. Move right past the four pillars to reach a grassy platform with two Tweeters bouncing along the top toward you. Pluck the plant at the platform's left edge for a Giant Vegetable to use against the Tweeters. If you take out five Beezos with the same shot, you get a 1UP.

To the grassy platforms' right are two pillars with two plants between them, both Small Vegetables. Pluck one of the Small Vegetables, carry it to the right, and use it to knock out the Panser under the first Ace Coin. Jump (or Super Jump) to grab the Ace Coin, then backtrack to the left slightly and pluck the second Small Vegetable.

Carry the Small Vegetable to the right, and use it to defeat the two Ostro-riding Shy Guys when they appear. If you hit a Beezo with the same shot, you get a 1UP. Above the Giant POW Block near the Ostros is the second Ace Coin. Jump (or Super Jump) to get it, then continue right.

After passing two pillars, you face a Snifit who's hopping on a third pillar. Jump on top of him, pick him up, and carry him to the right. Just before the screen's right edge is another Snifit. Take him out with the Snifit you're carrying. Until you enter a door or a pipe, all of the enemies on World 3-2's surface level are now gone, except for the Beezos near the beginning of the level.

Above and to the left of the grassy platform near the second Snifit is the third Ace Coin. Collect it, then pluck the leftmost of the three plants on the grassy platform to get a Magic Potion. Drop the Magic Potion on the grassy platform with the platform's right edge clearly in view to get a Mushroom.

The other plants on the grassy platform are Small Vegetables, good for defeating any nearby enemies that returned after you ducked through the Subspace door. To the left are two plants, both Bombs. Pluck one and drop it on top of the horizontal stone wall underneath the Ace Coin to open a passage to the level's subterranean part, then move down into it.

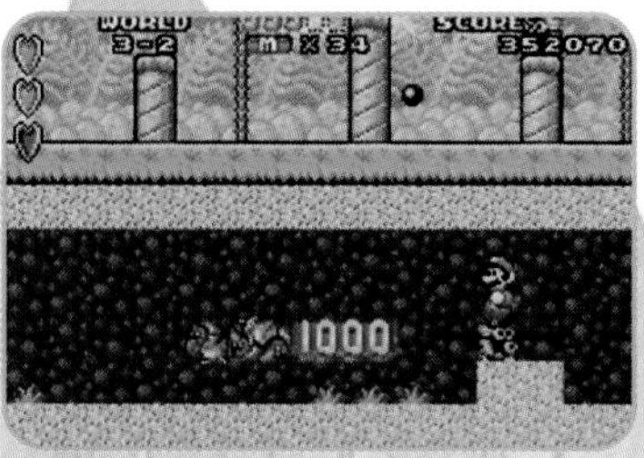

Move left and pluck one of the two plants you come across (both Small Vegetables). Use the Small Vegetable to knock out the Snifit and Tweeters a little farther to the left. If you don't hit them all with the shot, go back and grab the second Small Vegetable to finish the job.

Past the Tweeters to the left are three plants in a row. The two on the right are Small Vegetables, and the third is a 1UP Mushroom, so be sure to pluck it. At the subterranean platform's left edge is the fourth Ace Coin. Grab it, then backtrack to the right and descend the ladder.

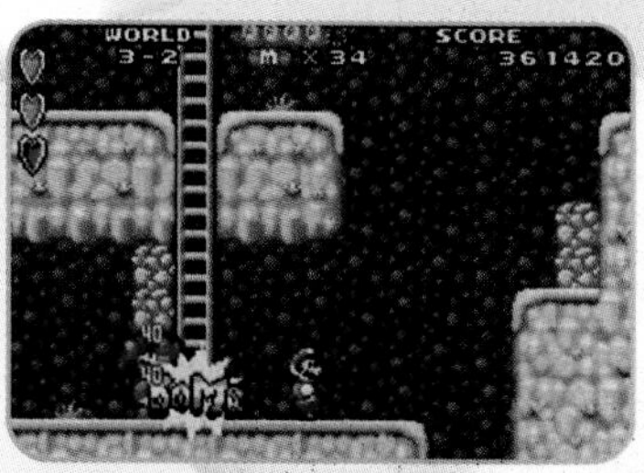

The ladder leads to a stepped platform with one plant (a Heart) on the left edge. Get the Heart if you need it, then jump left across the gap and onto the two parallel platforms with the ladders and stone walls. The three plants to the right of the upper-platform stone wall are all Bombs. Pluck the Bombs and destroy the upper and lower platforms' stone walls with them. Don't worry if you don't get the upper wall; you'll get another chance in a minute.

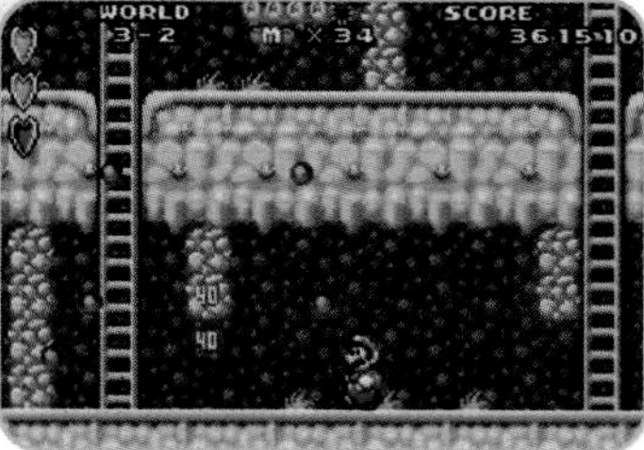

Remember: you can run while carrying a Bomb (or any other object) by pressing Ⓑ to pluck it and holding Ⓑ as you press ← or → to run. You can also hold Ⓡ while moving to run.

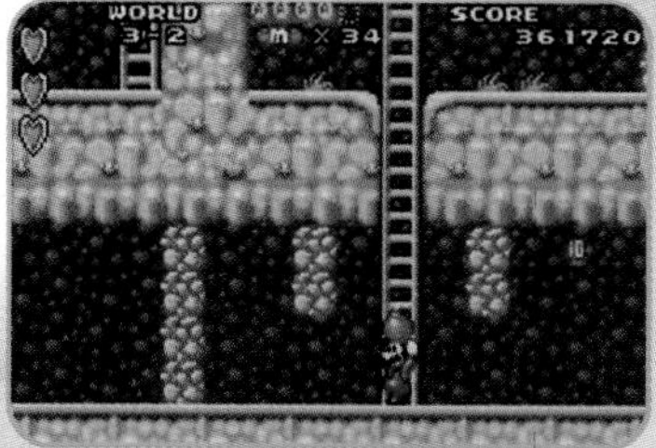

Once you Bomb open the three walls, climb down the ladder and walk left past the rightmost stone wall's remains. From left to right, the three plants to the stone wall's left are two Bombs and a Heart Radish. Pluck the Heart if you need it, then destroy the next two stone walls to the left with the two Bombs. Once you Bomb open the last wall, the three Tweeters on the other side are free to menace you. Get rid of them.

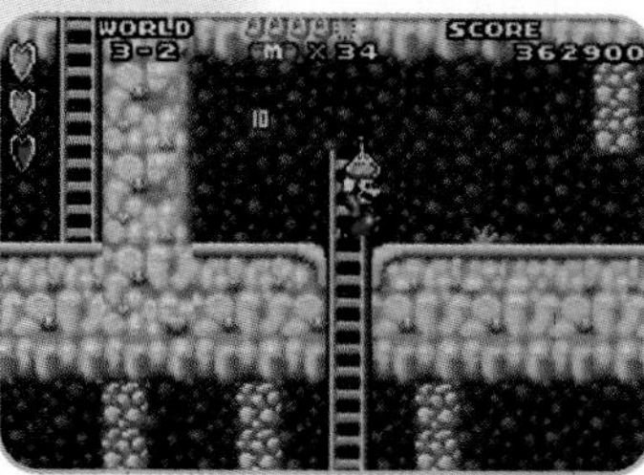

With all five stone walls destroyed, climb the now-accessible left ladder. The two plants to the ladder's right are Bombs, which come in handy if you didn't Bomb the upper platform's stone wall. The plant to the ladder's left is a Magic Potion, but don't pluck it until you take out the three Tweeters bouncing below.

Once the Tweeters are gone, pluck the Magic Potion and bring it to the left of the last Bombed stone wall on the bottom level. Drop it on the small grassy platform on the cavern's left side for a Mushroom. After getting the Mushroom, hop up onto the blue platform to the right, head right, then climb the ladder.

You appear in an upper area of the subterranean cavern below the Panser you passed on the upper level. The Panser's fireballs drop down in a straight line—avoid them. The plant to the ladder's top right is a Shell. Use it on the two Red Shy Guys marching toward you from the left, but be careful of the Shell's return bounce. The plant to the ladder's left is a Small Vegetable—good for eliminating the Shy Guys without a bounce-back.

After dispatching the Shy Guys, walk left and climb down the next ladder (the plant just before it is an unneeded Small Vegetable). At the bottom of the ladder are four grassy platforms separated by pits. A Blue Shy Guy patrols the third platform from the right, and the fifth Ace Coin hangs over the middle pit. Jump off of the second platform to grab the Ace Coin, land on the Blue Shy Guy's head, and pick him up. Toss the Shy Guy down a pit, then climb the ladder leading up from the leftmost platform.

The cavern you appear in is directly below the area on the surface where the Beezos annoyed you. They'll do the same here, even flying down into the cavern, so beware. Walk to the left to find another ladder leading down at the end of the cavern. The two plants in between are a Small Vegetable on the left and a Heart Radish on the right. Pluck the Heart if you need it, then descend the ladder to the left.

The ladder leads down past a grassy platform to the cavern floor, but you don't need to go any farther than the platform. The platform's three plants are all Bombs, and a stone wall is below and to the left of the platform. Pluck a Bomb, move to the platform's left edge, and drop the Bomb when it starts flashing. If your timing is good, it will detonate as it passes the stone wall, opening the passage. If not, you have two more chances.

Walk left past the bombed wall and climb the ladder to its left. If you take the ladder all the way up past the top of the screen, you arrive at the door to the Boss fight, but you don't need to do that yet. Instead, climb halfway up the ladder and head left across the grassy platform until you reach an area with two horizontal stone walls along the floor and two Porcupo cells beneath them.

Between the Porcupo cells are four plants. From left to right, they are: a Bomb, two Large Vegetables, and a Magic Potion. Pluck the Bomb and drop it on the horizontal stone wall to the right, then pluck the Magic Potion and drop it near the bombed wall to make the cell below visible. Enter the Magic Potion-created door to find a Mushroom in the cell under the wall you bombed.

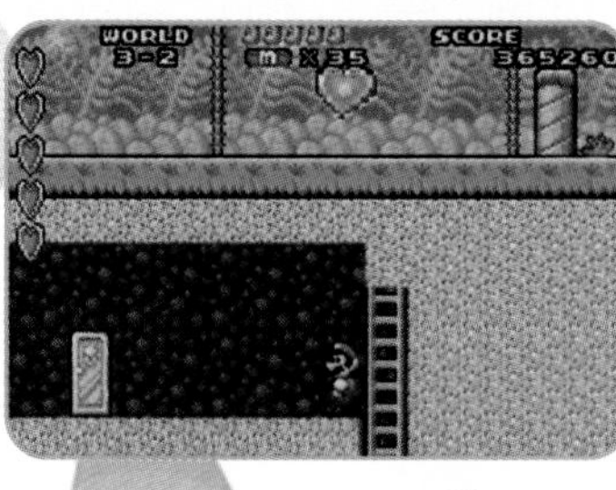

After getting the Mushroom, backtrack to the right, climb the ladder all the way up, and enter the door to Birdo's lair at the top of the ladder.

Boss Fight: Birdo (Red)

From the entrance to Birdo's lair, head left. Pluck the plant along the way if you need a Heart, then continue left to find Birdo. She still shoots eggs and fireballs, and you still need to grab her eggs in midair and hit her with them while avoiding the fireballs. Three hits and she's done for.

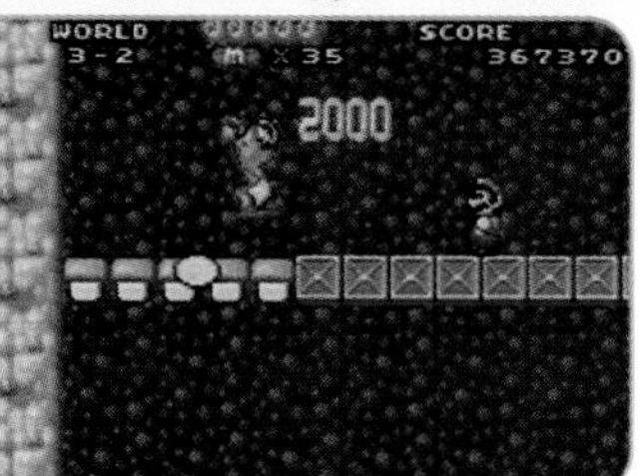

Once you defeat Birdo, grab the Crystal Ball she leaves behind, pluck one of the Mushroom Blocks from the floor to the left, and fall down to the ground below. Head to the right along the ground to find the gate. Walk through the gate to complete World 3-2.

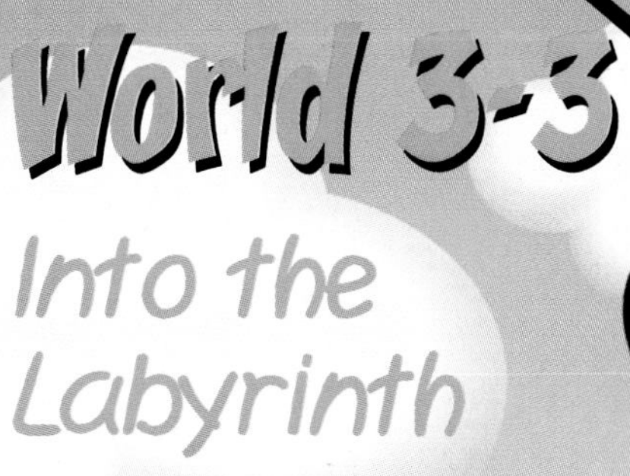

World 3-3

Into the Labyrinth

World 3-3 is a maze of doors and ladders, with Ninjis, Sparks, Shy Guys, and Snifits at every twist and turn. It's pretty intimidating at first; fortunately, every obstacle has a fairly simple solution. From the start point in World 3-3, head right. The first plant you come to is a Small Vegetable; the second is a Giant Red Shy Guy.

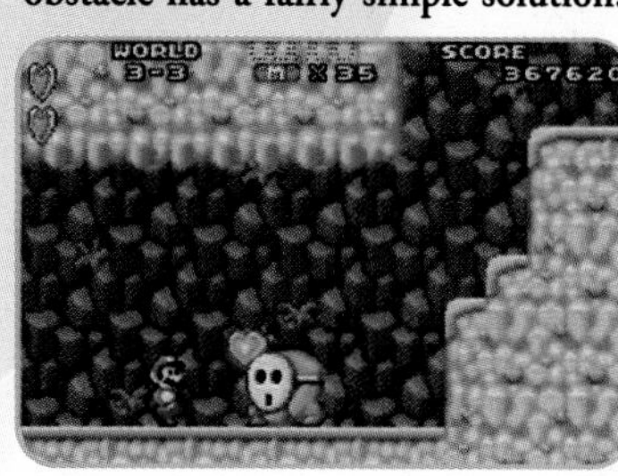

Pluck the Shy Guy and throw him. That won't defeat him, but he'll give you a Heart when he lands. Use the Small Vegetable to take him out and get another Heart for your efforts. Jump up the stepped platforms to the right to find the door leading into the next part of World 3-3.

The plant on the platform directly above the door you walk through is another Heart. Head right to see three pillars with plants between them and a POW Block and four plants to their right. The two plants between the pillars are Small Vegetables; don't pluck them yet. The first three plants to the last pillar's right are also Small Vegetables, and the fourth is a Magic Potion.

Don't pick up the POW Block, and don't pluck any plants except the Magic Potion. When you pass the third pillar, Albatosses carrying Bob-Ombs fly over you and try to drop their explosive cargo on your head. Avoid the Bob-Ombs and the Ostro-riding Red Shy Guy, and drop the Magic Potion near the tallest pillar.

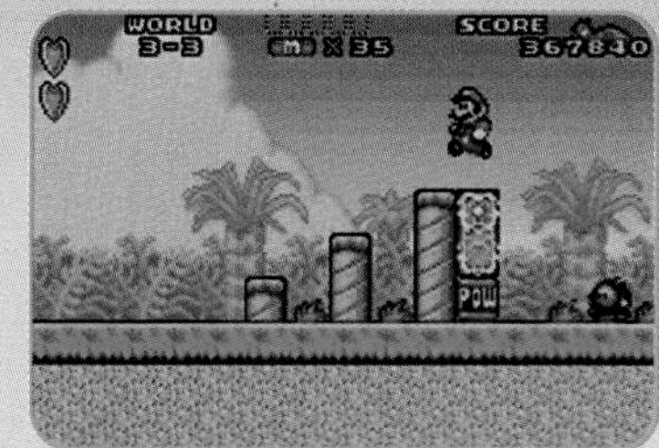

Enter Subspace to find a Mushroom on the tallest pillar. If you pick up the POW Block in Subspace and are still holding it when you return, you'll have two POW Blocks: the one in your hands and the one still on the ground. Use them to get rid of any pesky Bob-Ombs, Shy Guys, or Ostros, and head right until you reach another pillar.

Floating above the pillar is the first Ace Coin. Grab it, then continue right and go through the door just past the pillar to enter a subterranean cavern. To the cavern door's right is a Giant POW Block plant. To the door's left are three plants. From left to right, they are: a Bob-Omb with a very short fuse, a Magic Potion, and a Shell.

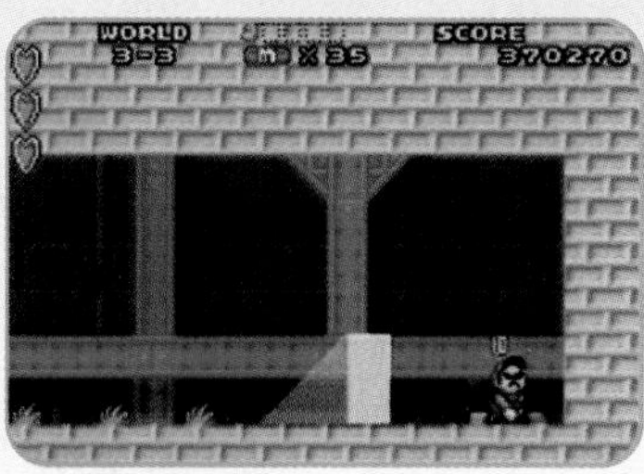

Pluck the Giant POW Block and carry it to the left. Throw it at the first two Ninjis who bounce toward you, then hold Ⓑ and run with the bouncing POW Block. By the third bounce, it should have taken out not only the two Ninjis but several other Ninjis and Sparks on the platforms overhead, and you should get at least one 1UP.

All plants and enemies return if you go through a door and reenter the area you left. You can perform the "follow the bouncing POW Block" trick, then run back to the right, go through the cavern entrance, and return to the cavern again to repeat the trick over and over and over, collecting 1UPs.

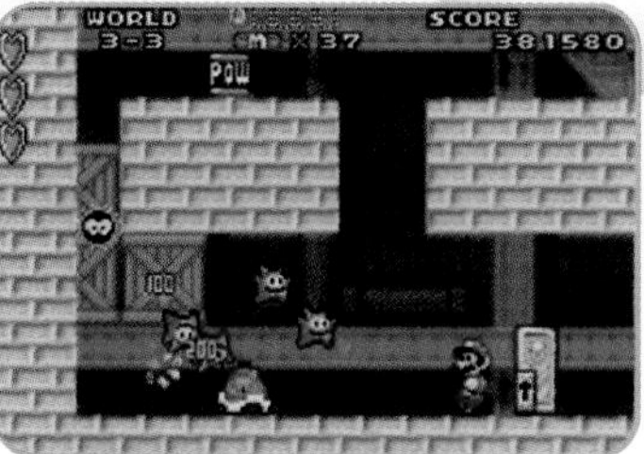

After using the Giant POW Block, backtrack to the entrance and pluck the Shell to the door's immediate left. Carry the Shell all the way to the cavern's left end and use it to knock out the four Ninjis there. Once they're gone, nothing on the cavern floor can harm you, with the possible exception of the Shell making a return trip.

Backtrack to the cavern entrance again and pluck the Magic Potion (the rightmost remaining plant). Carry the Magic Potion all the way to the cavern's left end and drop it to the ladder's immediate left. Make sure the ladder platform's entire left end is visible, then enter the Magic Potion doorway and climb the ladder in Subspace to snag a Mushroom from the platform.

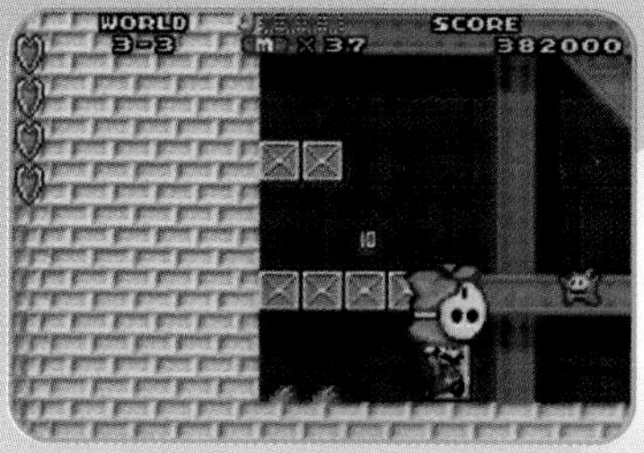

Enter the door to the ladder's bottom right. You appear at the bottom of a long vertical cavern with three plants to your left and a Ninji to your right. From left to right, the three plants are: a Small Vegetable, a Heart, and a Giant Red Shy Guy. Use either the Shy Guy or the Vegetable to eliminate the Ninji, pluck the Heart if you need it, then start jumping onto the platforms above.

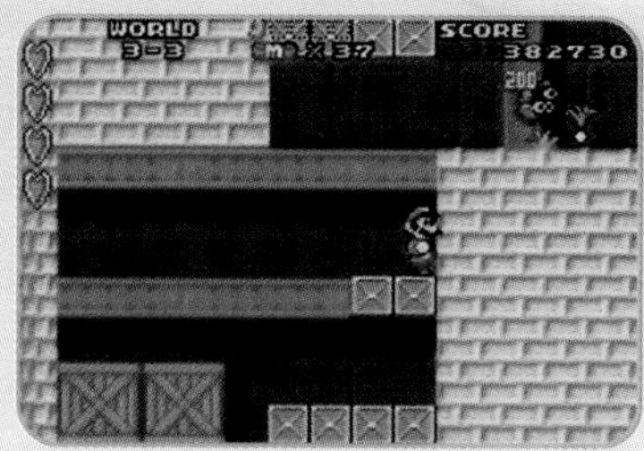

The platforms follow a repeating pattern: one long blue platform below a smaller blue platform below a ledge with an enemy and a plant on it. Jump onto the long blue platforms and study the enemy on the ledge's movement pattern. Time your next jumps so that you get onto the ledge safely and can grab the plant (usually a Small Vegetable) to use on the enemy. The third platform series has a 1UP Mushroom instead of a Small Vegetable.

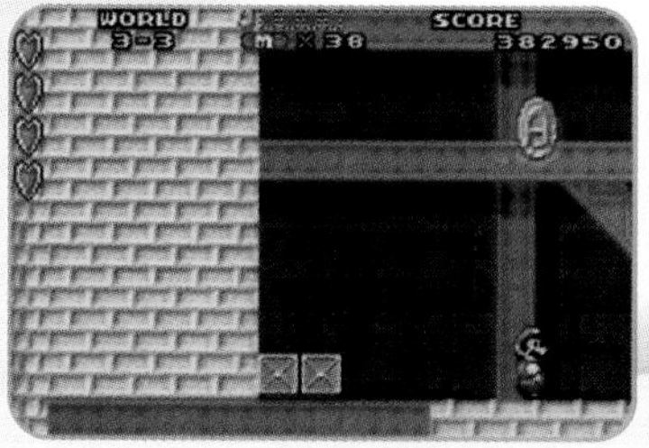

At the top of the platforms, the cavern extends up farther, but there's no way to get up there. The second Ace Coin floats above the last ledge. Grab it, then return to the bottom of the cavern and exit via the door you entered through. The enemies will have returned, so watch out for the Sparks and Ninjis.

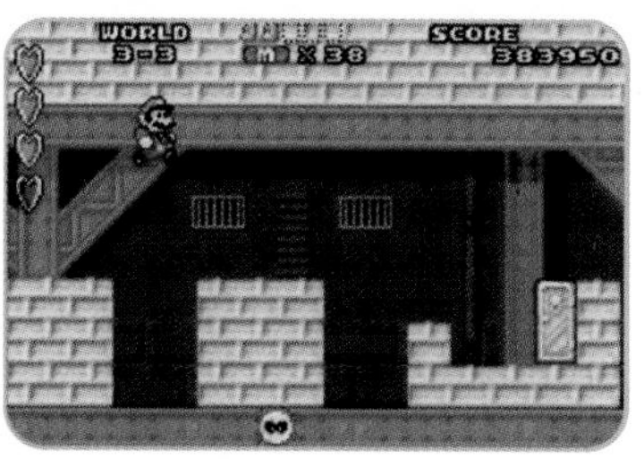

The other door on the ground is locked, and the only other door in the cavern is back to the right on the last upper platform. No one except Luigi can Super Jump to this platform. Luckily, there are two other ways of getting there. The first is to climb the ladder next to the door you just came through and jump along the platforms to the right until you reach the door. Use the Giant POW Block trick from before to clear out all Sparks and Ninjis on the upper platforms before you do.

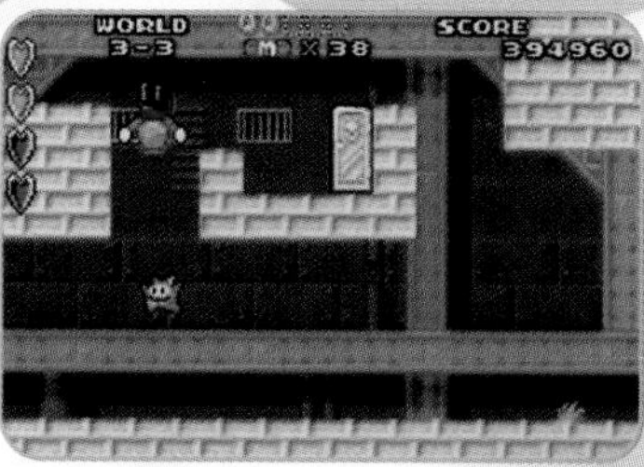

The other way to get to the door on the rightmost upper platform is trickier but works just as well. Take out the two jumping Ninjis to the right, then grab a stationary Ninji at the cavern's left end, carry him to the right. Below the platform with the door, drop him on the ground, jump on his head, and use the Ninji's jump to augment your own.

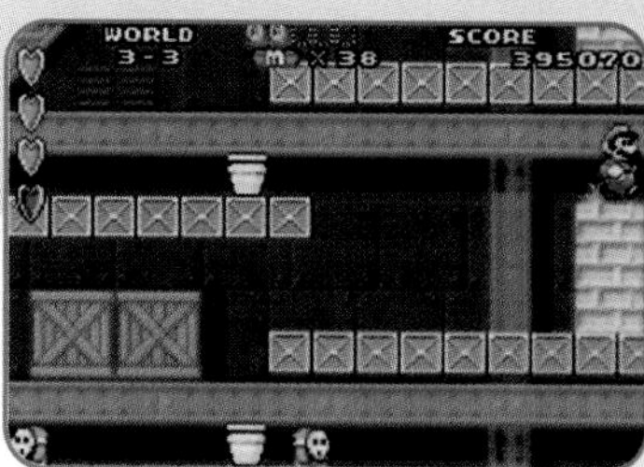

However you choose to get to the platform with the door, enter the door once you're there. Like the last vertical cavern, this one has a repeating platform theme: short stone platforms on the left with Shy Guy Generators that pump out Shy Guys, and long blue platforms to the right.

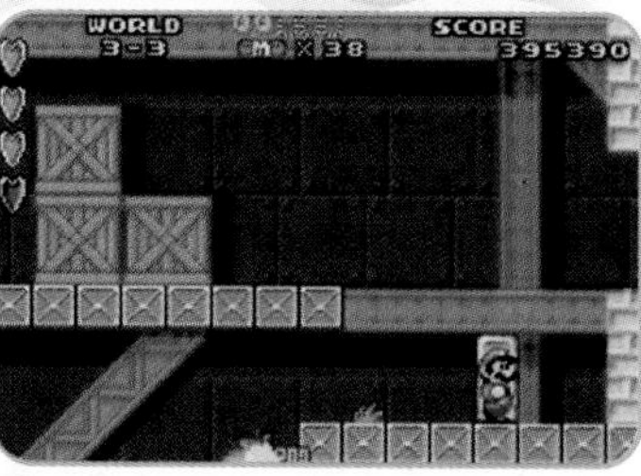

If you try to jump straight up from platform to platform, you'll likely run into many Shy Guys and lose many Hearts. Hop up onto a platform, run to the right until you appear on the screen's left side, then keep running right and jump onto the next platform. Repeat as necessary until you get to the top and find a door on the screen's right side.

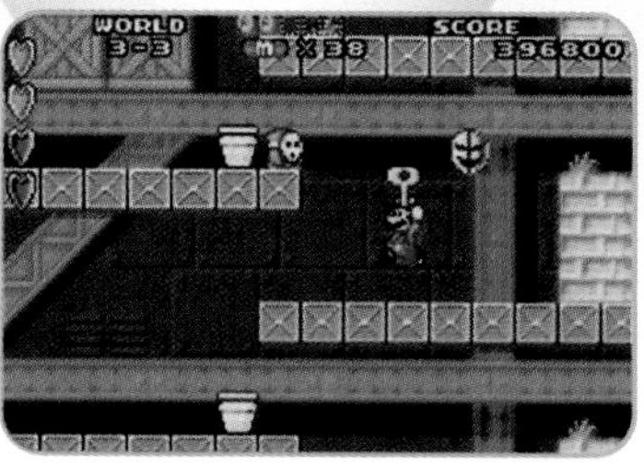

This door takes you to Phanto's lair and the Key you need to open the locked door you saw earlier. Grab the Key, leave the room, and drop the Key. Pluck the Shell next to Phanto's door and set it in motion. Pick up the Key and move as quickly as you can all the way to the bottom of the vertical cavern, keeping the Shell ahead of you. Make good use of the cavern's left-to-right wrapping structure.

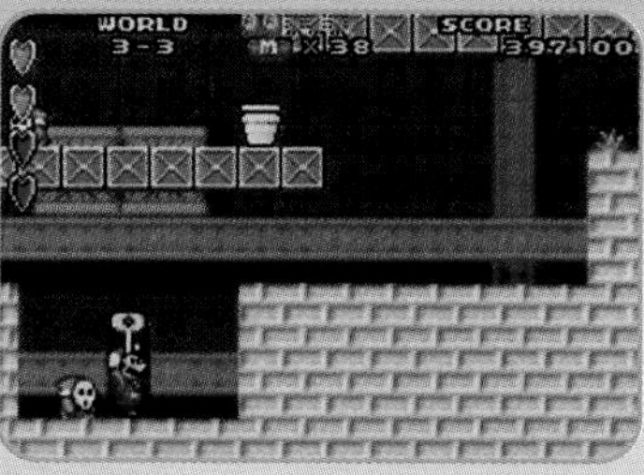

Once you reach the bottom, drop the Key and wait on the small ledge to the door's left. The Shell continues bouncing in front of the door, and the Shy Guy Generator keeps pumping out targets for it. Sit back, relax, and watch the Hearts and 1UPs roll in. Once you have four full Hearts and 99 chances, jump on top of the Shell, throw it up onto the platform to the right, then pick up the Key and get through the door before the Shell comes back to hit you.

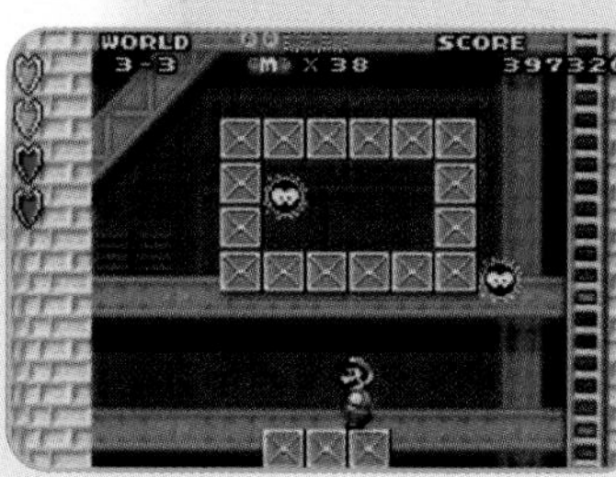

With Key in hand (drop it if Phanto gets too close, of course), return to open the locked door. The door takes you to another vertical cavern, with several cross-shaped platforms and lots of Sparks. Jump up from cross to cross, avoiding the Sparks, until you come to a blue box platform with a Spark inside and another outside. On the way up, you'll pass two plants—both are Heart Radishes, so pluck 'em if you need 'em.

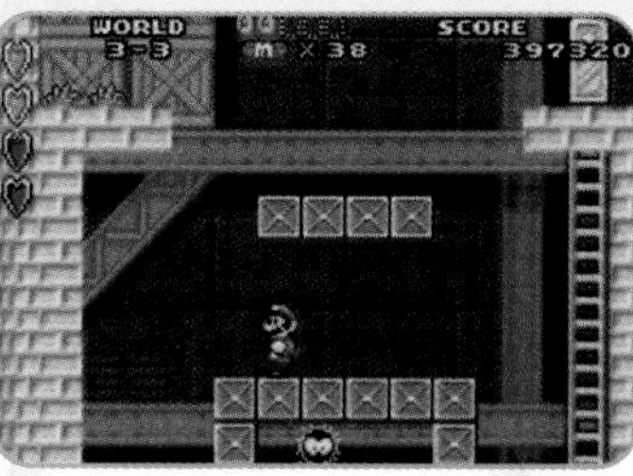

Jump up into the blue box platform and do your best to miss the Sparks. It's not easy (especially with the one inside the box), and you might lose a Heart or two. Even if a Spark hits you, the important thing is to jump to the top of the blue box platform and, from there, jump to the horizontal blue platform above it.

Above the horizontal blue platform is a cluster of blue blocks with Sparks and Ninjis patrolling it. To the left is a small ledge with two plants, both Heart Radishes. Jump up onto the blue blocks (the safest place to jump is right up into the middle of them). Two ladders are a little farther up—one along the right wall and one along the left.

Jump onto the right ladder and follow it up. If you accidentally jump onto the left ladder, climb all the way to the top and fall off to the right, snagging the right ladder as you do. From the top of the right ladder, jump onto the platform to the right and pluck the rightmost plant (a Magic Potion). For a Mushroom, drop the Magic Potion on the ladder's left side.

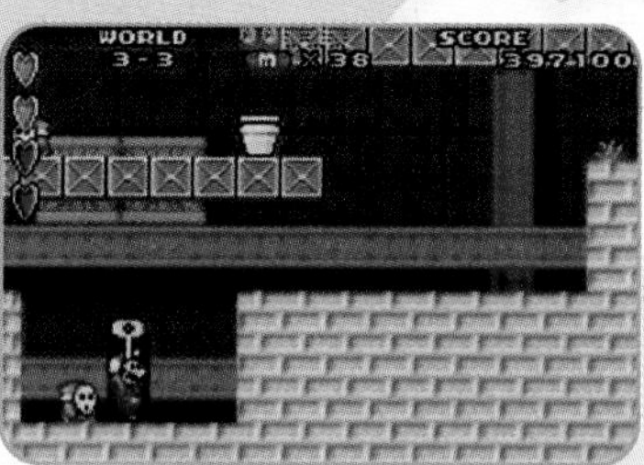

From left to right, the other four plants at the top of the ladder are: a Small Vegetable, a POW Block, another Small Vegetable, and a Heart. Grab the POW Block and fall down the ladder. Take out all five enemies and get a 1UP by dropping the POW Block just before you hit the cluster of blue blocks, then enter the door below and to the right of the blue blocks.

The door takes you to the same vertical cavern you entered earlier, to the area above the last platform you were able to reach. Jump up the blue platforms to the right and keep heading up until you get to a long brick platform to the left. There is a Shell plant here—perfect for getting rid of the meddlesome Shy Guys nearby.

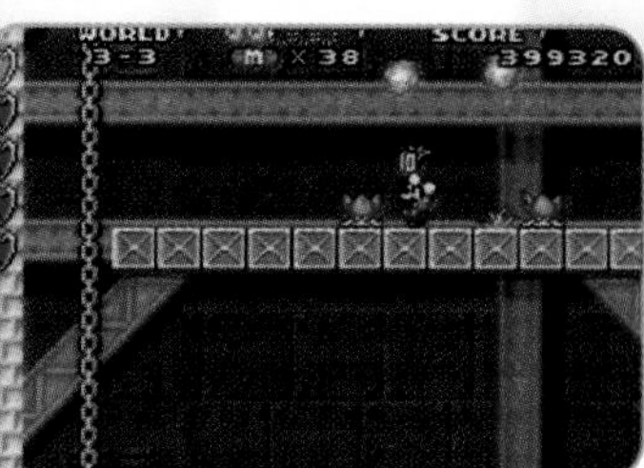

Fireballs appear to be raining from the sky. Two Pansers, high on the platform above, are launching their best volleys at you. Head to the brick platform's left end and climb the chain up to the Pansers' long blue platform. Wait until they fire, then hop over them and pluck the plants next to them to get Small Vegetables with which to take them out.

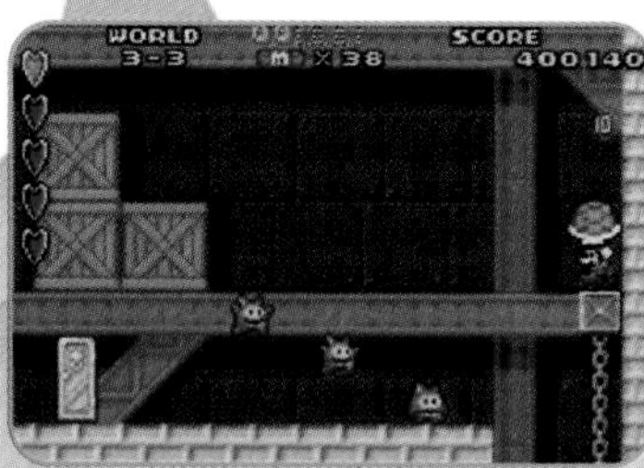

Once you've dealt with the Pansers, jump onto the last chain on the cavern's right side and climb to the top. On the brick platform to the left of the chain are three Ninjis, and on the tiny platform above the chain is a Shell plant. Use the Shell on the Ninjis, collect the Hearts they give up, then pass through the door on the platform's left side.

You're even farther up the vertical canyon now. Use the Small Vegetable plants to the door's left to dispatch the nearby Sparks, then head up the platforms. In this area are five Cherries; if you collect them all, you get a very handy Starman.

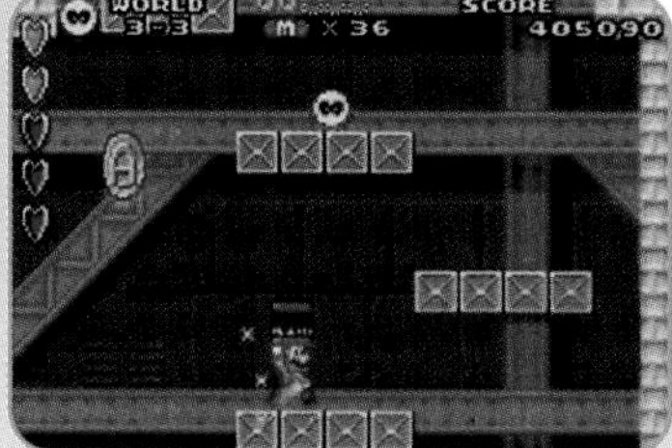

Inside the C-shaped blue platform is a POW Block. Pluck it and carry it with you as you move farther up the cavern. Drop it on the blue platform next to the floating Ace Coin to get rid of three Sparks, then run off the end of the platform to get the Ace Coin.

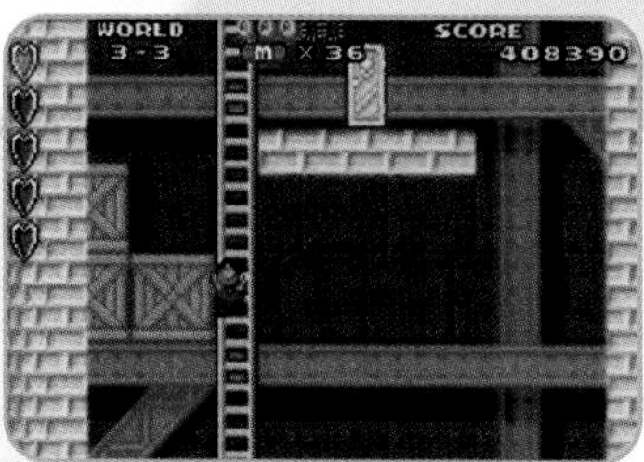

Keep jumping up along the platforms until you reach the ladder above the top one. Jump onto the ladder and climb to the top of the screen. To the ladder's upper right is a brick platform with a door in the middle. Jump off of the ladder onto the platform and enter the door.

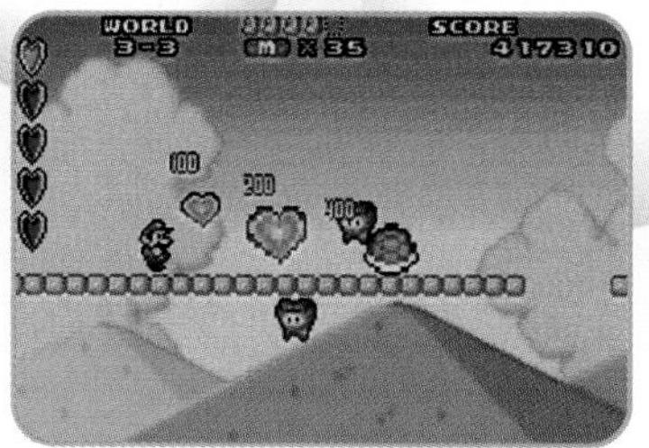

The door leads to the area just before the Boss fight. Jump up from the brick platform above the door to get the fourth Ace Coin. After getting the Ace Coin, head right and jump up onto the bridge. The plant at the beginning of the bridge is a Shell. Pluck it, toss it to the right, then run along behind it as it takes out Ninjis and then disappears down a gap in the bridge.

Jump over the gap and continue right until you come to a gate with a Crystal Ball in front. Above the brick wall to the gate's right is the last Ace Coin. Grab it, lift the Crystal Ball to open the gate, then proceed through the gate to fight Robirdo.

Boss Fight: Robirdo

Just when you'd gotten used to thinking of Birdo as a creampuff, along comes Robirdo—a mechanized, egg-hurling engine of destruction. Robirdo has three attacks: firing eggs (which are larger than Birdo's and take longer to lift), a full-body charge that runs you over, and a ground-pounding jump that sends shockwaves along the floor and leaves you stunned and vulnerable to Robirdo's eggs or charges.

Approach Robirdo to begin the fight, then run back to the leftmost chain hanging from the ceiling. When Robirdo launches an egg, grab it and throw it back at Robirdo. To avoid being stunned when Robirdo does a ground pound, jump just before Robirdo lands. When Robirdo charges, leap onto the chain, climb to safety, and leave the chain only after Robirdo runs under you, smacks into the wall, and backs up to its starting position.

Hit Robirdo with five eggs to defeat it. As soon as you hit it with an egg, jump onto a chain and climb, because Robirdo charges once it recovers. There are four Hearts in the room—one floating next to the chains and one on each side of the room. When you defeat Robirdo, an exit doorway appears. Go through to complete World 3.

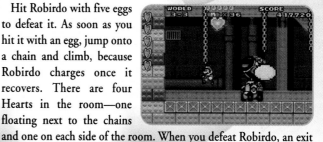

World 4-1

Ice Adventures

World 4 is a frozen wonderland with slick platforms and strange new enemies. You might want to play as Peach for this level, because her hovering jump can give you much greater control on the treacherous ice. World 4-1 starts you off on a long horizontal ice platform with two plants to the right. The first is a Small Vegetable and the second is a Giant Vegetable.

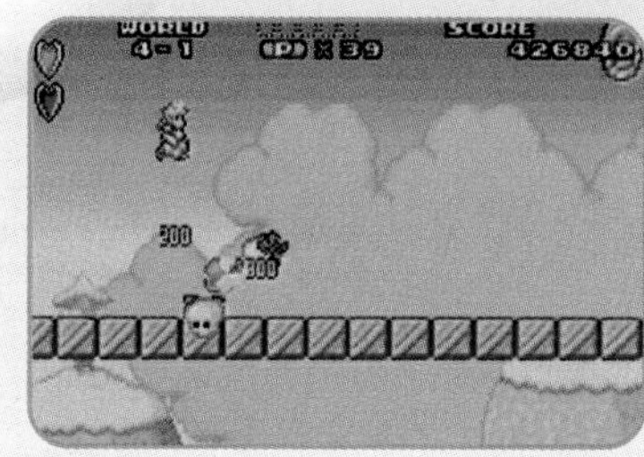

Head right, pluck a Vegetable "on the run," and throw it at the first of two Flurrys that start running toward you from the right. The first Ace Coin is just past the Flurrys, hovering over the first Trouter. Either knock out the Trouter and Super Jump to get it, or jump on the Trouter's back and jump up from there.

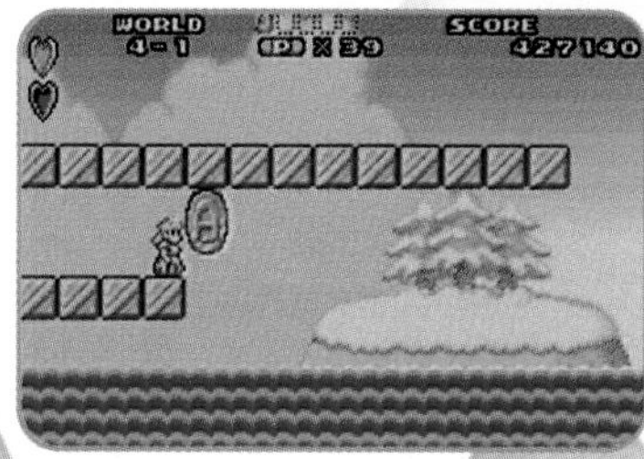

Continue right, avoiding Flurrys, Trouters, and gaps in the ice. When you come to two long, icy platforms running parallel to each other, stay on the bottom one until the end to get the second Ace Coin, then jump onto the upper platform and continue right.

Just past the end of the upper platform are two more parallel platforms, much shorter than the last pair. Hovering over the top one is a Heart. Collect it if you need it. Wait for all of the Flurrys to skate off of the lower platform and into one of the gaps, and then head down to the lower platform.

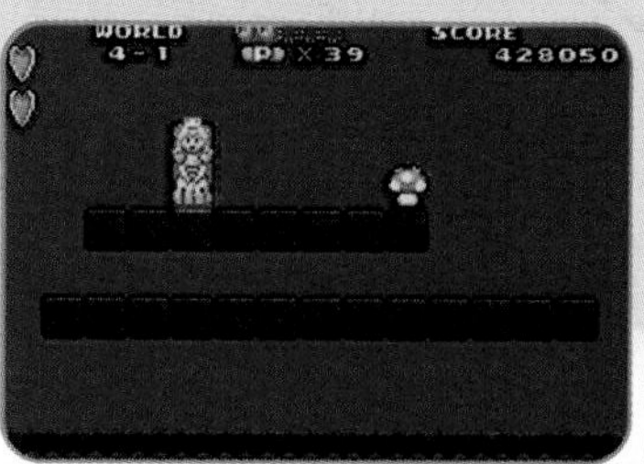

The only plant on the lower platform is a Magic Potion. Pluck it and drop it on the upper platform. Make sure the entire upper platform is visible on the screen, then enter the door and collect a Mushroom. Be careful when maneuvering around Subspace; the ground is still very icy, and it's not hard to slide off of the platform and lose a chance.

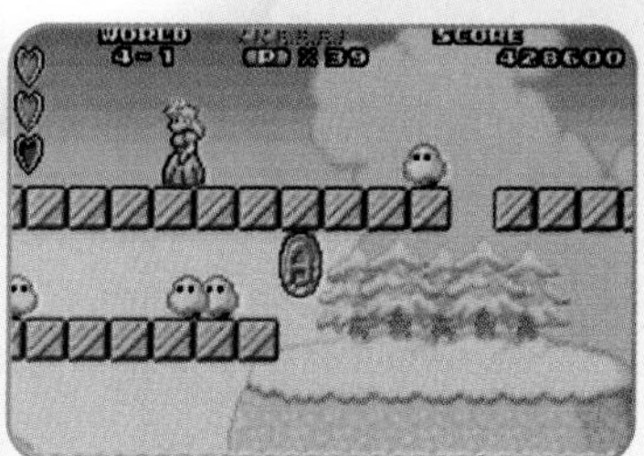

Upon returning from Subspace, continue right, staying on the lower of the two parallel platforms. Flurrys will attack you from both directions, so either use the five plants on the lower platform (most of which are Vegetables), or lure the Flurrys off of one of the platform's edges. At the end of the lower platform is the third Ace Coin; collect it, hop to the upper level, and continue right.

The platform ends in a set of icy stairs. Jump off of the stairs, over the gap, and onto the snowy ledge to the right. You'll be relieved to see that you have much better traction on the snow. The plant on the ledge is a Small Vegetable. On the snowy platform just up and to the right are two more plants: a Magic Potion and a Small Vegetable. Bring the Magic Potion to the lower left snowy ledge and drop it to find a Mushroom on the icy outcropping.

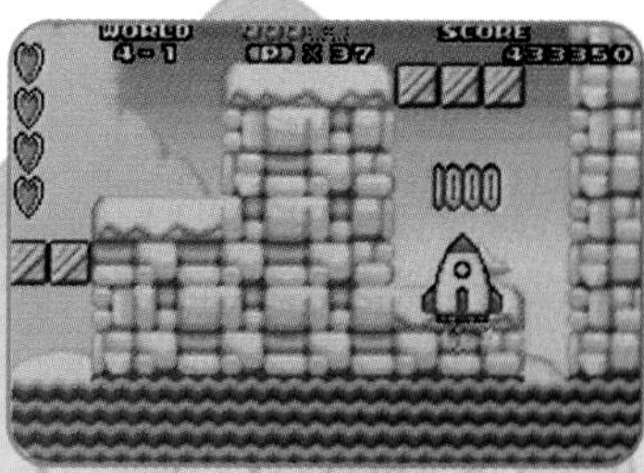

You've gone as far as you can to the right, and there doesn't seem to be anywhere else to go. Before you start backtracking to see if you've missed something, pluck the last plant on the right, just under the ledge where you found the Magic Potion. Instead of a Vegetable or a Heart, you pull a Rocket Ship out of the ground! It flies up and deposits you at the beginning of the second half of World 4-1 before detonating overhead.

The fifth and final Ace Coin is hovering far out of your reach over the icy platform. Fortunately, a Shy Guy obligingly rides his Autobomb down the stairs to the right and heads toward you. Jump on his head, then crouch down for a Super Jump. Jump to grab the Ace Coin as you pass under it, then head up the stairs to the right and onto the next snowy platform.

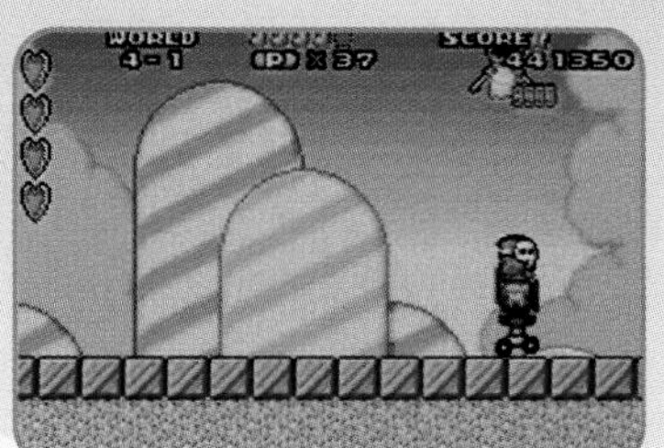

Run to the right along the icy ledge, onto the snowy ledge, and down onto a lower icy ledge. A Red Shy Guy riding an Autobomb rolls toward you from the right. The fourth Ace Coin hovers high overhead. You need a boost to reach it, and the Shy Guy is perfect for that. Jump on his head and soar upward to get the Ace Coin, then continue right, past the snow pillar and onto the snowy ledge.

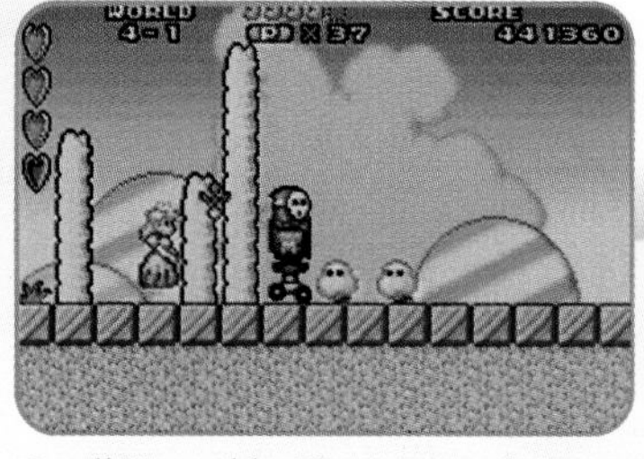

To the right of the snowy ledge is another drop-off and a series of snow pillars with two plants between them. The left plant is a Heart Radish; the right is a Small Vegetable. Grab the Heart if you need it, then pluck the Small Vegetable. Hop up on the second-to-last pillar and hit the Shy Guy on the Autobomb to the right.

With the Shy Guy and his Autobomb out of commission, hop onto the tall pillar to the right and jump off, leaping over the heads of the enemies below, and hightail to the right. Vault a few more pillars and Flurrys until you come to a long, flat icy platform with a set of ice stairs at the right end.

Two pipes are on this platform. The left one has a Shell in it, and the right one has a Small Vegetable and a 1UP Mushroom. Grab the 1UP, then the Shell. Throw the Shell off of the snowy platform's right edge; it'll knock out the Flurry below and start rebounding back and forth between the ledge and the bottom step of a snowy staircase.

Jump down to the platform that the Shell is skating along. A Shy Guy and Autobomb roll down the steps and charge you from the right. Leap over them and let the Shell take them out. Head up the steps and continue right.

Just right of the snowy steps is a Crystal Ball on a platform in front of a closed gate. Pick up the Crystal Ball to open the gate, and walk through it to complete World 4-1 without even having to fight a Boss!

World 4-2

Again, you'll probably want to pick Peach as your character because her floating jump gives you good control on ice. Pick up the Giant POW Block to the right of World 4-2's start point and use it to get rid of the Porcupos to the POW Block's right. Climb the vine at the screen's right edge to reach the upper level and begin the main part of World 4-2.

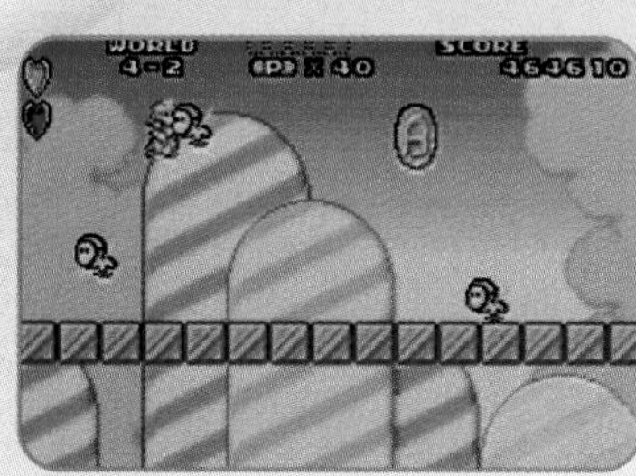

On the icy platform above and to the vine's top right are two plants, both Small Vegetables. Pluck one and carry it up to the next icy platform to the right before continuing right. Waves of Beezos come at you from the right, so stay on your toes and don't jump unless you must. The first Ace Coin hovers above this platform a little farther right.

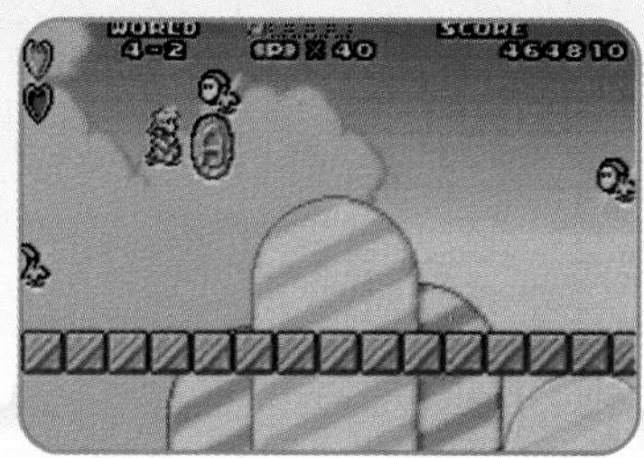

Continue right, and two Flurrys appear. Jump over them while avoiding the seemingly endless Beezos. Just past the point where the Flurrys first come into view is the second Ace Coin, hovering above the platform at the same height as the first one. Grab it and continue right.

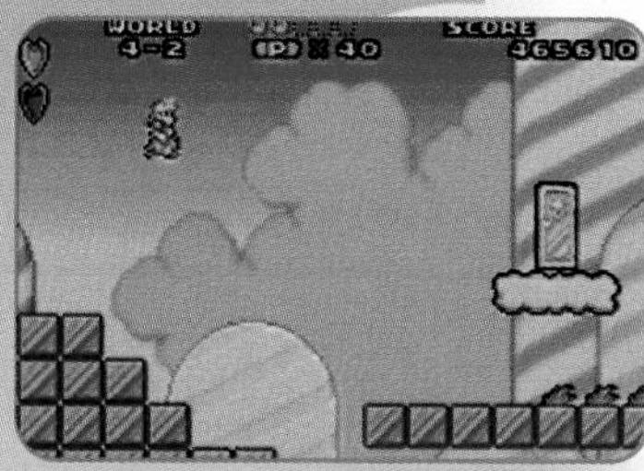

The icy platform ends, depositing you onto another overlapping one just below. Keep dodging Beezos and watch out for the Flurrys you passed; if you slow down, they might hit you from behind. When the lower platform ends, jump onto the one just above it and continue right until it ends at an icy staircase.

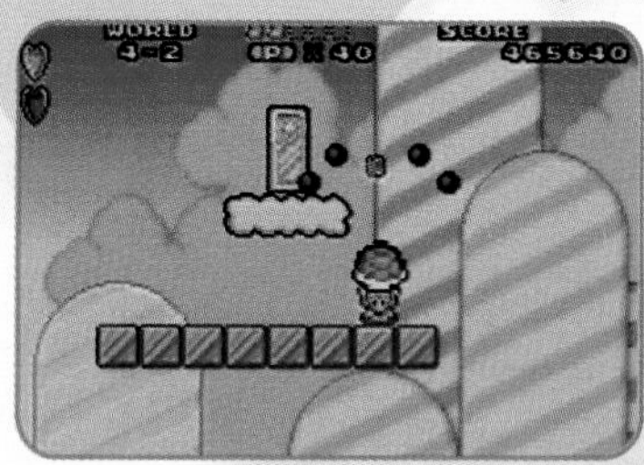

Leap across the gap following the stairs to reach a very short icy platform with three plants and a door hovering overhead on a cloud. From left to right, the plants are: two Small Vegetables and a Shell, none of which are terribly useful at the moment. Hop up onto the cloud and enter the door.

On the other side of the door is a similar cloud platform with a spouting whale below it. Three Blue Shy Guys and one Giant Blue Shy Guy walk along the top of the whale. If you need Hearts, pick up the Giant Blue Shy Guy and throw him so that he won't hit the others. Every time you do this, he will give you a Heart.

The whale itself is not dangerous, but its spout can be. You can ride on top of the water spray, but if you run into it from the side, you lose a Heart. The same is true for the several similar whales scattered throughout World 4.

Get rid of the Shy Guys, then jump over the gap to the whale's left to land on a non-spouting whale with three plants on its back. From left to right, they are: a Magic Potion, a Small Vegetable, and a Heart Radish. Pluck the Magic Potion and drop it where you found it to get a Mushroom (you'll find it sitting on the whale's tail in Subspace).

The next Ace Coin is on the last whale's tail, right next to a snowy platform with a pipe and a plant. Collect it and hop onto the snowy platform. The plant to the pipe's right is a 1UP Mushroom; grab it.

Once you have the Mushroom, move to the right and continue along the icy platforms near the top of the screen. Collect the Cherries hovering above the platforms. At the end of the second platform, drop off to the right onto the snowy platform with three plants. All three of the plants are Small Vegetables, perfect for popping the bubble around the 1UP Mushroom sitting on the whale's tail to the left.

Collect the 1UP Mushroom, then proceed to the next snowy platform to the right. The three plants on this platform are a Small Vegetable, a Heart Radish, and another Small Vegetable. On the next platform to the right, the three plants are (again, left to right): a Small Vegetable, a Giant POW Block, and a Magic Potion. Don't pluck them just yet.

Pluck the Magic Potion and drop it at the bottom of the broken icy stairs to the third snowy platform's right. The Mushroom appears on the very last ice step in Subspace. Grab it very carefully; it's very easy to misjudge the jump or slide off of the ice into the frigid waters below.

After getting the Mushroom, continue right and jump onto the second whale following the broken ice steps. If you're feeling confident, you might want to take the Giant POW Block and toss it in front of you while jumping from whale back to whale back, taking out Snifits and Shy Guys as you do. The third Ace Coin floats above the fifth whale's tail. Grab the Ace Coin and continue right.

Warp to 6-1

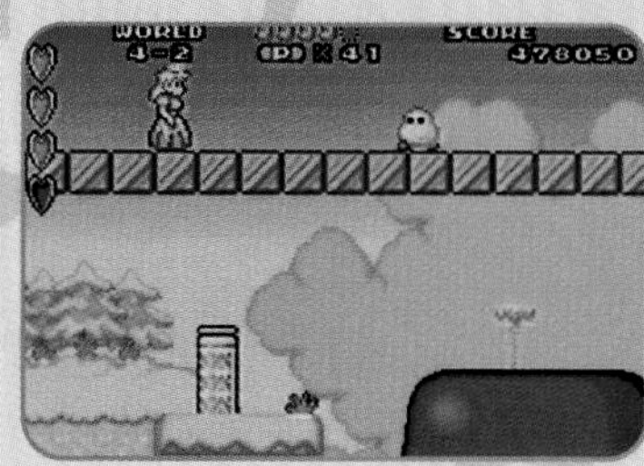

If you try to enter the pipe to the 1UP Mushroom's left, you'll find that you can't—it's a Warp Pipe. Grab a Magic Potion and drop it next to the pipe (the easiest one to bring over is the one you used to get the second Mushroom). When you enter the pipe from Subspace, you are transported to World 6-1. As with any Warp Pipe, skipping worlds means you won't get the Ace Coins in those worlds unless you go back for them, but this is a dandy way to get to the end of the game more quickly.

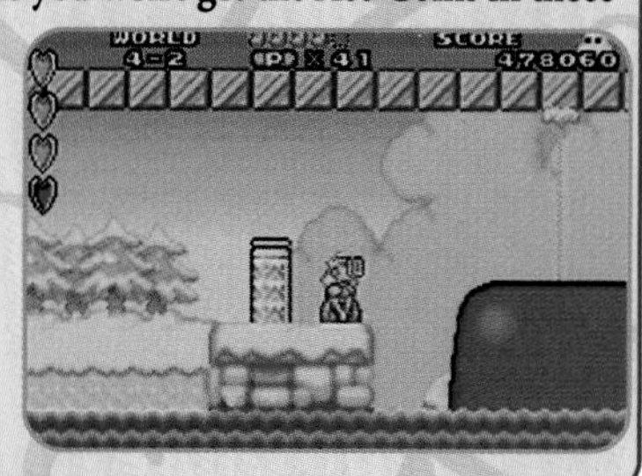

If you decide not to warp to World 6-1 (see sidebar above), Super Jump off the top of the pipe onto the icy platform above, watching out for that pesky Flurry. Move a short distance to the right and jump off of the end of the platform onto a steel platform with three plants. The left plant is a Small Vegetable, the right plant is a Heart Radish, and the middle plant is a Rocket Ship. Pluck the Heart first if you need it, then pluck the Rocket Ship to get to the next part of World 4-2.

Boss Fight: Birdo (Red)

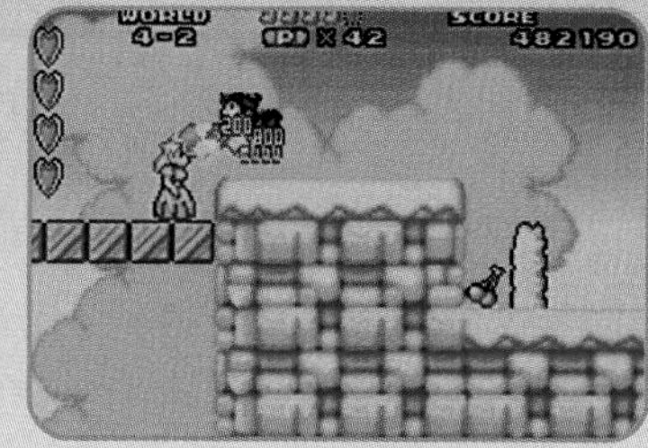

The Rocket Ship drops you onto an icy platform and explodes overhead. Pluck the Small Vegetable on the platform and use it to take out the three Blue Shy Guys on the snowy platform to the right. If you hit at least two of them with the same shot, you'll get a Heart.

To the snowy platform's right is a small drop-off and another snowy platform. A Red Shy Guy on an Autobomb patrols the platform, and the last Ace Coin floats overhead. Jump onto the Shy Guy and leap off of him to get the Ace Coin, then jump back onto his head and lift him off of the Autobomb. The Autobomb, deprived of its pilot, will roll off to the right.

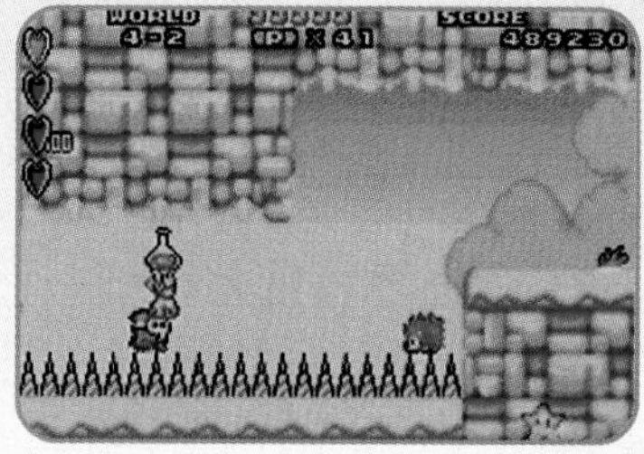

Drop the Red Shy Guy somewhere to the left, then grab the Cherry next to the drop-off from the last platform. Pluck the plant at the end of the snowy platform to get a Magic Potion. Jump onto the Shy Guy's back and ride him across the spikes to the snowy platform's right. Along the way, you collect four more Cherries, which results in a Starman floating up from the bottom of the screen.

Grab the Starman. You'll automatically knock out the Shy Guy you were riding when you became invincible, but the spikes won't harm you, so don't worry. Jump up onto the snowy platform at the right end of the spikes and run into the Porcupo (while invincible) to get rid of it; then, drop the Magic Potion. The last Mushroom is on this platform in Subspace.

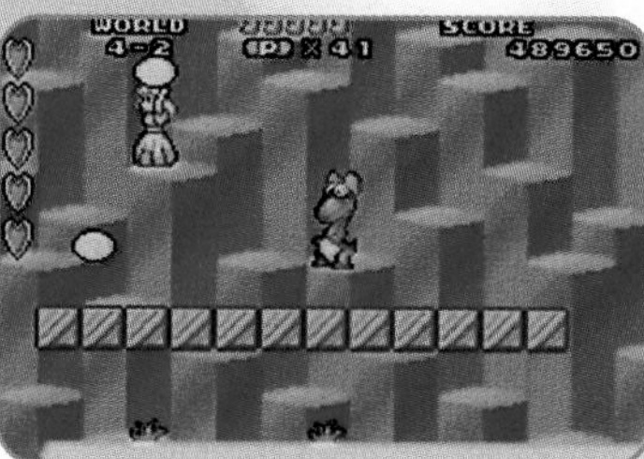

Hopefully, you're still invincible, but even if you're not, enter the door to the Boss's lair at the snowy platform's right edge (a Heart Radish is just before the door; pluck it if you need it). If you are still invincible, run right as fast as you can and straight into Birdo, knocking her out with one shot!

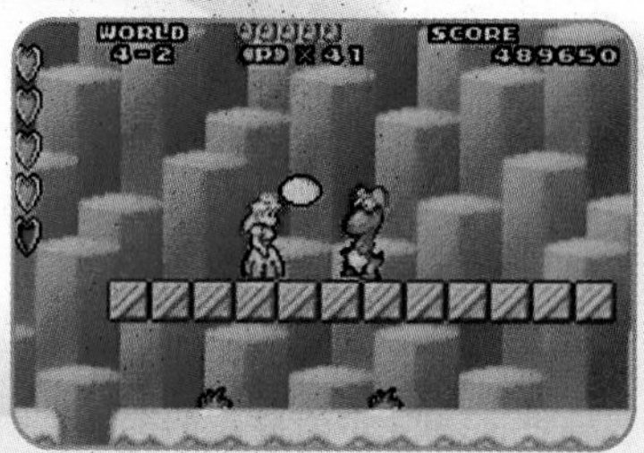

Even if you're not invincible, Birdo is still no more of a problem than she was before. Dodge her fireballs, pick up her eggs, and hit her with three of them to beat her.

Floating above the entrance to Birdo's lair is a Heart. The right and left plants under Birdo's icy platform are Hearts (grab 'em if you need 'em). The middle plant is a Bob-Omb with a very short fuse that you can use against Birdo, or it can blow up in your face and cost you a Heart. Once you defeat Birdo, grab the Crystal Ball she leaves behind and enter the gate to the right, completing World 4-2.

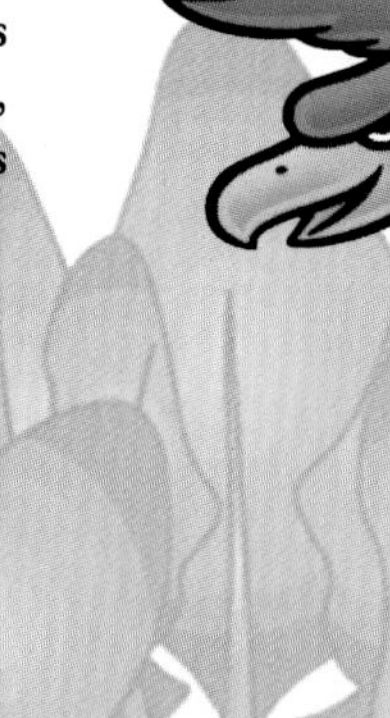

World 4-3

Peach is still the best character to use for this World. World 4-3 starts you out at the bottom of a small ice cavern with five plants and a ladder to the right. The middle plant is a Giant Red Shy Guy. Toss him around to your heart's content to fill up your life meter, then pluck any of the other four plants to get a Small Vegetable and take him out. Climb the ladder and enter the white doorway at the top of it.

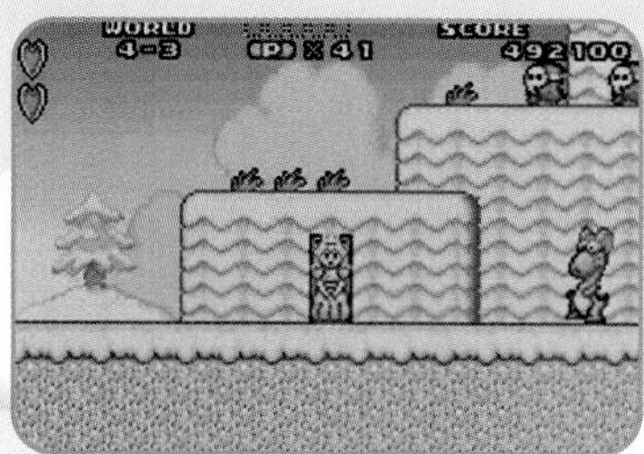

The door takes you to a series of snowy hills. Above the door are three plants (a Magic Potion, a Small Vegetable, and a Giant Vegetable, from left to right). Above and to the right of these is another Small Vegetable plant. Two Red Shy Guys move toward you from the platform with the single plant, and five more Blue Shy Guys pace along the platform above that one. Just so you don't get bored, Birdo is waiting to your right, on the same platform as the door.

First, pluck a Vegetable to take out the Red Shy Guys (or just use one of them against the other). Next, pluck the Giant Vegetable and throw it at the Blue Shy Guys. If your aim is true, you'll hit all five and get a 1UP. Finally, pluck the Magic Potion and take it to the three pillars at the screen's left edge. Ignore Birdo for now; she'll come in handy in a minute.

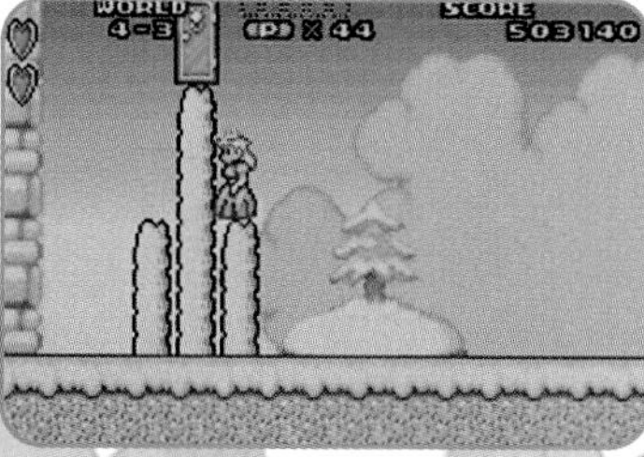

Drop the Magic Potion on top of the middle pillar (the tallest of the three). Enter the door to find the first Mushroom exactly where you're standing (you'll have to jump up to see it). You don't *have* to drop the Magic Potion exactly on that pillar to get the Mushroom, but the middle pillar can be tricky to reach in Subspace when there's a Mushroom on top of it, especially when your time is limited.

After grabbing the Mushroom, return to Birdo and stand to her right. When she fires an egg at you, jump on top of it and ride it to the right. Do not pick up the egg while riding it, or you'll drop into the water below and lose a chance. Birdo's egg will take you to a small, snowy stepped platform, and the first Ace Coin. If you're playing as Peach or Luigi, you can Super Jump off of the platform's left edge, hover over to the Ace Coin, and hover safely back to the platform. If you're playing as anyone else, Super Jump off the egg.

All six of the plants on the stepped platform are Small Vegetables, which come in handy for taking out the five Tweeters on the wooden bridge to the right. Hit all five Tweeters with one shot for a 1UP, then jump onto the bridge and move right until you come to a door. Enter the door.

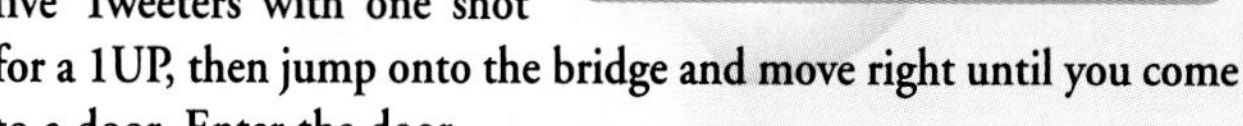

Super Shortcut

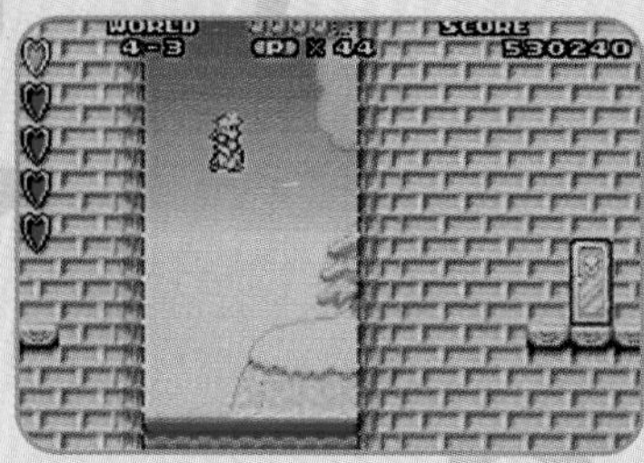

If you're playing as Peach or Luigi, you can skip almost all of World 4-3 by taking a running jump off of the right edge of the bridge. You'll land on the next bridge, which leads to two doors. The rightmost door leads to the cavern just before Fry Guy's lair. You'll miss out on the last two Mushrooms and the other four Ace Coins, but it's a good way to save time if you're confident in your abilities and just want to get to the Boss fight.

Assuming you didn't take the shortcut to Fry Guy's lair (see sidebar above) and instead entered the door, you appear in a cavern with ice platforms leading up and to the right. Hop up onto them, but watch out for the Flurry that comes bounding down from the upper right. Below and to the right of the third ice platform is a platform containing three plants. The middle one is a Small Vegetable, and the other two are Heart Radishes. Pluck 'em if you need 'em.

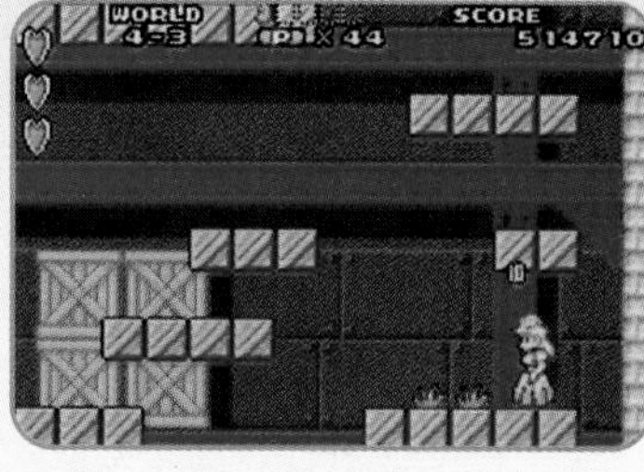

Keep jumping up the ice platforms, dodging the Flurries as they mercilessly zip down from above. You'll find the second Ace Coin along the screen's left side as you ascend the platforms. Grab it and keep heading up until you come to a pipe. Enter the pipe to get a 1UP Mushroom and a Heart Radish.

Leave the pipe, drop down to the left, then jump onto the platforms on the screen's left side and continue upward. The next two plants you encounter (located just above the pipe) are a Heart Radish and a Small Vegetable. Pluck the Heart Radish if you are not at full health, then keep jumping up the platforms.

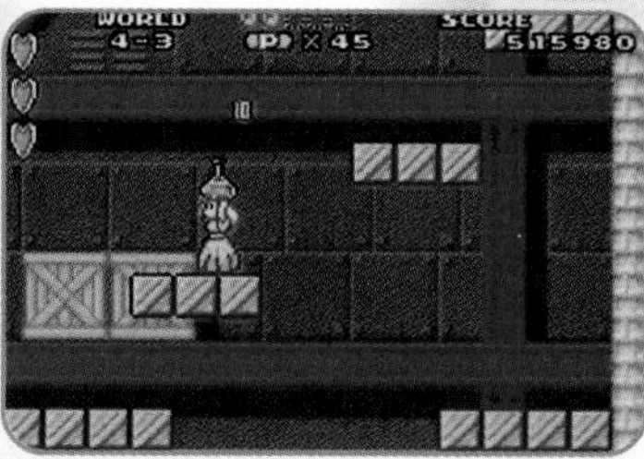

Once you pass a row of spikes on the screen's left side, you'll see an icy platform in the middle of the screen with a single plant on it. The plant is a Magic Potion; drop it where you found it to get another Mushroom. After getting the Mushroom, continue up.

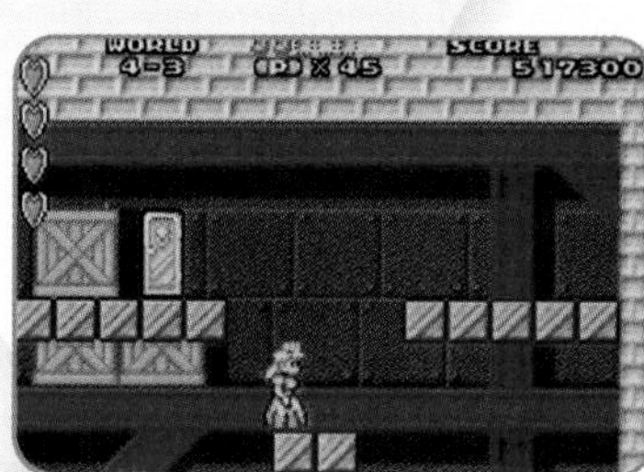

Above the platform where you found the Magic Potion is an area of very closely spaced horizontal icy platforms, complete with several Flurrys. You might be tempted to pluck the two plants on the left side of one of the platforms, but don't bother; they're just Small Vegetables, and you're better off avoiding the Flurrys altogether and entering the door at the top of the platforms.

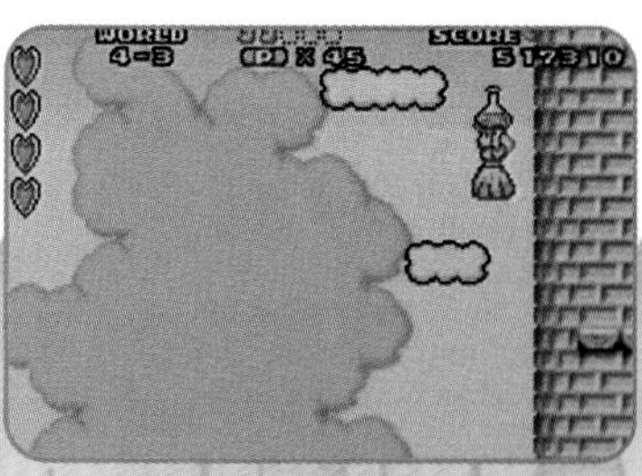

This door leads you outside onto another bridge. There is another door at the bridge's right end and two plants in between. The left plant is a Magic Potion; the right plant is a Small Vegetable. Pluck the Magic Potion, then ascend the cloud steps at the bridge's left end.

From the upper cloud, jump onto the castle's parapets, and keep jumping across to the right until you're on the second castle's very last parapet (from the cloud to the last parapet is 10 jumps). Drop the Magic Potion on that last parapet to get the third Mushroom of World 4-3. Once you do, jump back along to the left and drop safely down to the bridge below, then enter the door at the bridge's right end.

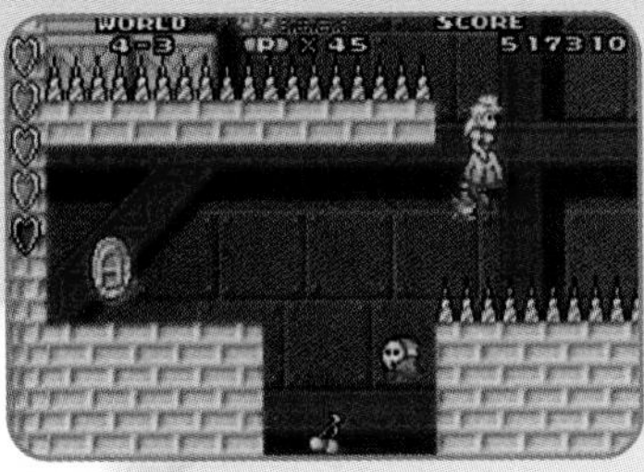

The door leads to the top of a vertical cavern. A Tweeter, a Red Shy Guy, and a Blue Shy Guy walk the platform just below the door. Jump onto the Red Shy Guy and ride him as he walks off of the platform's left edge onto a spiked platform, and stay with him as he walks off that platform's right edge onto another spiked platform. If you're playing as Peach, just before the Shy Guy walks off the second spiked platform's left edge, jump off and land on the brick platform to the left, where the third Ace Coin floats. All other characters must perform the jump after the Shy Guy falls off to reach the platform.

After getting the Ace Coin, walk off of the brick platform's right edge and try to stay in the middle of the screen as you fall. You'll land on an icy platform with a door that leads to Phanto's lair. Enter the door, get rid of the two Flurries on the platform overhead, and pluck the three Heart Radish plants if you need health. Jump up onto the next platform to get the Key, and exit the room with the Key in hand.

Still carrying the Key, run along the icy platforms below the door to Phanto's lair and continue down the screen, taking out Flurries with the Key if they become bothersome. At the bottom of the cavern is the locked door you need the Key to open, and to the right of that door is the fourth Ace Coin. Grab the Ace Coin, then enter the door.

The door leads to the left end of another bridge. At the right end is the door that leads to the room just before Fry Guy's lair. Between the two doors are Blue Shy Guys and Beezos. Defeat them, then enter the right door.

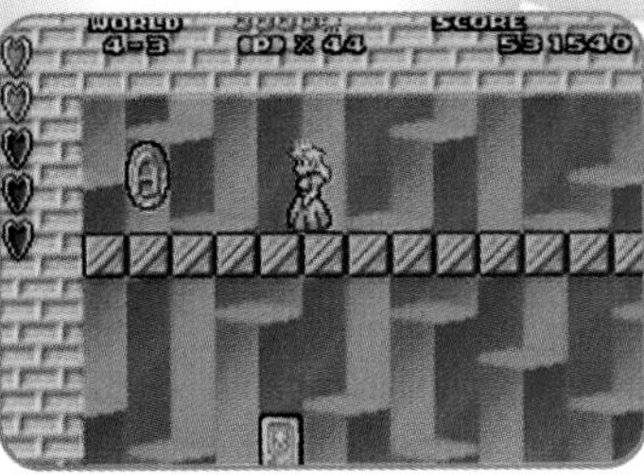

To the right, on the other side of the door, is a Crystal Ball on a pedestal. Two Flurries skate around on an ice platform overhead. Lure the Flurries into falling off of their platform's right side, then Super Jump onto the platform from the Crystal Ball. Move all the way to the left to find the last Ace Coin. Grab it, then drop back down to the Crystal Ball, pick it up to open the gate, and enter the gate to battle Fry Guy.

Boss Fight: Fry Guy

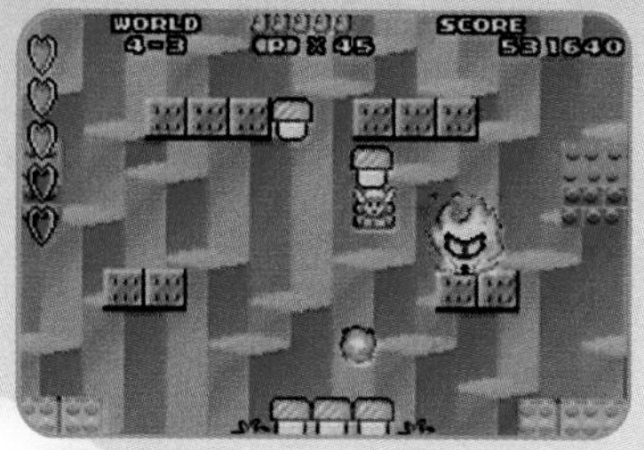

Fry Guy is a speedy ball of fire with a bad attitude who drops an endless supply of fireballs. Fry Guy moves in an arc and only fires down, so figure out where he's going and where he's shooting and make sure you're not there. One Heart floats near the entrance and two Heart Radishes are at the bottom of the screen if you need them—and you very well might.

The only way to hurt Fry Guy is with the six Mushroom Blocks scattered around his lair, so pick them up and throw them at him. The best way to hit him is to grab a Mushroom Block, jump up onto either of the green platforms in the top middle of the screen, wait for Fry Guy to swoop toward you, then throw the block so it hits him and stays on the platform. This keeps you from having to retrieve the Mushroom Block from the bottom of the screen and possibly get hit by a fireball or four.

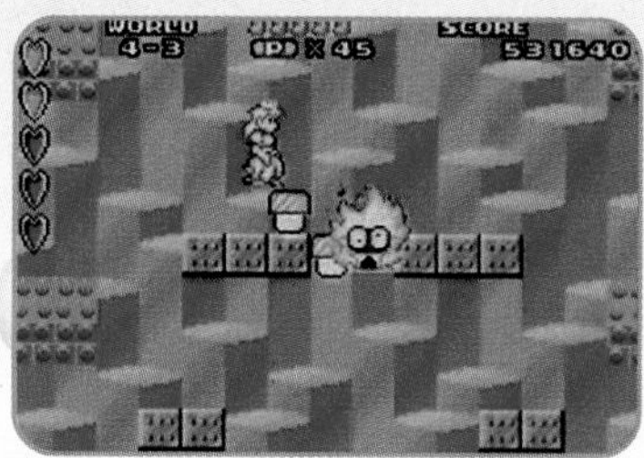

Once you hit Fry Guy with three Mushroom Blocks, he splits into four small Fry Guys. Fortunately, they move much slower than the big guy, they can't float (they only jump), and you only need to hit each of them once with a Mushroom Block to take him out. Unfortunately, with every small Fry Guy you get rid of, the others start moving faster.

Your best plan of action is to lure the small Fry Guys to the bottom of the screen and pelt them with Mushroom Blocks from above, because they won't be able to jump up to reach you. You can also stack two Mushroom Blocks on top of each other and make a wall that the small Fry Guys can't jump over. Stay out of their reach, aim well, and they'll be gone before you know it. Once you eliminate them, complete World 4 by entering the doorway at the bottom of the screen.

World 5-1

Water Follies

Most of World 5-1 involves jumping from one precarious perch to the next to cross huge waterfalls. When it comes to jumping, Luigi is the undisputed master, so unless you find Luigi's high-flying antics impossible to control, he's your best choice for getting through World 5-1.

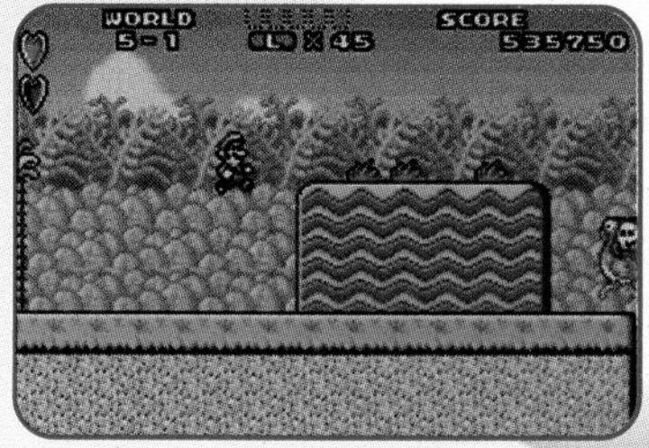

From the start point in World 5-1, head right to find a Red Shy Guy riding an Ostro. Jump on top of the Shy Guy and hurl him at the Ostro to get rid of both and pick up a Heart. Just past the Ostro is a small grassy platform containing three plants. The right and left plants are Small Vegetables, and the middle one is a Giant Vegetable. Don't use these on the Shy Guy and Ostro. They have a better use.

After defeating the Shy Guy and Ostro, press L to look down and see a 1UP Mushroom encased in a bubble below (if you can't see it, move farther right). Pluck a Vegetable, stand on the ground at the platform's right edge, and throw it to hit the 1UP Mushroom's bubble. Repeat once more, but save the third Vegetable.

After you've hit the 1UP Mushroom twice, pluck the third Vegetable and use it on the Panser to the right. Grab the Ace Coin floating above and to the left of the Panser, then walk off the platform's right edge to fall to the grassy platform below. The two plants on the lower platform are both Small Vegetables.

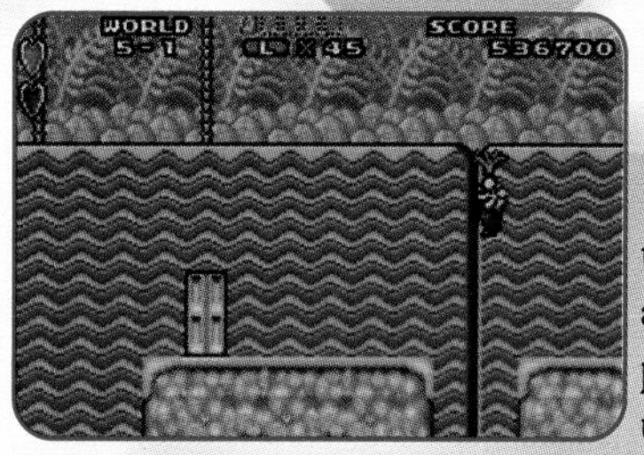

Pluck one of the Small Vegetables and hop across the platforms to the left until you see the 1UP Mushroom. Hop across onto the Mushroom's rocky platform, stand beside the Mushroom, and throw the Vegetable to burst the bubble and claim your prize. After you have the 1UP, jump back over to the right and enter the door.

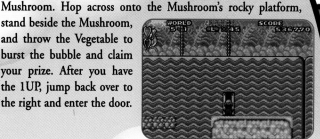

This door leads into a waterfall-filled horizontal cavern. Between the door and the first waterfall to the right are seven plants—two on the upper platform and five on the lower. From left to right, they are: a Bob-Omb, a Magic Potion, a Small Vegetable, a Giant Red Shy Guy, a Heart Radish, and two more Small Vegetables. Pluck the Heart Radish if you need it, and pluck and bounce the Giant Red Shy Guy if you need more Hearts.

Once you are at full health, pluck the Magic Potion and carry it across the waterfall and up onto the stepped grassy platforms to the right. To the grassy platforms' right is a wide waterfall with four descending logs and a Trouter between you and the other side. The second and third Ace Coins are also in the waterfall. The second is at the top, between the second and third logs, and the third is at the bottom, in the fourth log's path.

When crossing the waterfall, stay as close to the top as you can for the first three logs; this will ensure that you grab the second Ace Coin as you cross. When you jump onto the fourth log, however, ride it almost all the way to the bottom to pick up the third Ace Coin, then jump onto the grassy platform to the right.

To the grassy platform's right is a slightly narrower waterfall, but the only way to cross it is to jump on the two Trouters in it. If you're playing as Luigi or Peach, you can make these jumps by performing dashing jumps. Peach will need to use her floating technique. Drop the Magic Potion on this platform to get World 5-1's first Mushroom.

To the right of the platform with the Mushroom is—you guessed it—another waterfall. This one has three Trouters in it, with the fourth Ace Coin just to the first Trouter's right. If you're playing as anyone except Luigi or Peach, hop along all three Trouters when they're close to the top, grabbing the Ace Coin as you do, and jump off of the third one onto the upper platform with the two plants. If you're playing as Luigi or Peach, jump off of the third Trouter onto either the upper or lower platforms coming up and Super Jump to the upper platform if necessary.

The left plant on the upper platform is a 1UP Mushroom; the right plant is a Magic Potion. Pluck them in that order, then carry the Magic Potion as you jump down to the short grassy platform to the right. Drop the Potion on this platform for the second Mushroom.

Ride the Trouter past the Mushroom platform up to the next platform to the right. It's an easy jump to the following platform, but the fifth Ace Coin is floating in the middle of the narrow chasm between the platforms. To get it, jump on the Trouter between the platforms, ride it down until you get the Ace Coin, then jump straight up just before the bottom.

With any luck, the Trouter will reappear from the bottom and take you back up before you hit the bottom and lose a chance. Jump onto the narrow platform to the Trouter's right to get your feet on solid ground again. Whew!

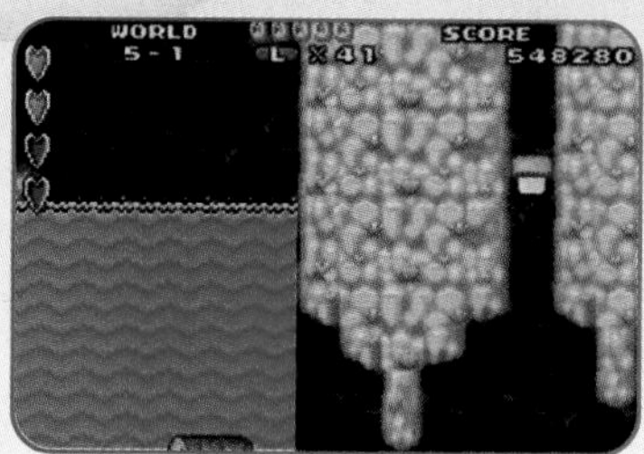

From the platform to the right of the fifth Ace Coin, jump along the two logs in the waterfall to the right. Stay as close to the top as you can. From the second log, jump off of the top of the screen and to the right. You land on top of the cavern ceiling and can't see your character, but the screen scrolls as you move.

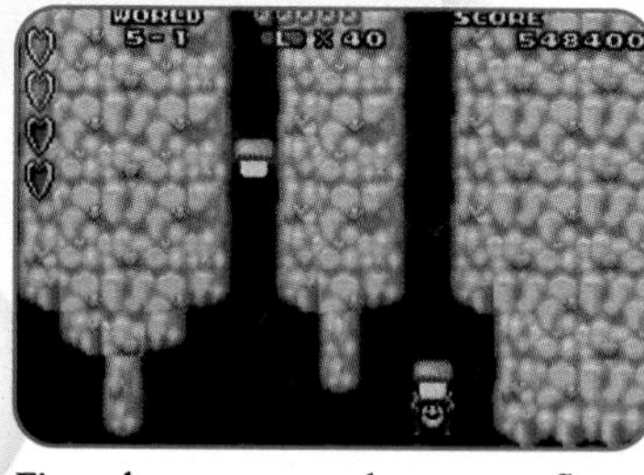

Two narrow vertical tunnels run through the cavern ceiling; Mushroom Blocks block both of them. Fall into the right tunnel and lift the Mushroom Block to get to the cavern floor. Discard the Mushroom Block. Five plants are on the cavern floor. From left to right, they are a Magic Potion and four Small Vegetables.

Pluck the Magic Potion and drop it under the tunnel you just unblocked. When you enter Subspace, a Mushroom falls through the tunnel and lands at your feet. If you hadn't unblocked the tunnel, the Mushroom would have stayed up there, out of reach. Grab the Mushroom and some Coins, then exit Subspace.

Boss Fight: Birdo (Green)

There's only one place go—into the door to the right of the plants on the cavern floor. This door leads to Birdo's lair for a Boss fight. Birdo has once again changed her color scheme and her attack. Instead of shooting eggs, or eggs and fireballs, Green Birdo launches only fireballs.

To defeat Birdo, pick up the Mushroom Block to the right of her starting position and hit her with it three times. Two Hearts are in her lair, but you probably won't need them. At the third hit, Birdo is knocked out and leaves the customary Crystal Ball behind. Pick it up to open the gate and exit World 5-1.

World 5-2

Night Life

World 5-2 is a nighttime version of the grassy lands of Worlds 1 and 3. Luigi is still a good choice for this level; his jumping ability is second to none, and you'll have plenty of opportunities to use it. From World 5-2's start point, use any of the three Small Vegetables to the right to defeat the Giant Red Shy Guy a little farther to the right (or, if you need more Hearts, pick up and throw the Shy Guy a few times, then hit him with a Small Vegetable).

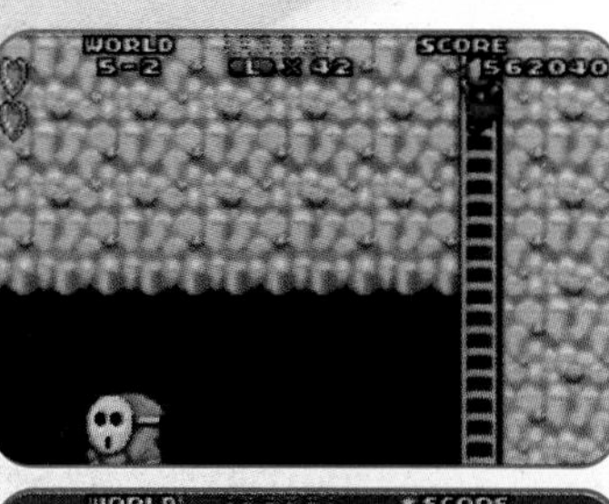

After taking care of the Shy Guy, climb the ladder on the screen's right to get to the next section. The four plants on the small grassy hill to the ladder's right are (from left to right): a Bob-Omb, a Small Vegetable, a Giant Vegetable, and another Small Vegetable.

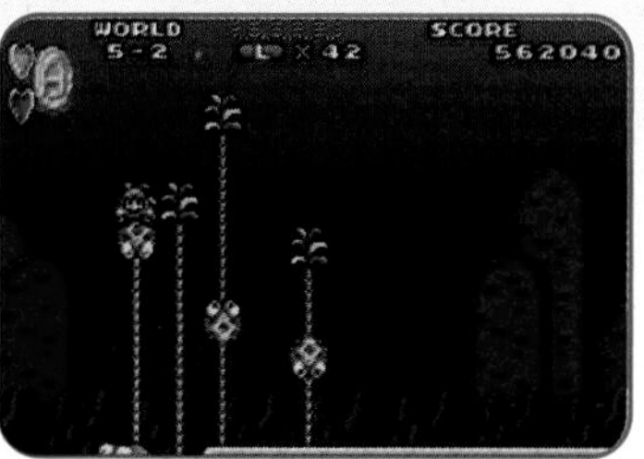

To the grassy hill's right are three Hoopsters traveling up and down three palm trees. Above the trees and to the left is the first Ace Coin. Ride the leftmost Hoopster up and jump off at the highest point to snag the Coin. Once you have the Coin, use the Hoopster or the Vegetables on the hill to the left to defeat all three Hoopsters and the Ostro-riding Red Shy Guy who appears near the Ace Coin.

To the three Hoopsters' right is a Large Vegetable plant, followed by three more Hoopsters. Use the Large Vegetable to defeat the Hoopsters and continue right. When you come to the pipe surrounded by plants, duck down it without plucking any of the plants.

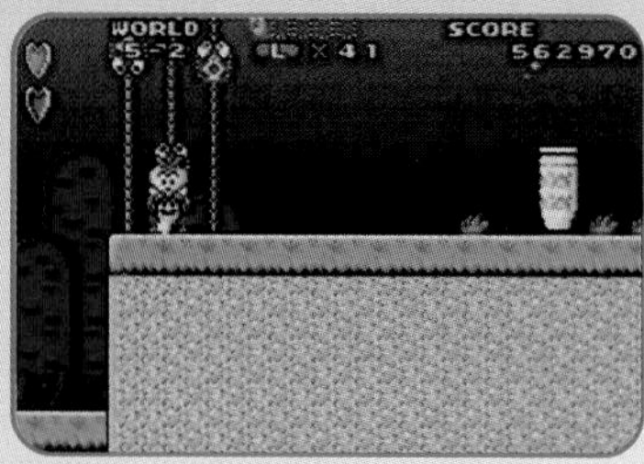

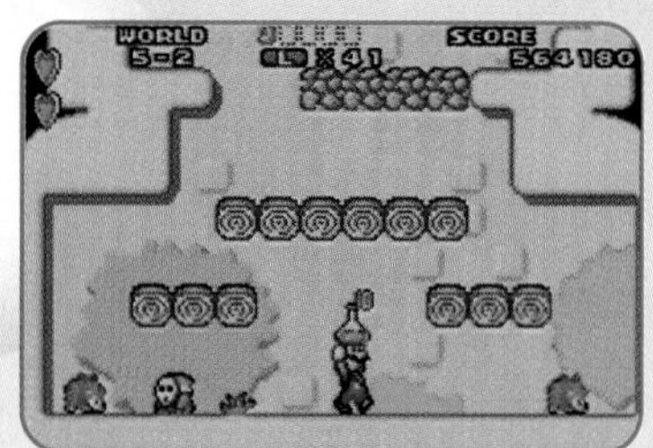

At the bottom of the pipe is a stone floor, a Bomb plant, and a Shy Guy. Use the Bomb to break open the floor (and, if you're really good, take out the Shy Guy too). Below the stone floor are two plants (the left one is a Large Vegetable, the right is a Magic Potion) and two Porcupos. Use the Large Vegetable to take out the Porcupos, then pluck the Magic Potion and carry it out of the pipe.

Drop the Magic Potion on the lower grassy platform to the right of the pipe beyond the narrow gap. A Mushroom will appear in Subspace on this platform. Once you've collected the Mushroom and returned from Subspace, feel free to pluck any of the rest of the plants. From left to right, the four on the top left platform are: a Bob-Omb, two Small Vegetables, and a Large Vegetable. From left to right, the two on the bottom right platform are a Shell and a Small Vegetable. The Shell is perfect for taking out the Shy Guy, Ostro, and Porcupos on the bottom level.

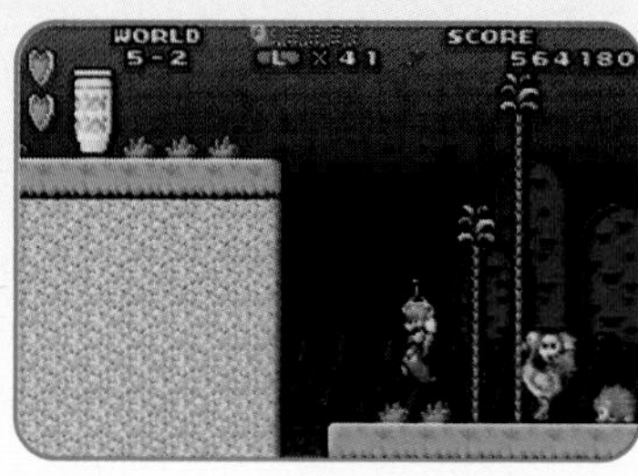

Before you get rid of the Shy Guy and Ostro, however, jump on top of them and Super Jump off to get the second Ace Coin that's floating high above. Once you grab the Coin, move right past the next Hoopster and jump down to the platform below the second Hoopster to pluck a 1UP Mushroom.

Jump onto the platform above and to the right of the 1UP Mushroom. Farther to the right are two more Hoopsters, with the third Ace Coin between them. Ride the left Hoopster until you can jump across to the other and grab the Ace Coin along the way, then jump onto the platform to the right.

To this platform's right are four very narrow platforms. The first is vacant, the second has a Hoopster, the third has a Green Panser, and the fourth has another Hoopster. Use the left Hoopster to take out the Panser and the right Hoopster, then pluck the plant that the Panser was sitting on to get a Magic Potion.

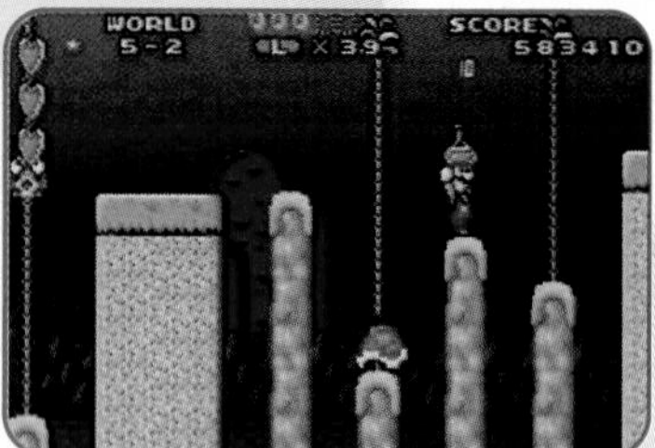

Jump onto the grassy platform to the right of where the second Hoopster used to be and drop the Potion near the grassy hill with the three plants on it. A Mushroom appears in Subspace at the edge of the grassy hill. The only plant of any interest here is the last plant (a Giant POW) to the grassy hill's right, just before the drop-off.

Jump down and to the right to the next platform, releasing the Giant POW Block just before landing. It will bounce and take out the Shy Guy, Ostro, and Porcupos on the platform and give you a 1UP in the bargain. After they're gone, climb the vine on the screen's right edge and keep climbing until you reach the Giant Blue Shy Guys in the clouds.

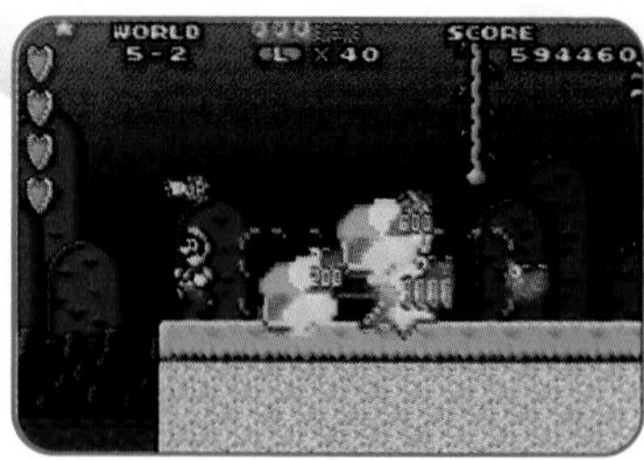

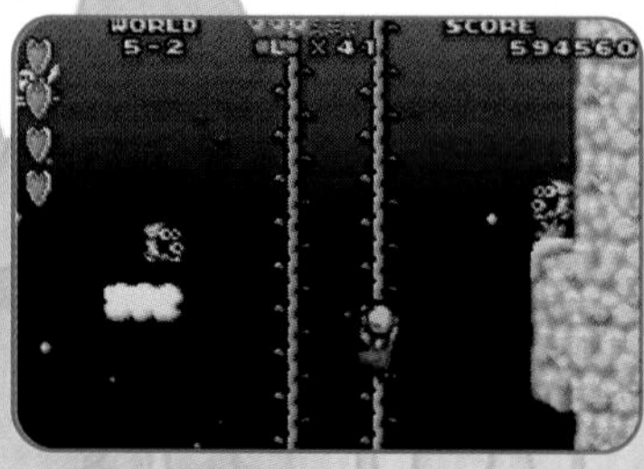

If you need Hearts, throw the two Blue Shy Guys around, then get back on the vine and keep climbing. When a second vine appears to the left, be careful; two Gray Snifits are just above, one on each side, and they're just waiting to knock you off the vine with a well-placed shot.

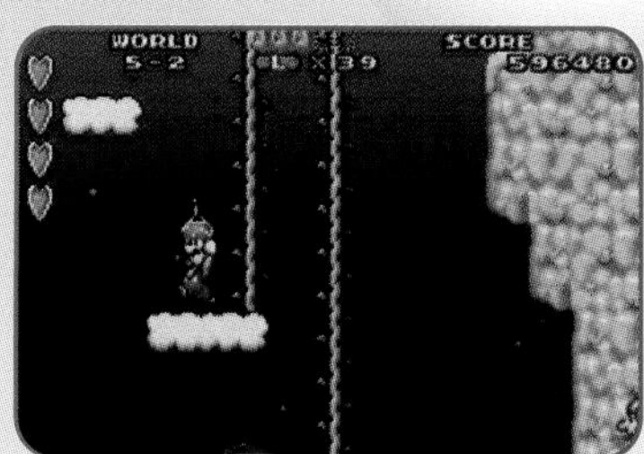

Take out the left Snifit any way you can (the easiest is to jump on his head and throw him off of his perch), then dispose of the right Snifit. **Do not** harm the Hoopsters. Under the right Snifit is a plant that reveals a Magic Potion when plucked. Pluck the Potion, then ride a Hoopster down to the cloud that is the left vine's base. Drop the Potion on the cloud and enter the door to Subspace to get the third Mushroom.

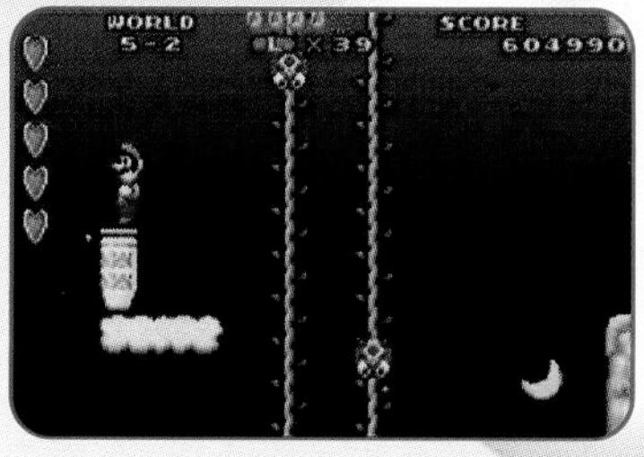

Upon returning from Subspace, keep climbing the vines. Watch out for Snifits, Hoopsters, and Beezos on the way up. If an oncoming enemy blocks your path, fall off of your vine in the direction of the other vine. You'll lose a little ground but keep all of your Hearts. When you come to the pipe on the screen's left side, jump off of the vine and onto the pipe's platform, then enter the pipe.

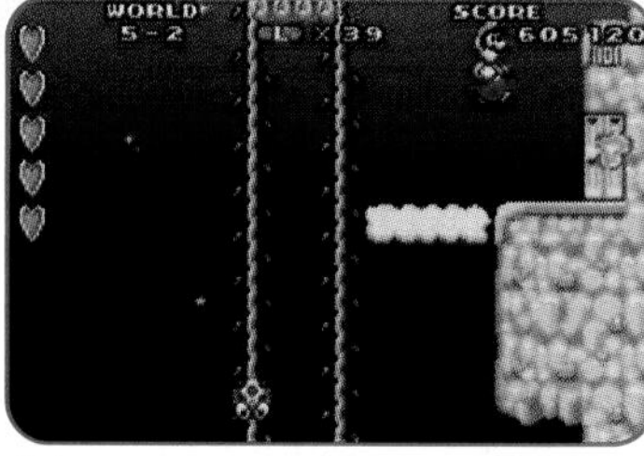

Inside the pipe are two plants. The left one is a Small Vegetable; the right one is a POW Block. There is also a bouncing blade in the right corner; don't hit it. Pluck the POW Block and exit the pipe, then Super Jump off of the top of the pipe to grab the fourth Ace Coin. Jump on top of a Hoopster to ride to the top of the vine in style.

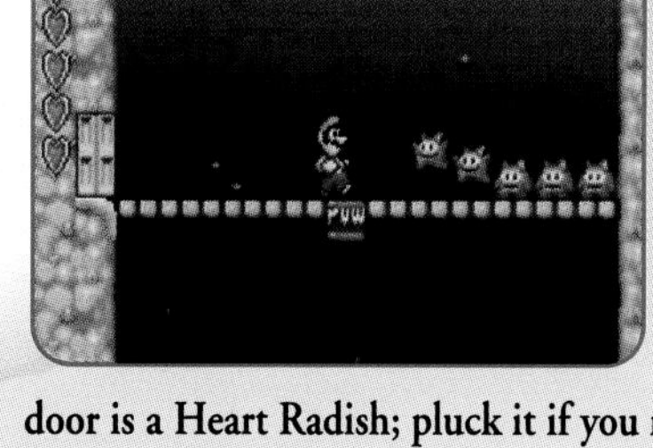

Once you reach the top of the vine, drop the POW Block to get rid of any remaining enemies, then enter the door on the screen's right side. The plant just above the door is a Heart Radish; pluck it if you need it. On the other side of the door is a bridge with five Ninjis and a POW Block in the middle. Pluck the POW Block and move to the left quickly to keep from falling. Drop the POW Block when all of the Ninjis are on the ground to get rid of all of them and pick up a 1UP.

Drop through the hole in the bridge where the POW Block used to be and steer your fall so that you stay near the screen's left side. All along the way down are small ledges with spikes on them; if you hit one, you lose a Heart. To avoid them, stay near the walls but not right up against them. When you're almost to the bottom, you see the fifth Ace Coin floating on the screen's left side. If you don't get it on the way down, there is no way to go back for it unless you restart the level or lose a chance.

At the left edge of the canyon bottom is a block of spikes. Don't land on it. To the right of the spikes is a Shell plant, which can take out at least one of the Trouters jumping up and down in the middle of the screen. On the canyon floor's right side is the door to the Boss room.

Boss Fight: Birdo (Red)

From the entrance to Birdo's latest lair, walk right and pluck the only plant in the room for a Shell. If you need Hearts, send the Shell to the right to take out the three Porcupos coming toward you. (Remember: every enemy you knock out with a Shell gives you a Heart.)

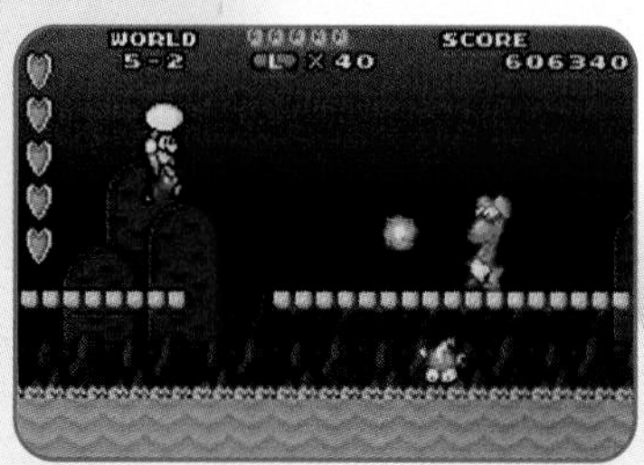

If you don't need Hearts, jump over the Porcupos, then jump over the gap in the bridge, and launch the Shell at Birdo. The ever-fashionable Birdo has changed her wardrobe again. She's back in red, meaning that she fires eggs and fireballs. As always, defeat her by hitting her three times with her own eggs, or any other projectile in the room (such as the Shell, or that Trouter that keeps jumping up and down around her).

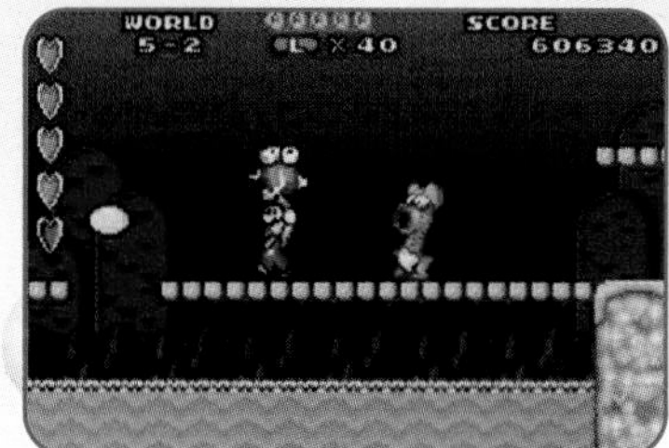

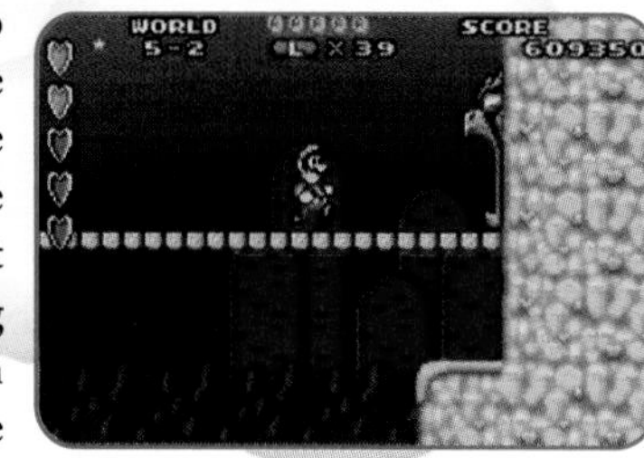

If you're going to try to catch her eggs, stand on the left side of the gap in the bridge so that you have more time to react and don't risk accidentally plucking the egg out of the air when you're over the gap. Once she's defeated, grab the Crystal Ball she leaves behind and exit World 5-2 through the gate to the right.

World 5-3

It's the Bomb

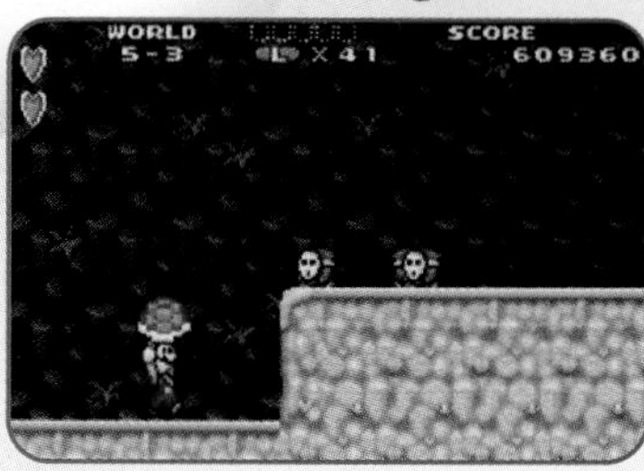

Luigi is still the best character to use in World 5-3, but no matter whom you use, this will be your most challenging level yet. You'll face Bob-Ombs at every turn and gaping chasms that call for split-second timing on the jump button. Even if your skills are sharp and you know what to do, you could easily lose a dozen chances or more on this level. World 5-3 is tough and is not for the easily frustrated.

From World 5-3's start point, head right and pluck the only plant in the cavern to get a Shell. Send the Shell flying on the upper platform to the right to take out the three Blue Shy Guys and pick up a Heart from each. Watch out for the Shell's return bounce, then climb the ladder on the cavern's right side.

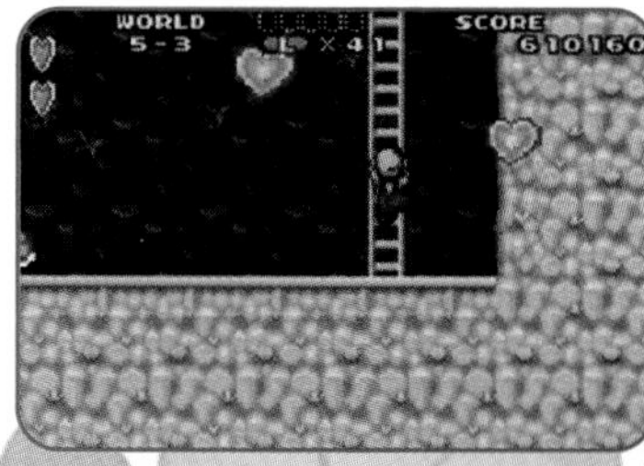

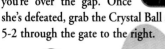

Warp to World 7-1

Directly above the top of the ladder leading out of the starting cavern is an overhanging platform with three plants and a pipe. If you're playing as Luigi, simply Super Jump onto the overhanging platform's right side. If you're playing as any other character, stand on one of the stone pillars a little farther to the right, jump on top of an Albatoss, and ride it over to the platform.

From left to right, the plants on the overhanging platform are two Large Vegetables and a Magic Potion. The first Ace Coin also floats over the platform's left side. Pluck the Magic Potion and drop it near the pipe, then climb down into the pipe to warp to World 7-1, forfeiting all Ace Coins for the rest of World 5-3 and all of World 6.

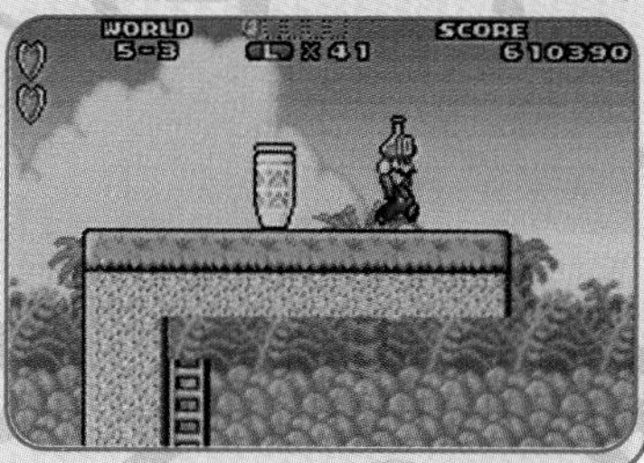

First, get up onto the overhanging platform directly above the top of the ladder (see the sidebar above for how to do this). Collect the first Ace Coin from the platform's left side, pluck the rightmost plant to get a Magic Potion, then hop back down to the ground.

To the ladder's right are several Bomb-able stone pillars and six plants. From left to right, the plants are: a Shell, a Magic Potion, two Large Vegetables, a Bob-Omb, and a Small Vegetable. Unless you didn't grab the Magic Potion near the Warp Pipe, you don't need these.

Drop the Magic Potion to the last pillar's right. Doing so is easier said than done; Albatosses swoop by relentlessly, dropping Bob-Ombs, and jumping over the pillars can be a challenge in itself. If you get the Potion past the pillars, however, you'll be rewarded with the first Mushroom.

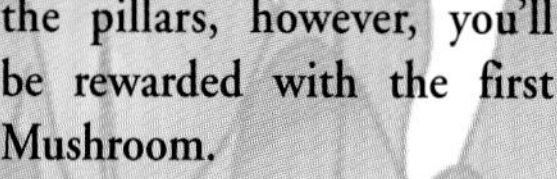

If you can trick a Bob-Omb into blowing away the left half of the first pillar, you'll uncover a Roulette. A Starman sure would come in handy about now.

Past the pillars is a grassy platform containing six plants. From left to right, they are: a Magic Potion, four Large Vegetables, and a Heart Radish. If you grabbed neither of the Magic Potions from the beginning of the level, use this one to get the first Mushroom. Even if you already got the Mushroom, though, use the Potion here anyway and pick up some Coins.

While you're standing on the grassy platform with the six plants, the Albatosses halt their Bob-Omb raid. The Albatosses resume their attack as soon as you reach either edge of the platform.

To the grassy platform's right is a T-shaped log structure with a plant on either side. The left one is a Bob-Omb, and the right one is a 1UP Mushroom. Grab the Mushroom and continue right. You'll pass under a log platform with a single plant; it's a Large Vegetable, which you don't need.

Super Jump off of the grassy platform to the right of the log with the Large Vegetable to get the second Ace Coin. If you want a Large Vegetable to help out with the Bob-Ombs swarming at the right, hop up on the log platform to the right and pluck the plant. Otherwise, wait for the Bob-Ombs to explode and take the low road to the right.

The first of two plants on the lower road is a Giant Red Shy Guy. The second is a Shell. Between these two items, you should be able to clear out the Bob-Ombs ahead of you and pick up enough Hearts to fully restore your health. Continue right and jump on top of the vertical stone wall that you come to.

To get the next Mushroom, blow open this wall. It's tough to trick the Bob-Ombs into doing it for you, so you'll most likely have to jump down, pick up a Bob-Omb, and throw him at the wall just as he starts flashing. Make sure the entrance is big enough to walk through easily (you must destroy two consecutive squares—preferably the bottom two).

Once the wall is open, hop to the upper platform to the wall's right. The three plants up there are, from left to right: a Bob-Omb, a Magic Potion, and another Bob-Omb. Drop the Potion near the bombed wall and enter Subspace to find the second Mushroom.

Once that's done, climb down the ladder to the right. If you approach the ladder from the left, another stone wall is in your way. The plant just before the wall is a Bomb, so you can blow the wall open, but a horde of Bob-Ombs will follow you in and probably cost you a Heart or two. Better to jump to the upper level, where you got the Magic Potion, then head right along the log, dodging the Bob-Ombs as you do. Drop off the log's right end to the platform below and head left to descend the ladder.

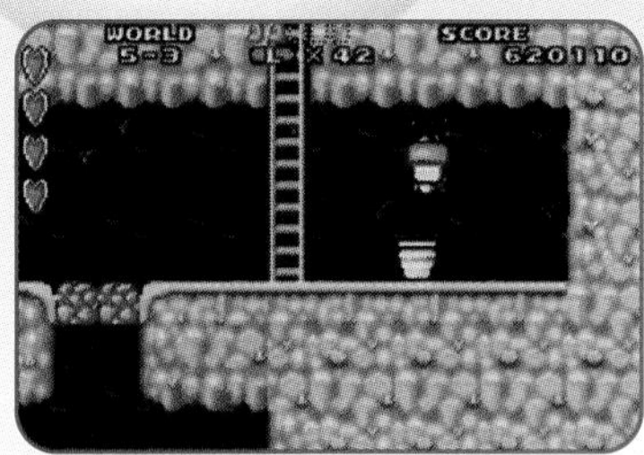

At the bottom of the ladder is a cavern. In the cavern, to the right are a Giant Blue Shy Guy and a Bob-Omb Generator with a Mushroom Block on top of it. To the left is a horizontal stone platform with two destructible blocks. Removing the Mushroom Block unleashes a steady stream of Bob-Ombs. Toss the Giant Blue Shy Guy around for a few Hearts if you need them, then lift the Mushroom Block and drop it on the left destructible block.

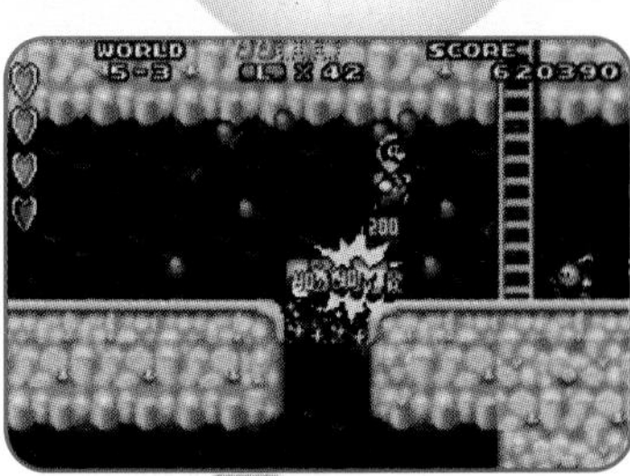

The Bob-Ombs pour out of the Bob-Omb Generator. Stand on top of the Mushroom Block and wait for them to blow open a gap in the floor. Bob-Ombs also approach from the left, but if you're on the Mushroom Block and it's on the left destructible block, you have nothing to fear. Note that this only works if you stand on the left edge of the Mushroom Block; otherwise, you take damage from the Bob-Ombs.

As soon as the floor underneath the Mushroom Block is open, pick up the Mushroom Block to fall down the gap and head left. The Bob-Ombs from the Bob-Omb Generator will bounce harmlessly to the right, and the Bob-Ombs from the left won't even make it down the hole.

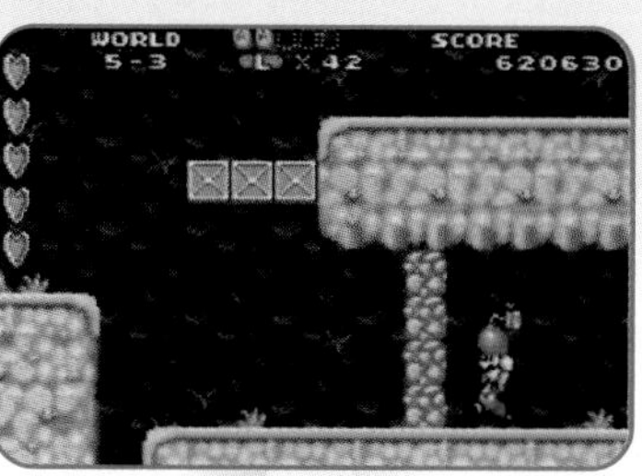

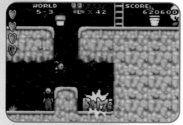

Drop the block to the left of the gap and pluck the rightmost plant on the bottom level to get a Magic Potion. Drop the Magic Potion where you found it, making sure that the little alcove that the Bob-Ombs are bouncing into is visible. Enter Subspace to collect the third Mushroom.

The rest of the plants along the cavern's bottom level are, from right to left: four Large Vegetables, a Heart Radish, and a Bomb. Use the Bomb to blow open the stone wall immediately to the left and move left through the hole.

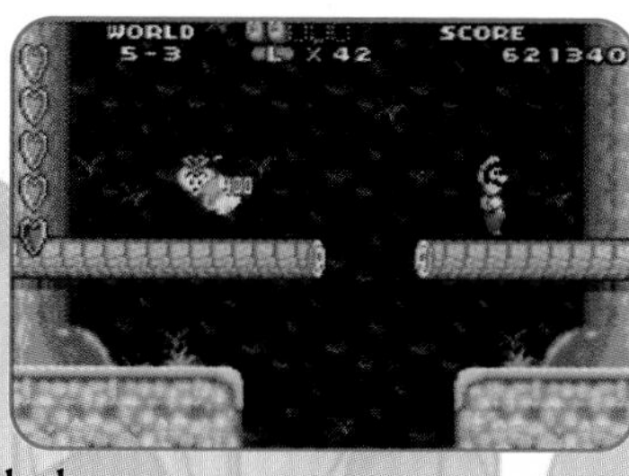

The first plant to the left of the wall is a Shell. You don't need it. Jump up and to the left onto the next platform, and pluck the Large Vegetable to use on the Bob-Ombs approaching from the left (if you plucked the four Large Vegetables to the right of the wall, this will be a Time Stop instead—also helpful).

Hop up onto the log steps and head left along the log platform. Throw a Vegetable or a Bob-Omb at the Panser to the left of the gap, then jump the gap, run off the log's left end, and double back slightly to the right to grab the Heart Radish under the log.

There is another plant under the log on the right side of the gap. The only character who can get it is Peach, with her floating jump. Don't waste time or chances trying to get it, though, because it's only a Small Vegetable, which isn't good for anything except luring gullible players into throwing chances down a hole (literally).

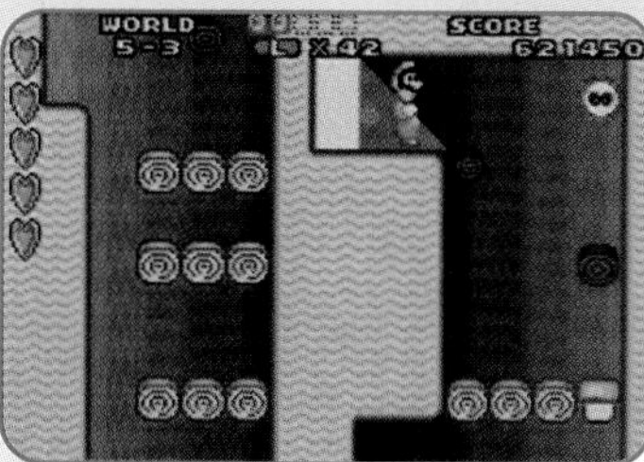

Enter the door to the logs' left. You appear on the right side of a vertical cavern. There's a Spark running around, but as long as you stand in the doorway, you're safe. Once the Spark passes by, move to the right and lift the Mushroom Block to open a passage through the bottom platform.

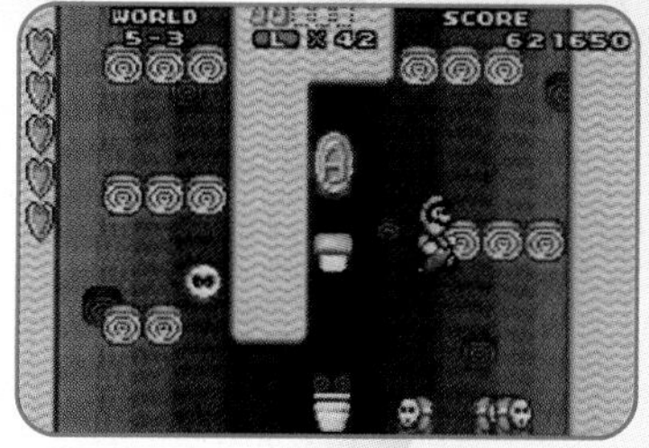

Head down through the gap, carrying the Mushroom Block, and throw it off of the left edge of the platform below so that it hugs the wall on the way down. It will land on top of a Shy Guy Generator and block it before it can spit out too many enemies. Walk off the platform's left edge, and make your way down to the platform that the Shy Guy Generator is on.

In the floor to the right is another gap with a Mushroom Block stopping it up. Once again, lift the Mushroom Block out of the gap and head down. With a few minor variations, this is all you must do to get to the cavern's bottom right side. Whenever possible, use the Mushroom Blocks to stop up Shy Guy Generators or get rid of enemies below, then make your way to the bottom of the cavern.

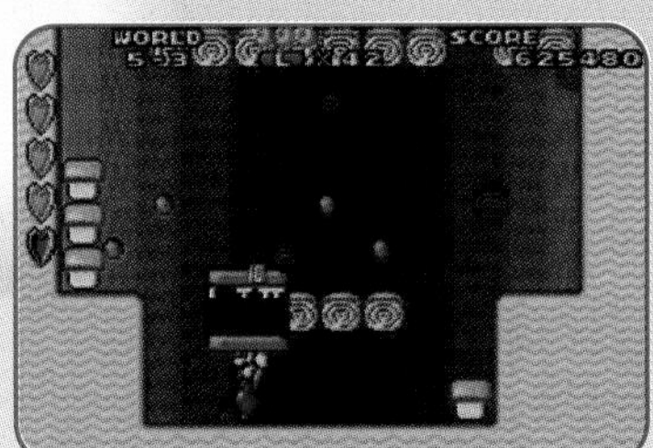

At the bottom of the cavern are two plants. The left one is a Giant POW Block, and the right one is a Small Vegetable. Pluck the Giant POW Block and carry it as you ascend the cavern's left side. Think of it as an insurance policy; use it when there are too many enemies to deal with onscreen.

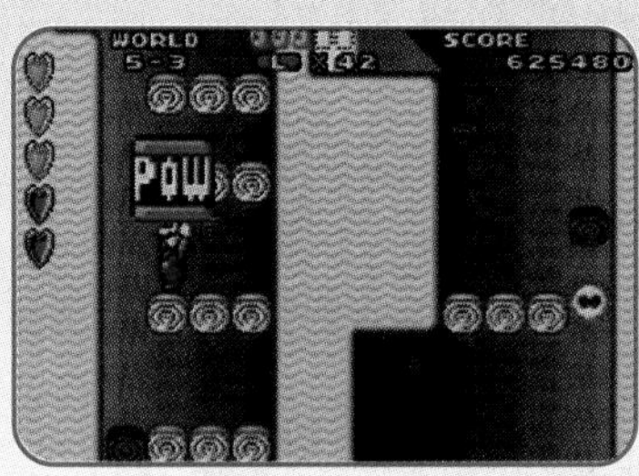

Continue up the cavern's left side. For the first half of the trip, you won't have to do much more than jump straight up from platform to platform, dodging enemies as they come. Don't be shy about using that POW Block if you need to; that's why you've got it. You'll find another (regular-sized) POW Block in the only pipe on the way up.

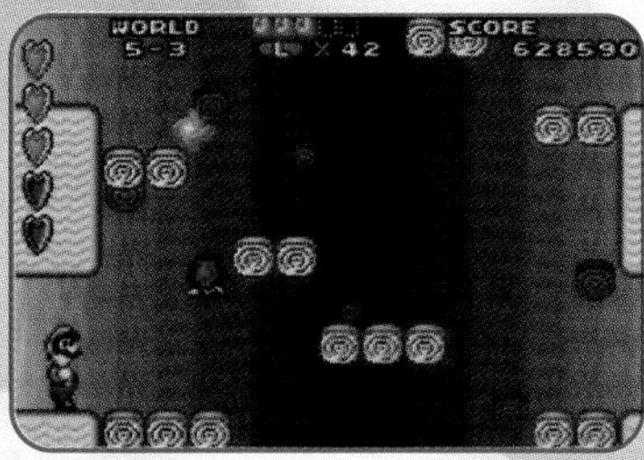

The second half of the upward journey is a series of stepped log platforms with "wrapping" horizontal gaps in the walls and Blue Pansers descending the platforms while shooting fireballs. Lovely, isn't it? Start at the bottom of each stepped platform and keep jumping up and to the left, dodging or eliminating Pansers as you go. When you reach the top, walk through the left gap in the wall to "wrap" around to the right side, and repeat the process for the next platform.

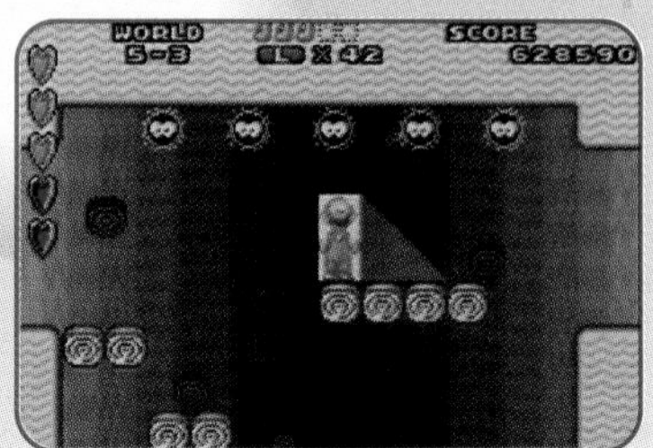

When you reach the top, use a POW Block (if you have one) on the Sparks running along the ceiling. If you don't have one, wait for them to pass overhead, jump onto the platform in the center of the cavern, and walk through the doorway in the center of the platform.

You reappear outside, on the first of a series of horizontal log platforms extending to the right. The Boss music is playing, so you know you must be near the end. Two Giant Blue Shy Guys walk the platform you appeared on; toss them around for some Hearts if you need to, then get rid of them. The five plants to the door's right are, from left to right, four Large Vegetables and a Shell.

Pluck the Shell and head right. Use the Shell on the Blue Snifit when you find him. Next to the Snifit is a Pidgit on a flying carpet. When he swoops down toward you, jump on his head and throw him off to seize control of the carpet. Head right, keeping to the upper part of the screen.

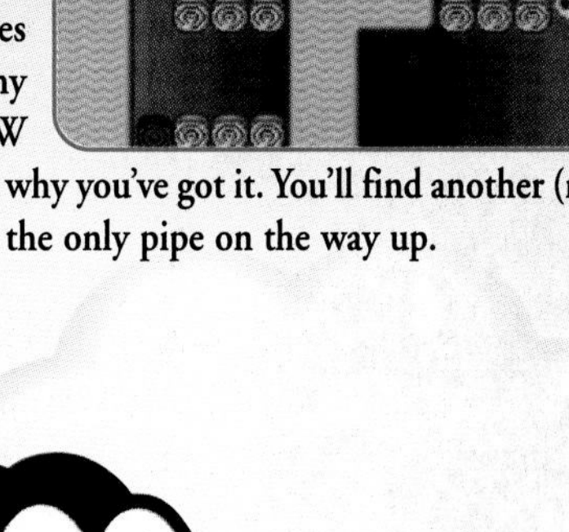

The fourth Ace Coin appears about two-thirds of the way across. Grab it, then steer toward the log platform to the right, past the second Pidgit. Once you're on the ground, steal the second Pidgit's carpet and head down and left to get the final Ace Coin. Return to the log platform once you have it.

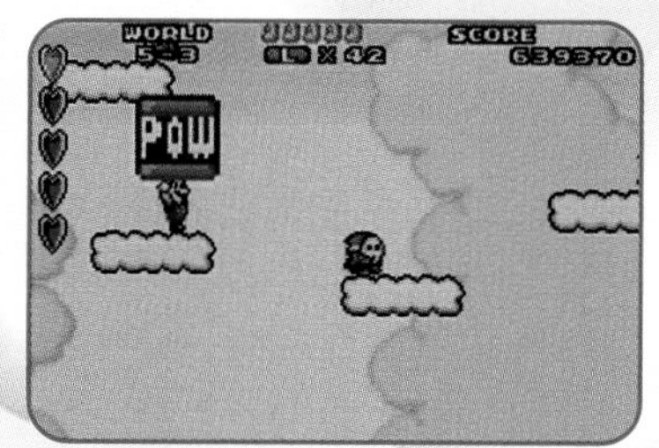

The three plants on the log platform are all Large Vegetables. Use them to defeat Blue Shy Guys and Beezos as you cross the cloud platforms to the right. Pick up the Giant POW Block when you come across it, but resist the temptation to use it immediately. Instead, carry it to the right as you continue hopping from cloud to cloud.

At the end of the clouds is a series of log structures, and waiting on one long horizontal log to the right is your old pal Birdo, the red fireballs-and-eggs version. Drop the Giant POW Block as soon as you start fighting her; this should give you one or two of the three hits required to defeat her—before she even gets an egg off.

Defeat Birdo using the same strategies you've used before, and pick up the Crystal Ball she leaves behind. The gate to the right opens; hop up the stepped platforms and enter it to begin the fight with Clawgrip.

Boss Fight: Clawgrip

Clawgrip is a giant crab with a fondness for throwing boulders at Mario and his friends. He's quick on the draw, too, so if your reflexes aren't sharp, you're going to have a tough time. Upon entering Clawgrip's lair, grab the two floating Hearts and pluck the one Heart Radish (if you're not at full health).

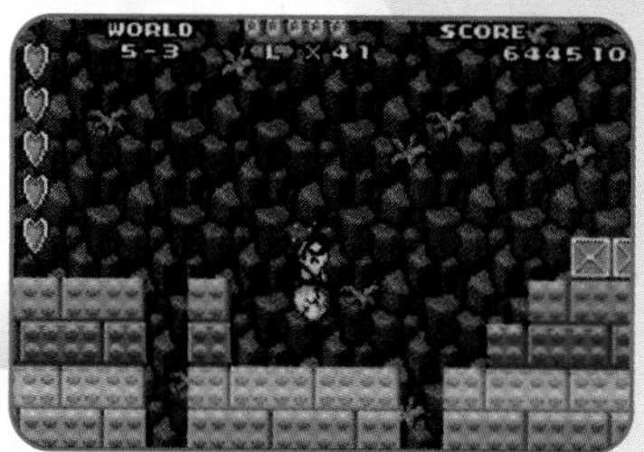

When the fight begins, stand in the corner of the L-shaped platform to the left of Clawgrip's pedestal. As his rocks fly toward you, jump up, land on them, and press Ⓑ to pick them up. Once you have a rock in hand, jump up to Clawgrip's pedestal and chuck it at him by pressing Ⓑ. There isn't a lot of strategy here...it all comes down to raw speed and reflexes. Hit Clawgrip five times to crack his shell. To complete World 5, walk through the doorway that appears when you defeat him.

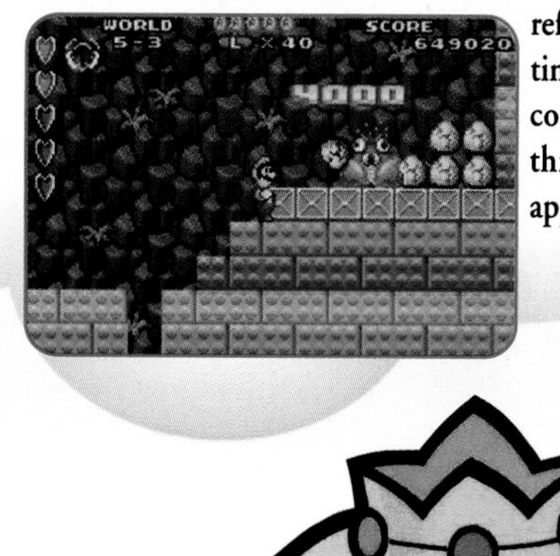

World 6-1

Mario of Arabia

Similar to World 2, World 6-1 is a desert land filled with quicksand, cacti, and Cobrats. Use whichever character you used for World 2 (Mario and Toad are both good choices). From World 6-1's start point, jump up onto the closed gate to the left and Super Jump up to grab the Heart floating overhead.

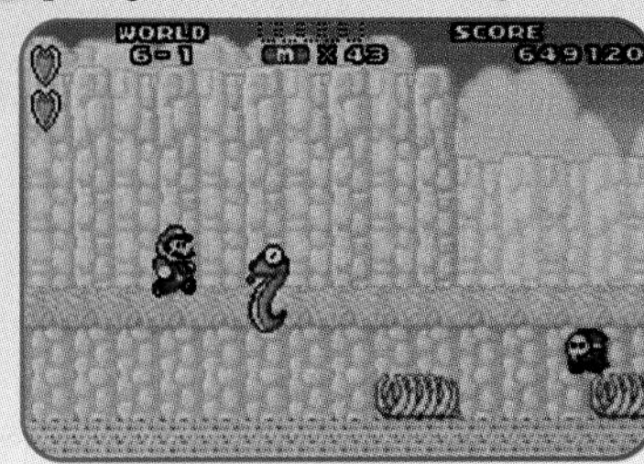

To the right is an expanse of quicksand with a Cobrat lurking just under the surface. Approach the Cobrat to lure him out, then pick him up and move to the right. Throw the Cobrat at the Blue Shy Guy pacing back and forth along the bone platform. If you time your throw correctly, you'll also hit the Cobrat on the right side of the Shy Guy's platform and get another Heart.

Continue right and pluck the Cobrat out of the first pipe you see. Enter the pipe to pluck a Magic Potion from the bottom. Leave the pipe carrying the Potion and continue right. Jump up onto the bone platform to the pipe's right and drop the Potion on the platform's left side.

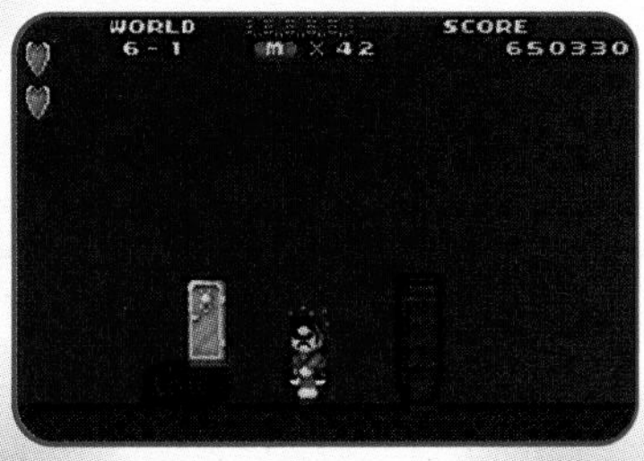

Before you enter the door to Subspace, make sure that the bone platform is on the screen's right side and the pipe is visible. The first Mushroom falls next to the door and sinks into the quicksand. Grab it before it's totally submerged. When you return from Subspace, stand on the bone platform's right side so the screen scrolls right, and wait for a Pokey to approach you from the screen's right side.

Jump onto the Pokey's head and ride him across the quicksand to the right (make sure to stand just right of center on the Pokey's head, or he'll take you all the way back to the left). At the first pair of cacti you come across, Super Jump up to grab World 6-1's first Ace Coin.

Keep riding the Pokey over the treacherous quicksand pits. None of the enemies below can touch you. Another pair of bone platforms is after the two pairs of cacti where you found the Ace Coin. Super Jump straight up at the left platform for the second Ace Coin.

Past the bone platforms is a short patch of solid ground and then another bone platform and two pipes to its right. Pluck Pokey's head to dispatch the Cobrats in the pipes, and use Pokey's other segments to get rid of the rest of him.

Both pipes contain Shells. Get one of them and take it out of the pipe with you (watch out for the other Cobrat when you exit the pipe). Jump over the two Cobrats in the sand to the right and up onto the grassy platform with the seven cacti. Two Pokeys approach from the right. Hang onto the Shell and jump on top of one of the Pokeys.

To get the third Ace Coin, Super Jump off of the top of the Pokey as it passes to the seventh cactus's right. Then, throw the Shell to the right of the seventh cactus. It bounces between that cactus and another farther to the right and takes out both Pokeys as they approach, giving you several Hearts and a couple of 1UPs.

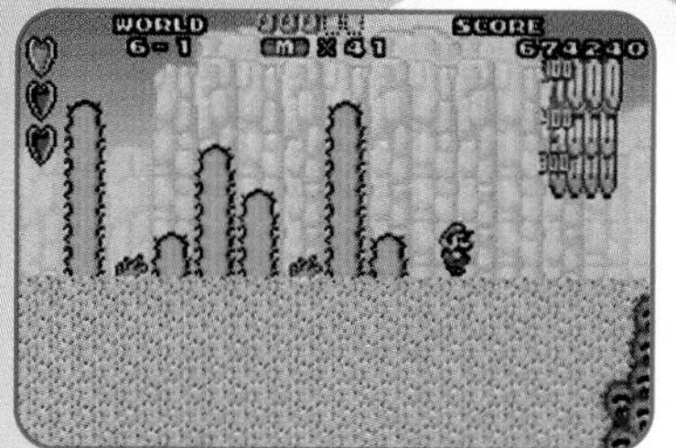

Backtrack slightly to the left and return to the seven cacti. Two plants are between the cacti: the left one is a Large Vegetable and the right one is a Magic Potion. Use the Large Vegetable to take out the Blue Panser to the right, then grab the Potion and take it with you as you move right.

Carry the Magic Potion all the way to the screen's right side and drop it on top of the sandy blocks above the door for the second Mushroom. The single plant among the cacti to the Panser's right is just a Small Vegetable, as are the four plants on the sandy blocks, so there's no reason to pluck them. Enter the door to reach the next area.

The door leads into a horizontal cavern with two Mushroom Blocks to the right. Lift the left one to get a Roulette. Grab a Mushroom Block and carry it off the ledge to the right to reach a row of 21 pipes—a few containing Cobrats.

Get rid of the Cobrats in the pipes, head left, toss the Giant Red Shy Guy around for some Hearts if you need them, then eliminate him with a Mushroom Block. The fourth Ace Coin is right near the Shy Guy, and the fifth Ace Coin hovers over the sixth pipe from the right. Get both of them before going any farther.

Wondering what's in those pipes?

Wonder no longer (pipes are numbered from left to right):

- *Pipes 1, 2, 8, 11, 13, 14, 15, 18, and 19 each contain one Shell plant.*
- *Pipes 4, 5, 6, 9, 12, 16, 20, and 21 each contain a 1UP. After you pluck a 1UP Mushroom in any of these pipes, the plant will become a Small Vegetable.*
- *Pipes 3, 7, and 10 have a sand floor and are filled with Red Shy Guys. If you dig through the sand to the bottom, you'll find four plants. The first time you enter any of these pipes, they will contain a 1UP Mushroom. After you pluck the 1UP Mushroom from any of the pipes, the four plants become Small Vegetables.*
- *Pipe 13 is a Shy Guy Generator. If you remove the Mushroom Block over it, Shy Guys pop out.*
- *Pipe 17 holds the Key to the locked door underneath a sand floor. Dig through the sand to get it.*

Once you have both Ace Coins, head to the cavern's far right, where you'll find a locked door with two plants on the platform above it. The left plant is a Heart Radish, and the right plant is a Magic Potion. Take the Potion back to the pipes and drop it near the tallest one (seventh from the left). The Mushroom appears on that tall pipe in Subspace.

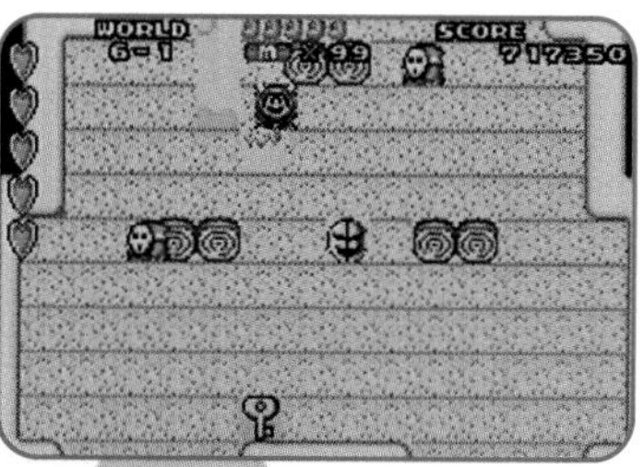

Once you get the Mushroom and return from Subspace, it's time to unlock that door. The Key is at the bottom of the fifth pipe from the right, under a layer of sand. Dig through the sand to reach it, and avoid the Red Shy Guys. Unlock the door and enter Birdo's lair for the World 6-1 Boss fight.

Gimme Another Chance (or 99 of Them)

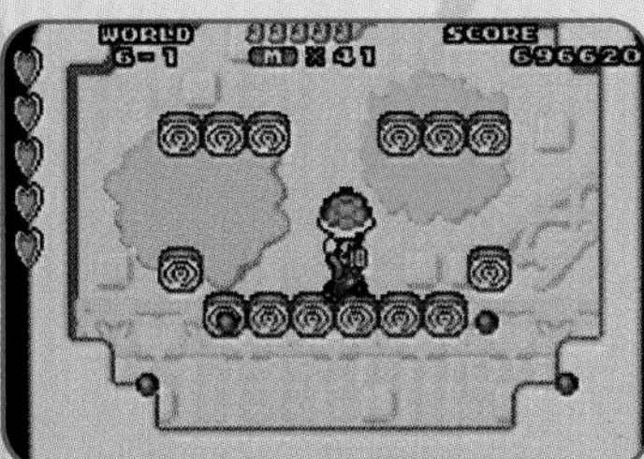

In this cavern are Mushroom Blocks, Shells, and a Shy Guy Generator—a recipe for as many chances and Hearts as you can hold. First, make sure you're near full health, because you might lose a Heart or two performing this trick. Next, pluck the Shell from pipe 8 and bring it out with you. Set it bouncing between pipes 7 and 13 and get rid of the returning Cobrats.

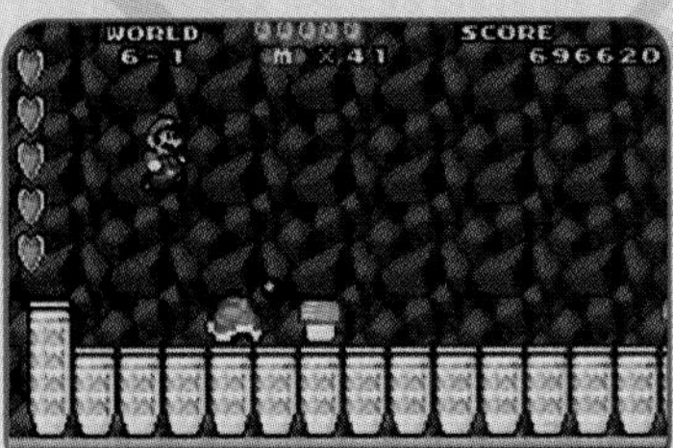

Finally, remove the Mushroom Block from pipe 13, drop it to the right, and stand on it. Shy Guys pour out of pipe 13, only to get smacked by the Shell. Watch the show until you have 99 chances and enough Hearts to fill your life meter, then head to the Boss fight.

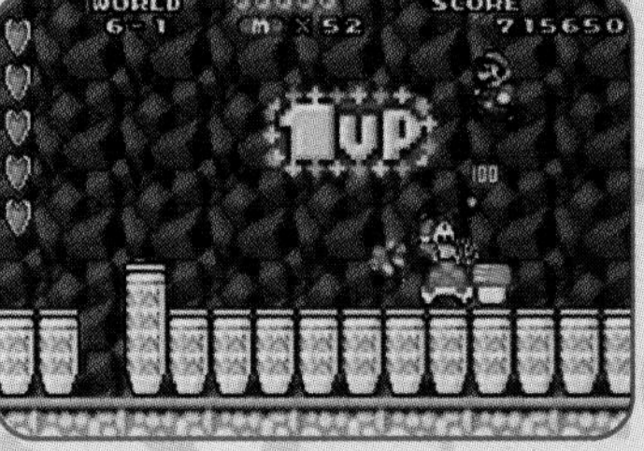

Boss Fight: Birdo (Green)

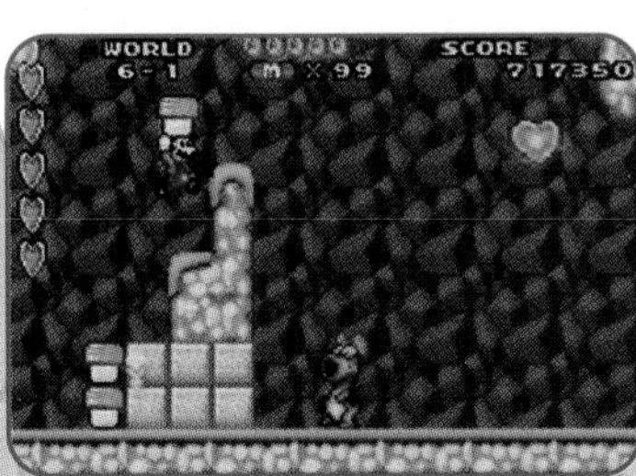

Birdo's latest lair is a horizontal cavern with two floating Hearts and three Mushroom Blocks. Because Birdo is green this time, she only shoots fireballs, so there's none of that mucking around with flying eggs.

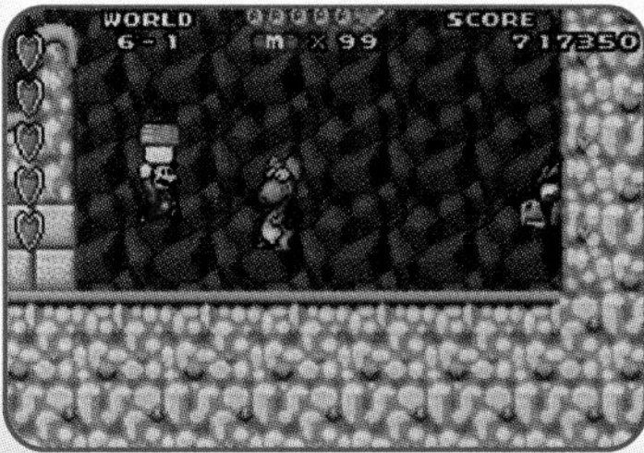

Birdo's fireballs can penetrate everything in the room except Mushroom Blocks, so your first order of business is to approach the three Mushroom Blocks arranged horizontally to the entrance's right. Stack the left and center Mushroom Blocks on top of the right one to make a vertical wall immediately to the tall grassy platforms' left.

Take the top Mushroom Block to the top of the grassy platforms and drop it immediately to their right, then do the same with the second, making sure it falls right on top of the first. You should see that you're gradually moving a wall of Mushroom Blocks toward Birdo—a wall that her fireballs can't pass through.

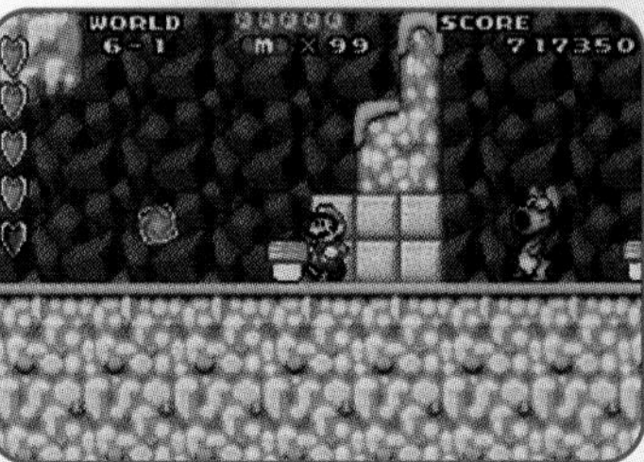

Grab the last Mushroom Block and carry it up to the top of the grassy platforms, then drop it on top of the stacked Mushroom Blocks below. As long as you're standing two blocks above the ground and Birdo is on the ground, her fireballs can't reach you.

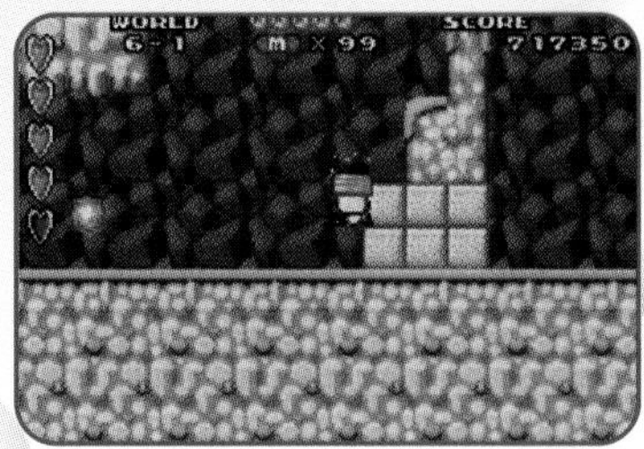

Wait until she gets close, then throw the Mushroom Block at her and follow up as fast as you can with the other two Blocks you're standing on. If you can press Ⓑ quickly (especially if you're using Toad), you should be able to throw all three Mushroom Blocks before Birdo can retaliate with even a single fireball. Collect the Crystal Ball she leaves behind and walk through the gate to the right to complete World 6-1.

World 6-2

Let's Travel By Albatoss!

World 6-2 resembles World 5-2's nighttime level, with one important exception: there is almost no solid ground anywhere in the level. To make it through, you must execute a series of precision jumps onto and off of about a dozen Albatosses. Choose Luigi as your character—his high jumps and slow descents help a lot.

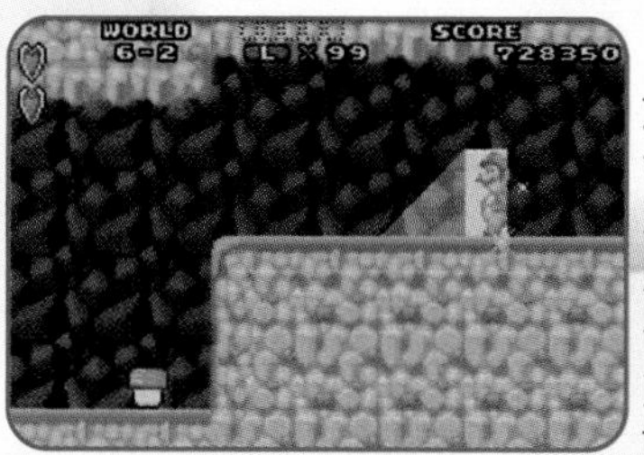

When World 6-2 begins, you're standing in a horizontal cavern with two Mushroom Blocks to your right. Pick up the right Block to reveal a Roulette. Drop the Roulette to get a Starman or a Heart, use the Mushroom Blocks to get rid of the Ninjis and Blue Shy Guys in the rest of the cavern, then exit through the doorway at the right end.

Here's where it gets fun (and by "fun" we mean insanely difficult). Pluck the plant to the right of the door you just came through to get a Large Vegetable, then jump onto the back of the Albatoss flying from left to right just below you. Keep holding onto the Vegetable.

When the next three Albatosses fly by from right to left in a staircase formation, hop up on each of them and ride the top one to the left until *another* Albatoss flies toward you from the left. Hop on that Albatoss's back and ride him to the right.

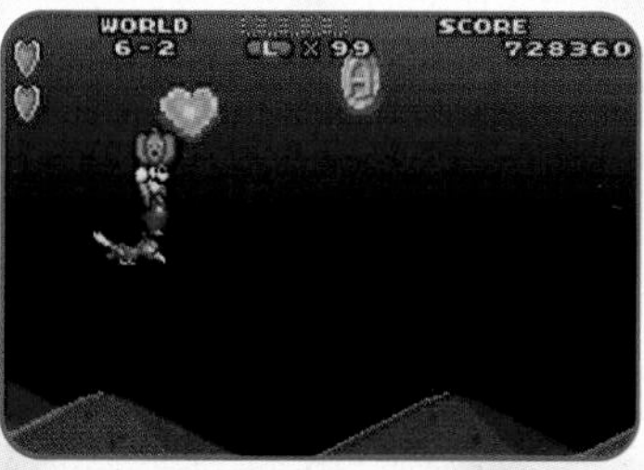

Continue riding the Albatoss to the right to reach the first Ace Coin. You have to hop up to get it, so make sure you land back on the Albatoss, or it's a lost chance for you. A short while later, you pass over the second Ace Coin (past the fireball-spitting Panser on the ledge below). Fortunately, some Albatosses are going in the opposite direction. Hop on one of them.

Ride the Albatoss all the way back to the beginning and hop off onto the platform near the door. Jump on the back of the first Albatoss you rode (the bottom one traveling from left to right). When you reach the Panser, hit it with the Large Vegetable you are (hopefully) still carrying.

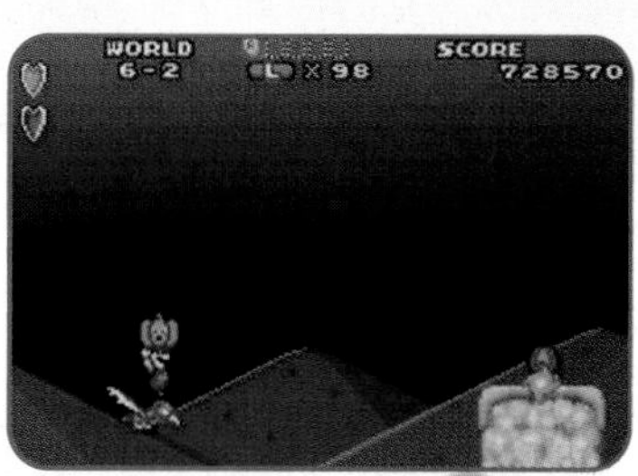

If you're standing on a platform and miss your chance to jump onto the Albatoss that you must ride, try walking back and forth on the platform. When you make the screen scroll, the Albatosses usually return.

Once you've defeated the Panser, jump onto its platform and pluck the plant to get a Magic Potion. If you're playing as Luigi, you should have just enough time to pluck the Potion and jump back onto the Albatoss's back. If you're playing as anyone else, hitch a ride on a right-to-left-flying Albatoss to return to the start, then get on the lower left-to-right Albatoss again to backtrack to the Panser's platform. Hop up onto the platform and then back onto the Albatoss as it continues moving right.

The Albatoss takes you to the next Ace Coin and a Heart. If you're playing as Luigi, crouch down and prepare to Super Jump as soon as you get the Ace Coin. When the next platform comes into view, jump up onto it. If you're playing as any other character, jump onto the right-to-left-flying Albatoss and ride it until you can jump onto a left-to-right-flying Albatoss above you. Jump off of that Albatoss and onto the platform past the second Ace Coin.

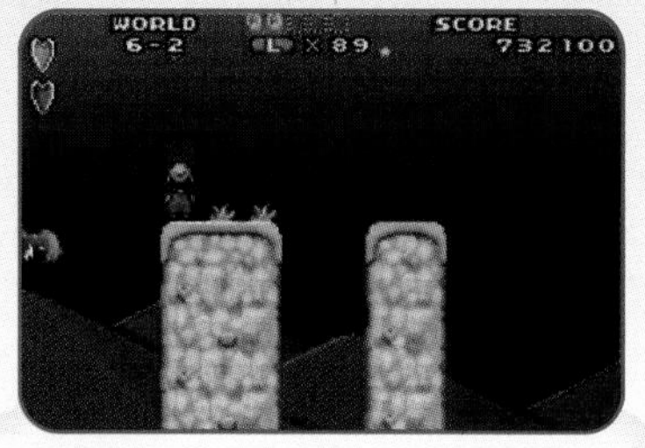

Drop the Magic Potion on the platform so that the narrower platform to the right is also visible. Enter Subspace to find the Mushroom on the narrower platform. When you return from Subspace, pluck the right plant on the wider platform for a Large Vegetable. The left plant is another Potion, in case you forgot to bring one.

Ride a right-to-left flying Albatoss back to the beginning, then ride the upper left-to-right-flying Albatoss past the platforms with the Mushroom. When the three Albatosses flying in vertical formation appear from the right and head toward you, jump onto the top one. Ride it for a short distance, then jump up to get the third Ace Coin. Ride the Albatoss until you can get onto a left-to-right-flying Albatoss.

Take that Albatoss to the right until you meet the three right-to-left Albatosses flying in the vertical formation. Jump over them, then onto the one following them, and then onto the one following that one. Jump off of the last Albatoss's back to get the fourth Ace Coin. Ride the Albatoss all the way back to the beginning.

Once again, get on the lower left-to-right-flying Albatoss and ride it to the platforms where you got the Mushroom. Super Jump onto the platforms, then run across them and jump back down to the Albatoss as it passes the platform's right end. Ride it until you reach the final Ace Coin.

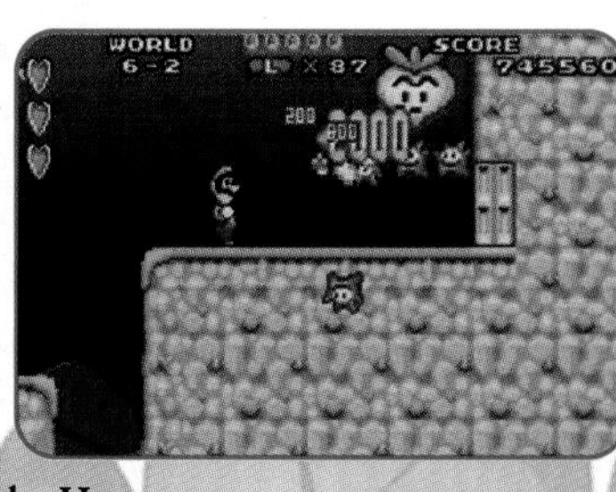

After grabbing the fifth Ace Coin, get ready to jump up onto the platform just past it. Pluck the plant on the platform for a Giant Vegetable, jump up onto the next platform to the right, and hit all five Ninjis with the Huge Vegetable, snagging a 1UP and a Heart.

Boss Fight: Birdo (Green)

Enter the door at the second platform's right end to enter Birdo's lair. Head right until you see the two Mushroom Blocks, the Giant Blue Shy Guy, and Birdo herself. Once again, she's sporting green, which means she will only be shooting fireballs—no eggs.

Hop up onto the platform above her and move toward her to begin the fight. Pick up the Mushroom Block and drop it on her head once she moves into the proper position.

Drop down to the lower platform on the left, then drop onto the Giant Blue Shy Guy's head when he walks under you. Pick him up (Birdo's fireballs can't hurt you while you're lifting), and throw him at Birdo. The Shy Guy should do at least one hit's worth of damage to Birdo, and will quite possibly do two hits worth, defeating her.

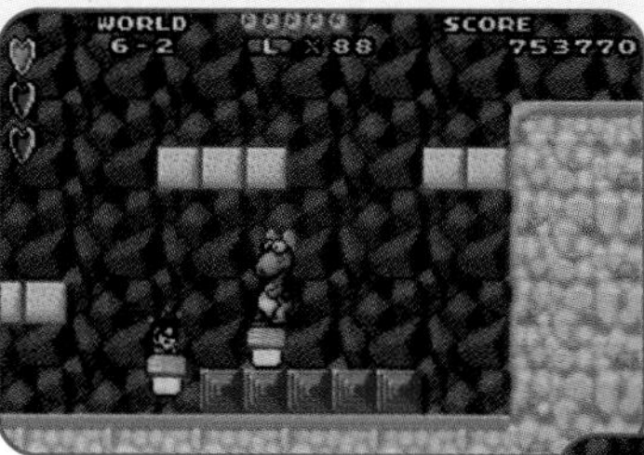

If she's still kicking after the Shy Guy attack, pick up the Mushroom Block next to where the Shy Guy was and throw it at her. Pick up the Crystal Ball she leaves behind to open the gate.

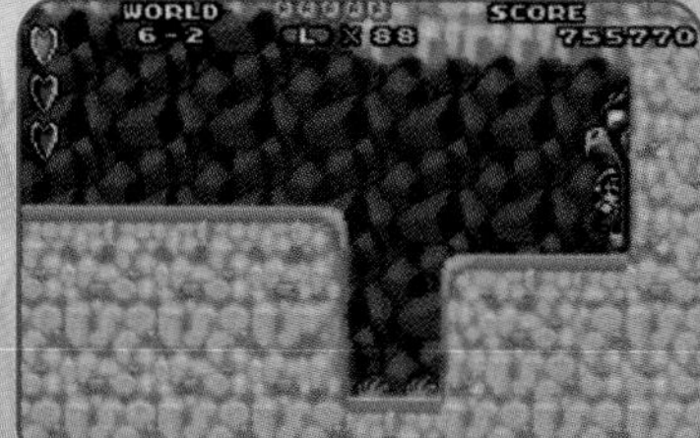

The plant on Birdo's pedestal is a Heart Radish, probably too dangerous to pick up during the fight. On the way to the gate, you'll pass two other plants. The left one is a 1UP Mushroom, and the right one is a Bob-Omb. Pluck the Mushroom and leave World 6-2 via the gate.

World 6-3

Return of Mouser

And now, the good news: compared to either 6-1 or 6-2, World 6-3 is a walk in the park. The Ace Coins and Mushrooms are all fairly easy to find, the enemies aren't overly tough, and the Boss is Mouser, whom you've already defeated once before (he's no tougher this time). Any character will do for World 6-3, but Mario is strongly recommended—he's the most well rounded character.

You begin World 6-3 in a sandy subterranean cavern with ten plants lining the floor. With that many plants, you'd think there must be something of interest here, but you'd be wrong. The only useful plant is the Heart Radish, which is second from the right. The others are all Small Vegetables. Pluck the Heart Radish, then climb the ladder to reach the next section.

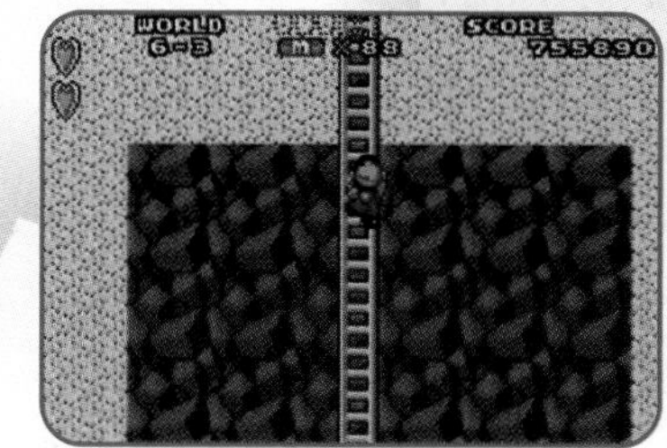

To the top left of the ladder is a patch of quicksand and a stone wall (see the next sidebar to learn the secret of the quicksand). To the right is a plant, followed by three cacti and another plant. The left plant is a Magic Potion, the right one is a Heart Radish. Pluck the Heart Radish if you need it, but leave the Potion alone for now.

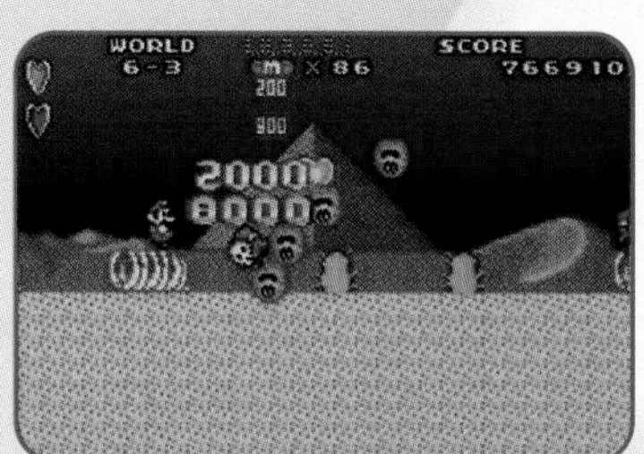

Move to the right past the cacti and jump up onto the second of two bone platforms. Pick up the Blue Shy Guy pacing on the platform and throw him at the Pokey appearing from the right. With both enemies defeated, go back to the Magic Potion, pluck it, and drop it on the second bone platform, making sure you can see the two stubby cacti to the right. The level's first Mushroom appears on the farther cactus in Subspace.

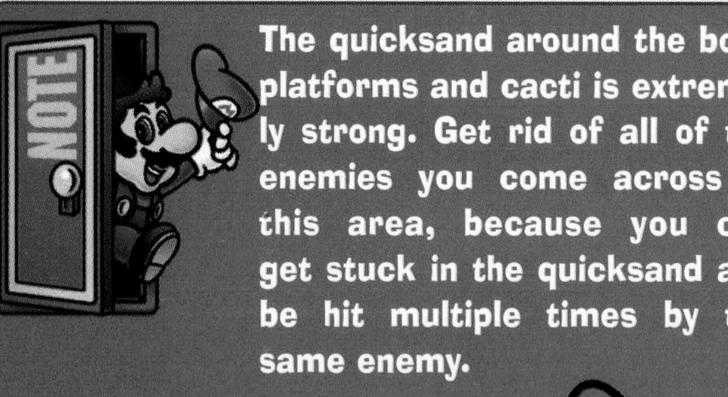

The quicksand around the bone platforms and cacti is extremely strong. Get rid of all of the enemies you come across in this area, because you can get stuck in the quicksand and be hit multiple times by the same enemy.

Quicksand Shortcut

If you don't care about getting all of World 6-3's Ace Coins and Mushrooms, you can skip about three-quarters of the level by taking a shortcut. From the top of the ladder leading out of the start point, walk into the quicksand to the left, and keep walking left.

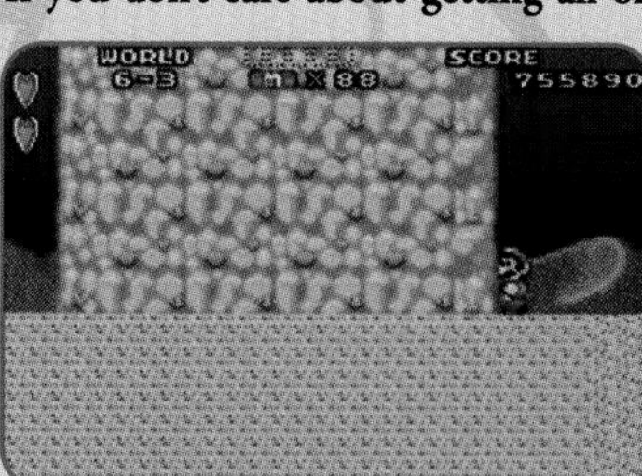

Keep pressing ← once you're up against the rock wall and sinking into the sand. Just before you are completely submerged, you start walking underneath the rock wall! Press Ⓐ rapidly and repeatedly as you hold down ← to walk left under the wall. If you don't keep jumping by pressing Ⓐ, you'll sink into the sand and lose a chance.

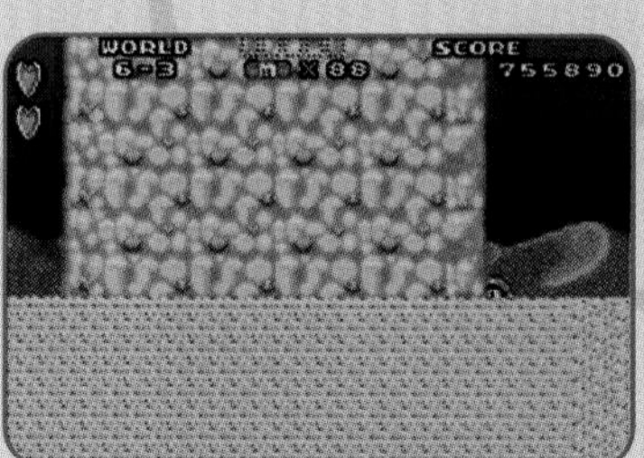

On the other side of the wall is a door that leads to a series of horizontal cloud platforms to the left. Hop across them, and when you reach the last one, jump down and to the left to find yourself in front of the door to Birdo's lair!

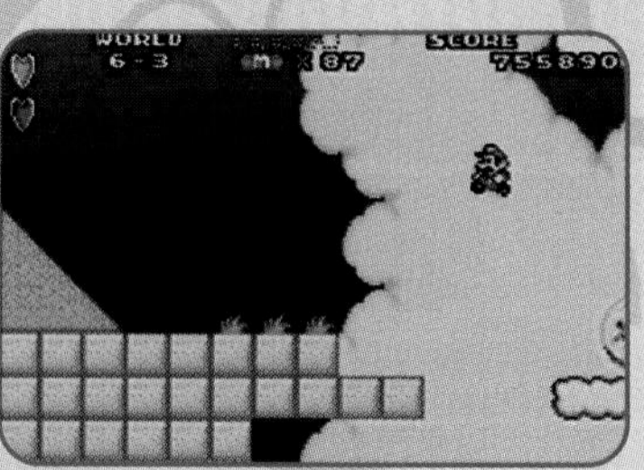

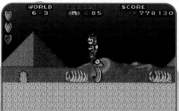

After getting the Mushroom, continue right. Past the two stubby cacti are two more bone platforms, with a Blue Shy Guy on the left one and a Cobrat lurking in the strong quicksand between them. Jump onto the Shy Guy's platform and pick him up, but don't use him to take out the Cobrat—you need the Cobrat in one piece for now.

Jump toward the Cobrat to lure him out from under the sand, then jump up on his head and crouch down for a Super Jump. When the Cobrat is in the middle of the space between the two bone platforms, jump straight up for the level's first Ace Coin. Once you have it, you can get rid of the Cobrat.

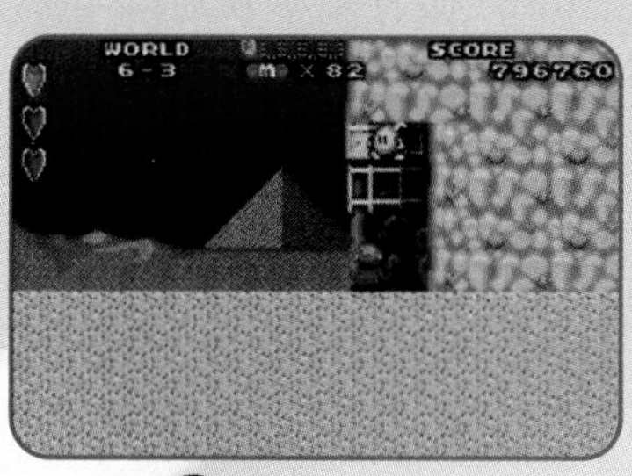

To the right of the second bone platform is a Bob-Omb plant and, more importantly, solid ground. Move all the way to the right to find a large gated doorway. Enter it as you would any other doorway (that is, by pressing ↑ while standing in it).

Bob-Omb Cavern

You probably guessed from the Bob-Omb on the outside gate that you'd find a few explosive enemies inside. This horizontal cavern is filled with things that go BOOM! Fortunately, Bob-Ombs are not the brightest baddies in the game. From the entrance of the cavern, jump up to get the two Hearts floating overhead and to the right if you need them, then proceed to the right.

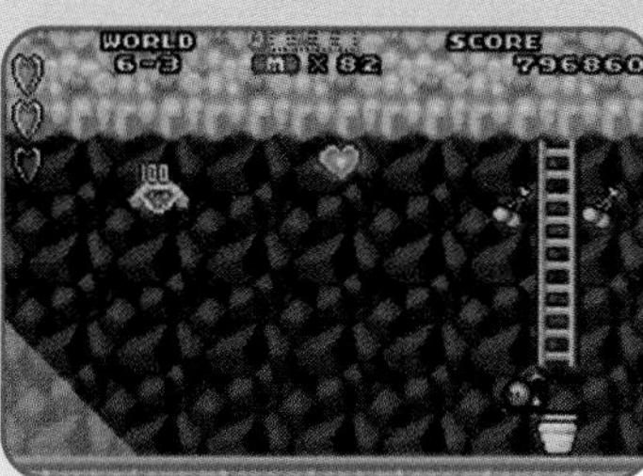

Along the ceiling are ladder fragments that seem to go nowhere. Directly below the first one you find is a Bob-Omb Generator. Jump onto the ladder and hang there for a while. The Bob-Ombs popping out of the Generator wait right underneath you and then explode, taking out the Generator and each other.

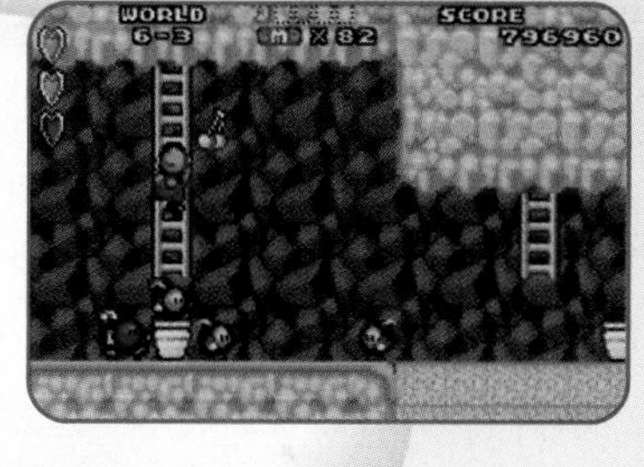

Move to the right and repeat the process when you reach the next Bob-Omb Generator, on top of a sand pit a short distance from the last one. The last Generator is in another sand pit just to the right of the one before it.

With all three Bob-Omb Generators destroyed, backtrack left to the beginning of the cavern and pick up the two Cherries on either side of the first ladder and in each of the sand pits. When you have all four, move to the right and jump up onto the grassy platform above.

Stand at the top of the sand pile immediately to the grassy platform's left and dig down four blocks. The sand you're standing on is even with the sand on the other side of the stone wall to your right. Hop back up to the upper platform.

Pluck either of the two plants on the upper platform; they're both Bombs. Drop the Bomb down the tunnel you just dug to destroy the stone wall to its right. Walk through the blown-out wall and collect the Cherry on the other side of it. This should be your fifth Cherry, and a Starman should appear.

Catch the Starman to become invincible, then take out as many of the ten Ninjis and Shy Guys to the right as possible. If you get rid of all of them, you'll get a nice handful of 1UPs to go with your new enemy-free cavern.

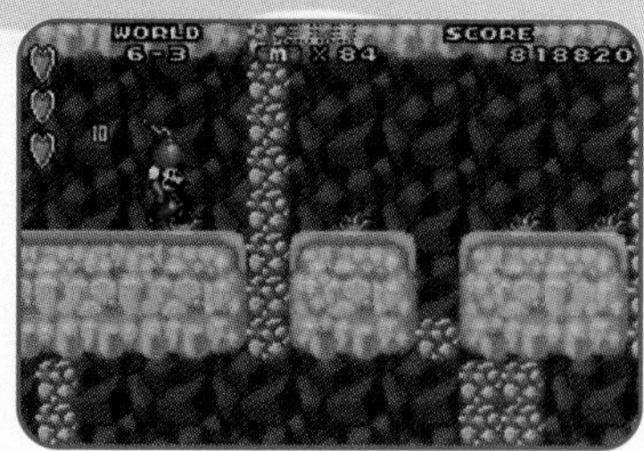

Head right past the huge sand pit where you took out all of those Shy Guys and move onto the grassy platform level with it. From left to right, the three plants on the platform are a Heart Radish and two Bombs. Pluck the Heart Radish if you need it, and then use one of the Bombs to blow open the wall to the right.

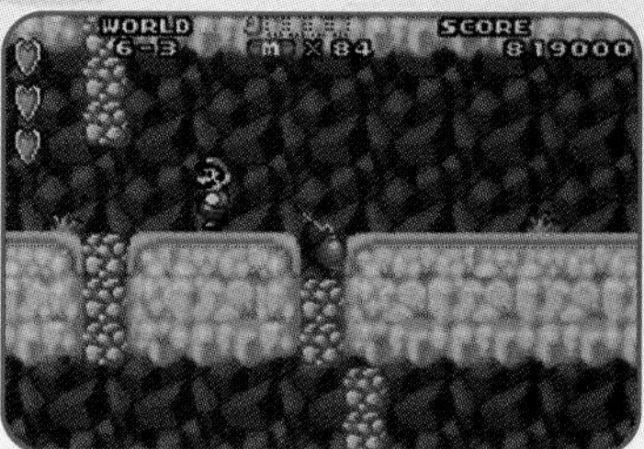

On the other side of the Bombed wall are three plants: a Magic Potion and two Bombs. Pluck the first Bomb to blow open the next wall to the right. Past this wall is a two-block vertical stone wall embedded in the platform. Use the second Bomb to get rid of the top block. Pluck the next plant to the right to get a Bomb, and use that Bomb to destroy the last block in the embedded wall.

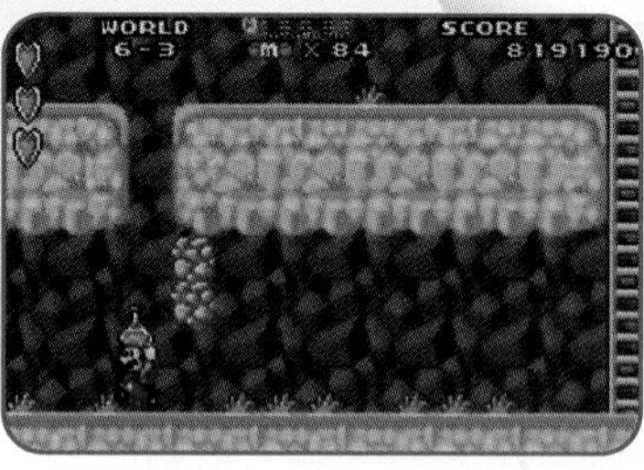

Pluck the Magic Potion and drop it down the gap you just created, but don't go through the door yet. At the bottom of the gap, to the left of yet another stone wall, are two Bomb plants. Use one to blow open the stone wall to the right, and then enter the door to Subspace. That will let you get the Mushroom (which appears right next to the door) and pluck the Coins past the last stone wall you Bombed.

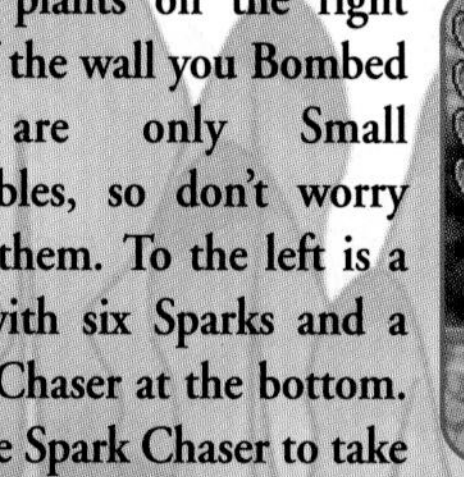

The plants on the right side of the wall you Bombed last are only Small Vegetables, so don't worry about them. To the left is a pipe with six Sparks and a Spark Chaser at the bottom. Use the Spark Chaser to take out the Sparks and get a 1UP or two if you do a good job.

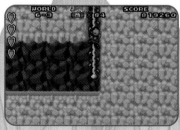

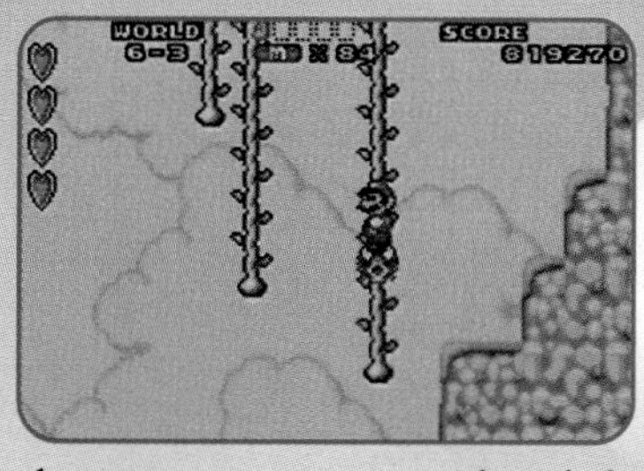

Continue right. Climb the ladder to reach the grassy platform to the right, then climb the vine at the grassy platform's right end to reach the next area—a canyon with a whole jungle of vines and a Hoopster on nearly every one.

Start climbing the vines. Get on top of the first cloud platform you come to and Super Jump up to grab the second Ace Coin. From that same platform, carefully jump to the narrow ledge on the screen's right side and walk right, "wrapping" around to the left to find a plant. Pluck it to get a 1UP Mushroom.

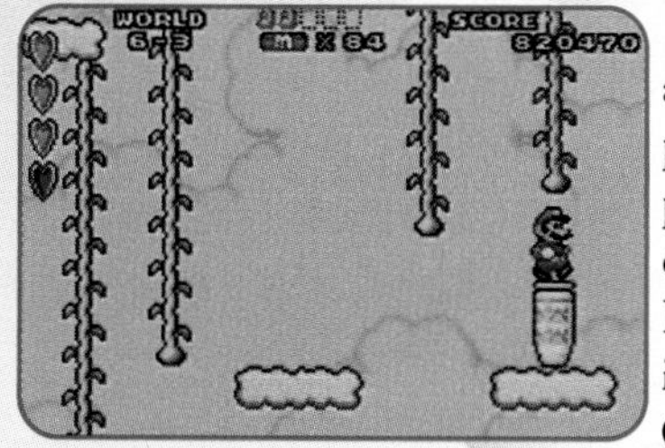

Continue climbing vines and jumping across cloud platforms until you reach a pipe sitting on top of a cloud on the screen's right side. Head to the pipe and down into it while avoiding the Gray Snifit to the pipe's left. Pluck the plant at the bottom of the pipe to get a Magic Potion.

Carry the Magic Potion out of the pipe and jump to the left onto the cloud platform where the Gray Snifit was (he shouldn't have reappeared after you left the pipe). Drop the Potion on this cloud to get the third Mushroom. Then, jump onto a vine on the left side of the screen and resume climbing.

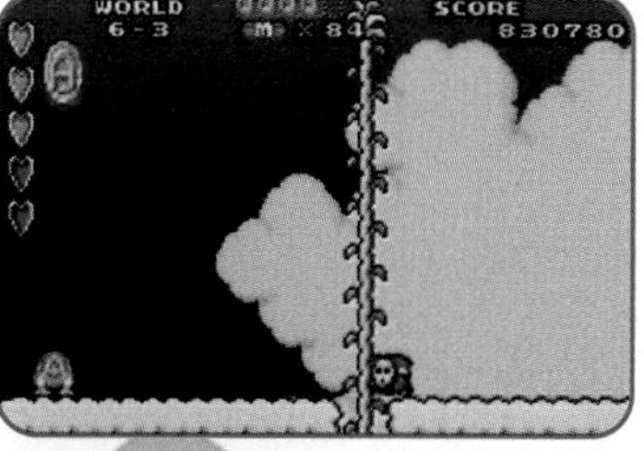

The third Ace Coin is just a couple of screens above the pipe. It's floating next to a vine on the screen's left side and isn't tough to spot or pick up. Underneath the right Mushroom Block on the same screen as the Ace Coin is a Roulette. Grab it if you want it, then continue upward.

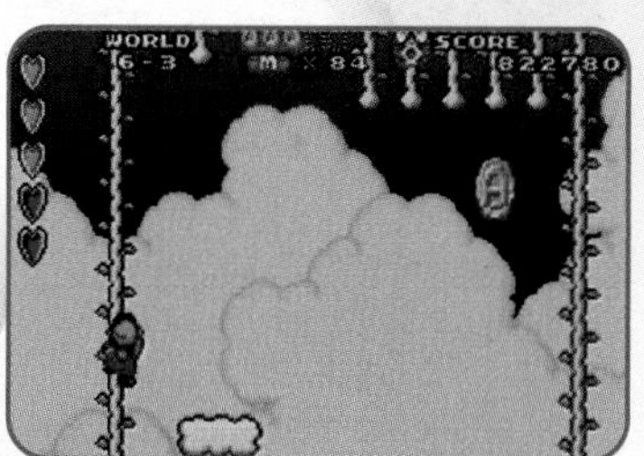

The fourth Ace Coin is on the screen's right side just past a number of closely spaced vines with Hoopsters on them. It isn't hard to find or acquire. Get the Coin, then—you guessed it[—keep climbing.

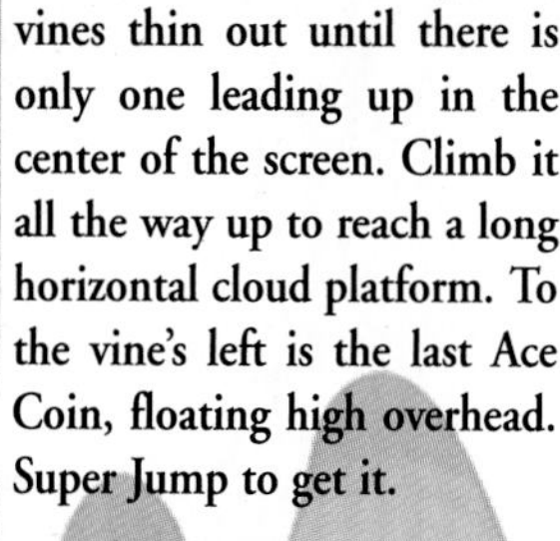

As you near the top, the vines thin out until there is only one leading up in the center of the screen. Climb it all the way up to reach a long horizontal cloud platform. To the vine's left is the last Ace Coin, floating high overhead. Super Jump to get it.

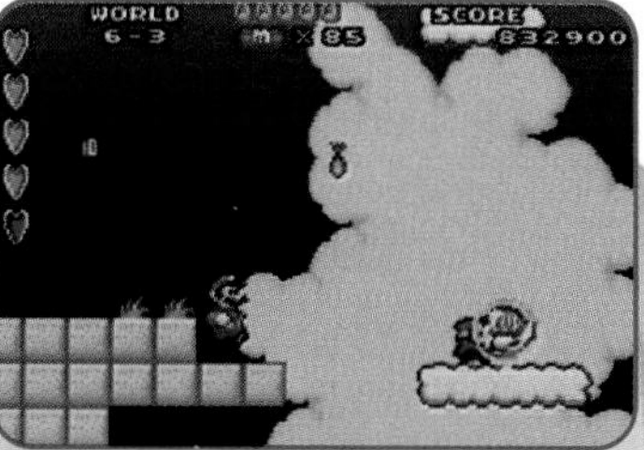

Once you have all five Ace Coins, head right. Watch out for the Blue Shy Guys and Tweeters (who don't put up much of a fight). The door to the Bosses' lair is in the middle of a pyramid to the right, and just past that is a 1UP Mushroom in a bubble, with three Small Vegetables next to it.

The cloud platforms you can just barely make out over the 1UP Mushroom are the platforms you jump across after taking the shortcut from the beginning of the level.

Boss Fight: Birdo (Red) and Mouser

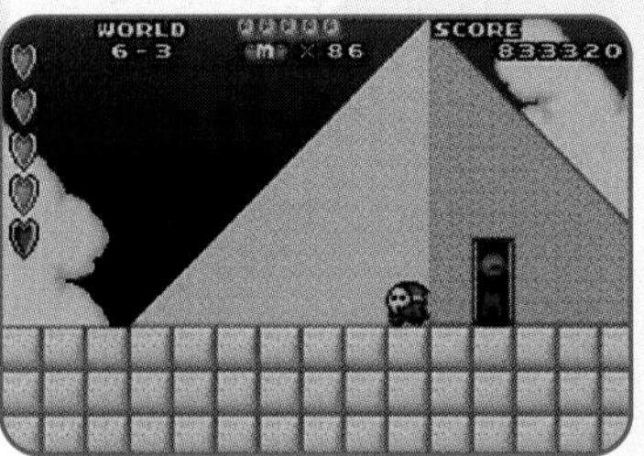

Use the three Small Vegetables to pop the 1UP Mushroom's bubble, grab the Mushroom, then head back to the left and enter the door to the Bosses' lair. The first Boss you face is Red (eggs and fireballs) Birdo. By now, you should be able to beat this Birdo blindfolded and with both hands tied behind your back.

Pick up the Crystal Ball Birdo leaves behind to open the gate to the right, and enter the gate to begin the main event: the fight with Mouser. He's learned very few new tricks since you first fought him. You need five hits to defeat him now, and two Sparks are in the lair with him. Everything else is business as usual.

Grab the two floating Hearts, then run to the right to begin the fight with Mouser. He's standing on his pedestal, hurling Bombs down and to the right. Drop to the floor beneath his pedestal and catch his Bombs in midair by jumping under them as they soar overhead.

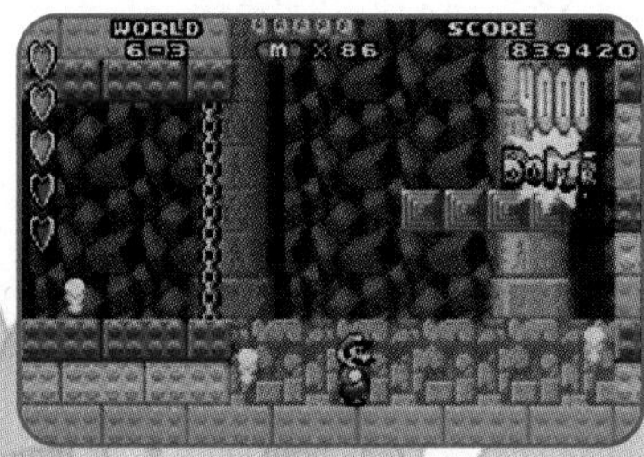

Once you have a Bomb, run toward Mouser's pedestal, jump, and press Ⓑ to drop it at his feet. Place the Bomb on the right side of his pedestal; that's usually where he'll be when it blows. As mentioned before, it takes five Bomb blasts to defeat Mouser and open the doorway out of World 6-3.

World 7-1

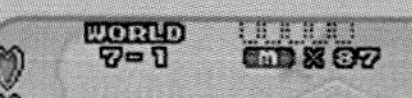

The …
of th…

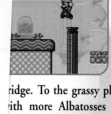

Babbage's

0077-Genesee Valley Center

3331 Linden Rd.
Flint, Michigan 48507
(810)733-3155

08-10-2001 13:59 0077-2010810-020 GAD

831001 VGHint 1 @ 14.99 ea 14.99
Super Mario Advanced Off Stgy Gd (Pr

Merchandise	$	14.99
Sales Tax @ 6%	$	.90
Total	$	15.89

Payments
Mall Certificate $ 20.00

Change
Cash $ 4.11

A receipt is required for all returns.
Returns must be made within 7 days.
Game systems replaced with same item.

Don't forget to trade your games!

some of World 6's … fine in World 7-1, … is always a good ch…

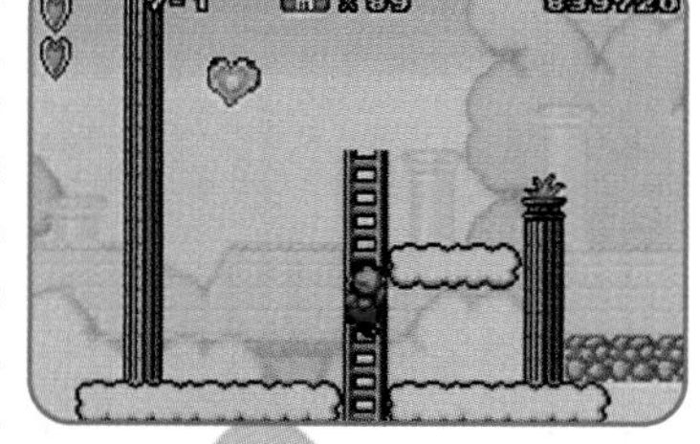

your reward. Jump up … the third one.

The ladder brings you to a cloud city with Grecian columns. To the left is a very tall column with a Heart floating to its right; grab the Heart if you need it. To the right are two short cloud platforms, followed by a short pillar with a plant on it (a Small Vegetable) and a horizontal stone bridge. Albatosses fly by dropping Bob-Ombs that detonate and open gaping holes on the bridge.

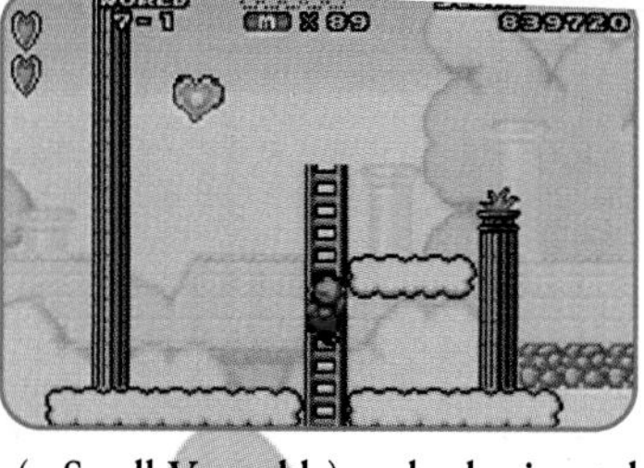

Run to the right across the stone bridge and continue past the grassy platform …ridge. To the grassy platform's right is another …ith more Albatosses and Bob-Ombs. On the …idge's right end is a pillar with a plant on it. Pluck … a Magic Potion, then bring the Potion back to the … and drop it to get the level's first Mushroom.

The right and left plants on the grassy platform are Small Vegetables. The middle plant is a Heart Radish. You won't need any of them if you just got the Mushroom, so double back to the right and keep running. Jump up on the first …latforms to the right of the pillar where you plucked …ion.

…y Generator …d Shy Guys on …loud platform. …e Mushroom … first platform …Generator with …r the door to … the Shy Guy

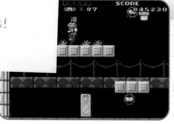

The door leads into a small room with two platforms and two Sparks. Jump up onto the higher platform and pluck the third plant from the right to get a Magic Potion. Drop the Potion where you found it, then enter Subspace to get the second Mushroom and a bunch of Coins. From left to right, the other plants are four Large Vegetables and two small Vegetables.

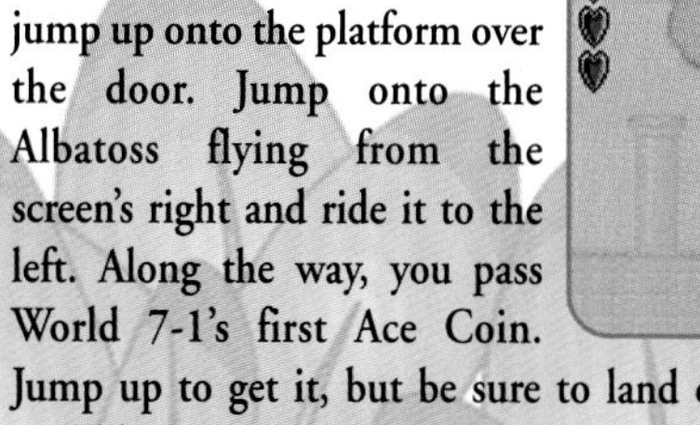

After you have the Mushroom, exit the room and jump up onto the platform over the door. Jump onto the Albatoss flying from the screen's right and ride it to the left. Along the way, you pass World 7-1's first Ace Coin. Jump up to get it, but be sure to land on the Albatoss; otherwise, you'll have to go back to the door and do it again.

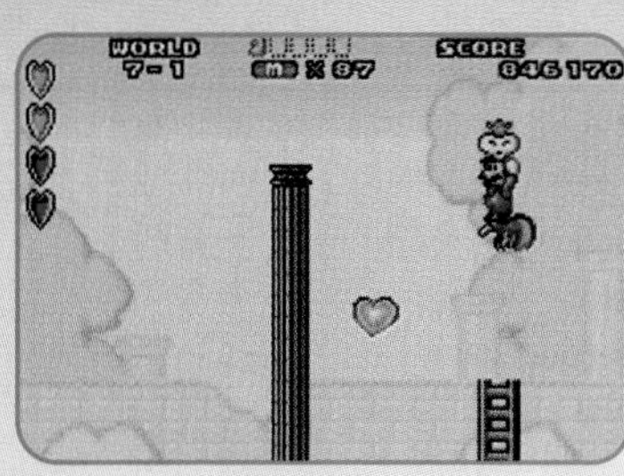

The Albatoss takes you past the first ladder you climbed, but the column to the left is too tall for you to ride past. The Albatoss can pass through it, but you'll be pushed off of its back if you don't jump over the column.

You'll also have to jump the next column, which has a 1UP Mushroom plant on top of it that you can grab if you're quick. Be sure to jump back onto the Albatoss after getting it, or you'll have to go back to the door and catch another ride.

The second Ace Coin is to the left of the column where the 1UP Mushroom was. Jump up to get it and continue riding to the left. There is only one more column to jump, and you don't have to land on the Albatoss afterwards. Instead, drop to the ground to the left of the column.

In the middle of the small brick platform you land on is a plant. Pluck it to get a Rocket Ship ride up to the next area—another series of cloud platforms extending to the right. Jump onto the pillar to the left of where the Rocket Ship dropped you off and Super Jump to get the third Ace Coin. The plant to the column's left is a Heart Radish.

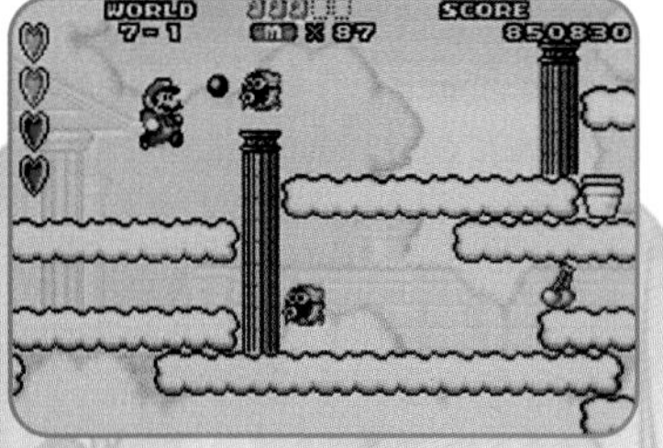

After getting the Ace Coin and the Heart Radish, head right to find several closely spaced horizontal cloud platforms with Snifits, Shy Guys, and Tweeters roaming across them. Move right along the bottom cloud platform to grab the first of five Cherries in this area, then jump up to the Gray Snifit on top of the column. Grab the Cherry over his head, then pick him up and toss him to the column's left.

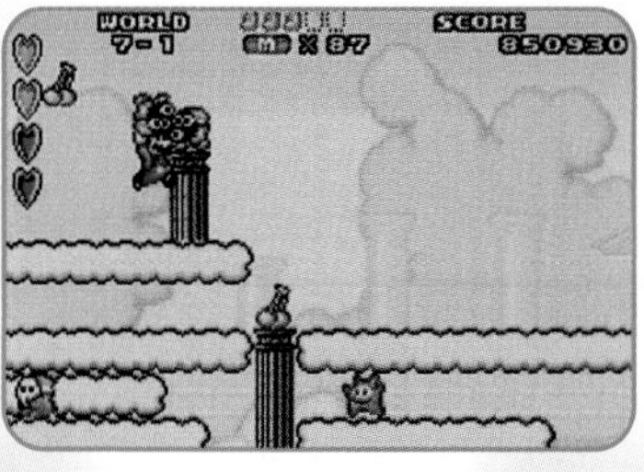

Jump over the next column to the right and move right along the following cloud platform. Grab the Cherry floating overhead. At the cloud's right end is another pillar with another Gray Snifit. Pick this one up too and throw it to the column's left, then drop off of the column and grab the Cherry below.

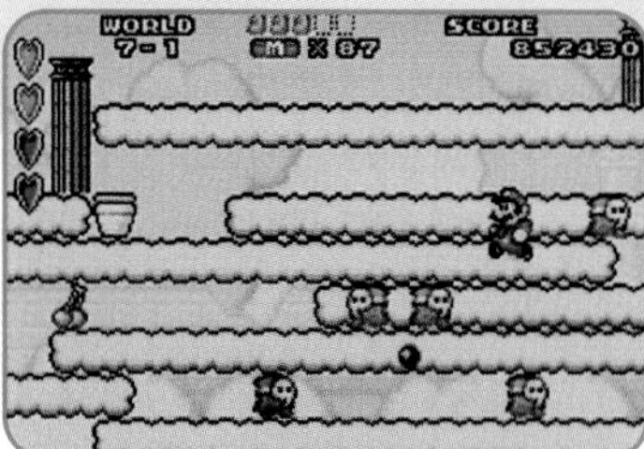

Run left until you reach the Shy Guy Generator, then drop onto the cloud platform just below the one you were on. Run to that platform's right end, keeping a careful watch on all of the Snifits and Shy Guys that could harm you, then drop down two more platforms.

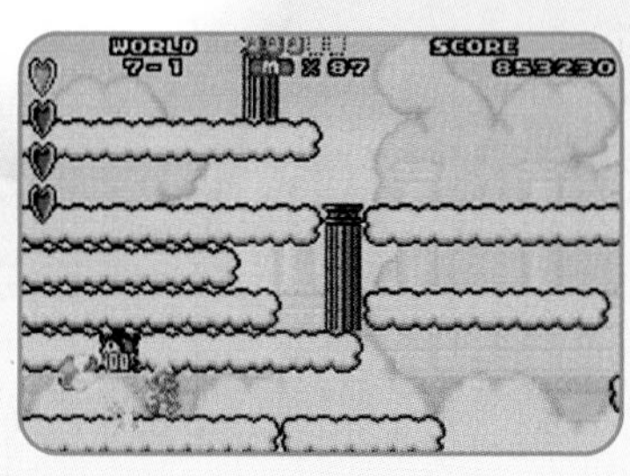

Head left until you get the fifth Cherry. Then, jump up to the platform above the Shy Guy Generator and grab the Starman once it reaches you. As soon as you become invincible, zigzag down the clouds as fast as you can, hitting every enemy along the way.

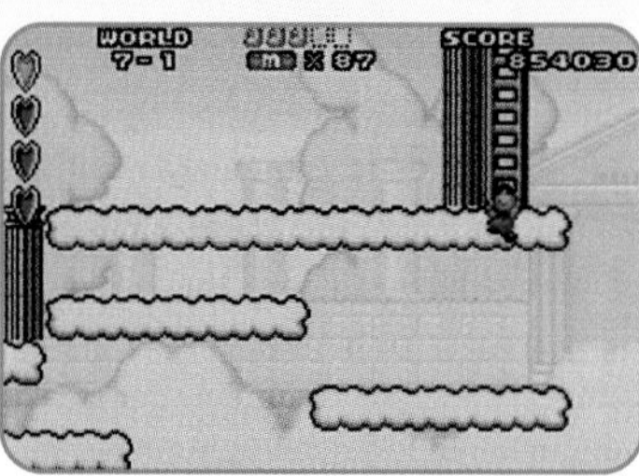

When you reach the bottom cloud platform's right end, jump up and to the right and then take out the Ninji hopping on the cloud to the column's right. After that, run off of the right edge of that cloud onto the one below and to the right, and get rid of the Gray Snifit.

From this last cloud platform on the bottom right of the screen, jump up to the ladder above and start climbing. The ladder leads to another area with long horizontal cloud platforms and "wrapping" sides (if you run off of the left edge of the screen, you appear on the right, and vice versa).

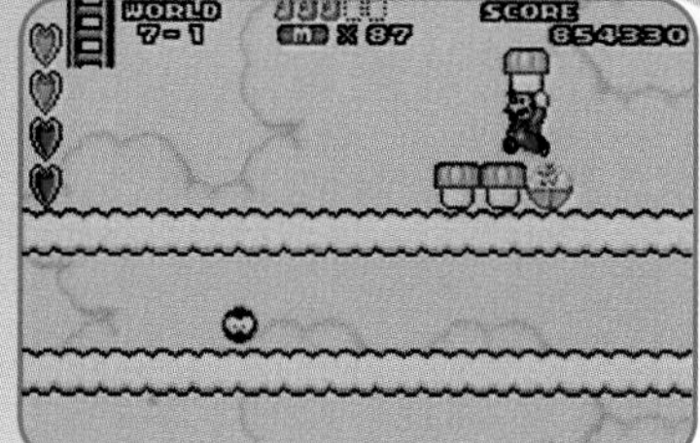

Jump up the cloud platforms, being careful to avoid the Sparks speeding by, until you reach the cloud with the three Mushroom Blocks. The right Mushroom Block has a Roulette under it and a Heart floating over it. Get the Heart if you need it, use the Roulette to get a Starman, and then climb the ladder on the left side.

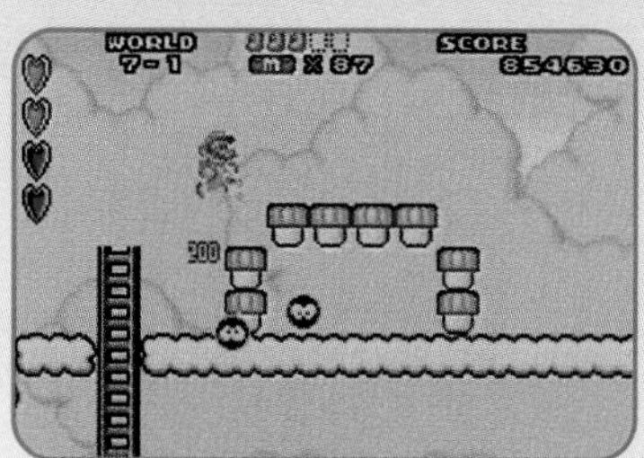

The ladder leads to another cloud with a bunch of Mushroom Blocks in a horseshoe formation and two Sparks zipping around—one inside the Mushroom Block formation and one outside of it. Quickly, before your invincibility wears off, pick up one of the blocks and get rid of the Spark on the inside, then eliminate the other Spark.

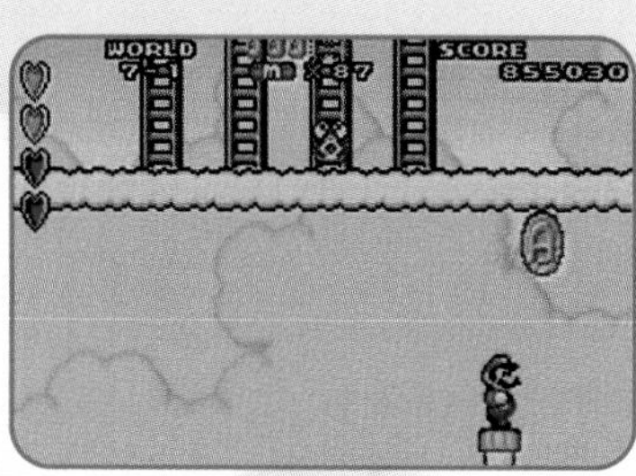

After the Sparks are gone, stack the Mushroom Blocks four or five high on the screen's right side and leap off of the top of them to get the fourth Ace Coin and reach the next cloud platform.

The cloud platform above the Mushroom Blocks has four ladders; the middle two have Hoopsters roaming up and down. Climb the rightmost ladder to get to the pillar on the next screen up, and pluck the plant on top of the pillar to get a Magic Potion.

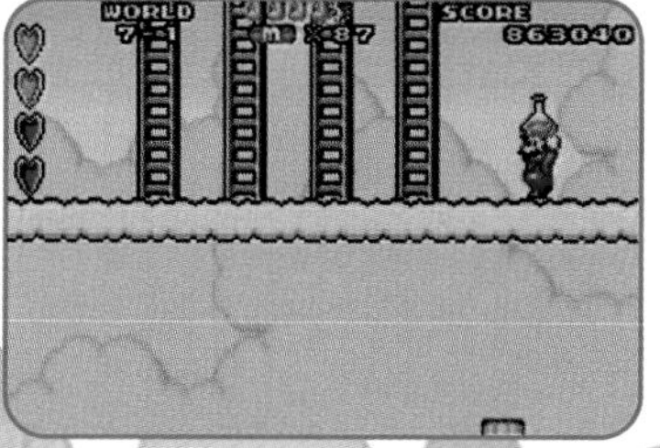

Drop off of the pillar and fall down to the base of the ladders. Toss the Magic Potion anywhere on this cloud platform *except* directly on top of a ladder. Remember: if you place the door to Subspace over a ladder, pressing ↑ while standing in the doorway will make your character climb the ladder, not enter the door. The Mushroom appears between the ladders.

Once you have the Mushroom, climb back up the right ladder and keep going up until you reach the door under the small grassy platform surrounded by two pillars. The plant on the left pillar is a Small Vegetable, the plant on the right pillar is a Large Vegetable, and the plant on top of the grassy platform is a Heart Radish. Get the Heart Radish if you need it, then enter the door to battle the Boss.

Boss Fight: Birdo (Green)

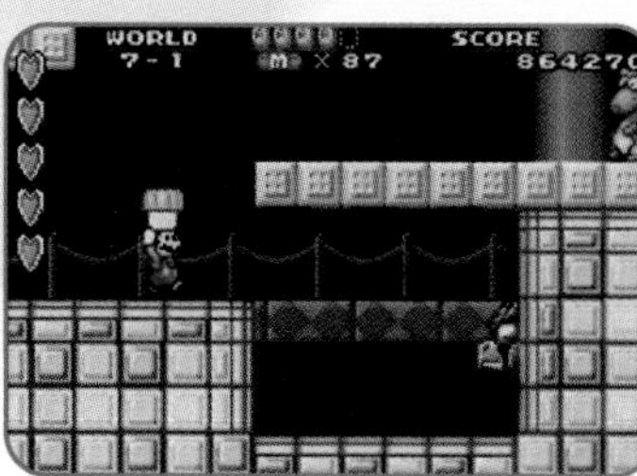

This is the green Birdo, so expect a lot of fireballs (no eggs) to shoot from her mouth.

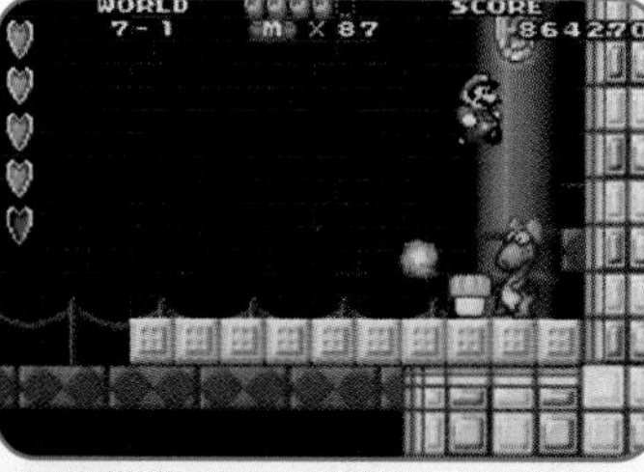

You have one Mushroom Block (to the right of the entrance) to use against her. Hit her three times to beat her. The only other item of interest in this room is the fifth Ace Coin, which hovers to Birdo's upper right. After you defeat Birdo and grab the Ace Coin, open the gate with the Crystal Ball, then head through.

World 7-2

The Final Showdown

World 7-2 is not only *Super Mario Advance*'s final level, it's also the hardest. It's a maze filled with conveyor belts, doors, and just about every enemy you've faced so far. Completing it requires split-second timing, almost superhuman dexterity, a lot of patience, and a quick eye. Luigi's jumping skills are best suited for World 7-2, so choose him as your character.

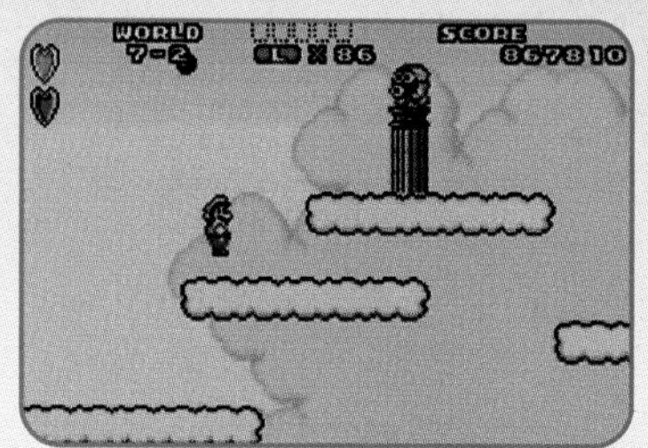

From the cloud platform on which you start, jump up and to the left to pluck the Heart Radish from the ledge above. Jump to the cloud platform with the Gray Snifit on the pillar. Pick up the Snifit and throw him at the other Gray Snifit below and to the right.

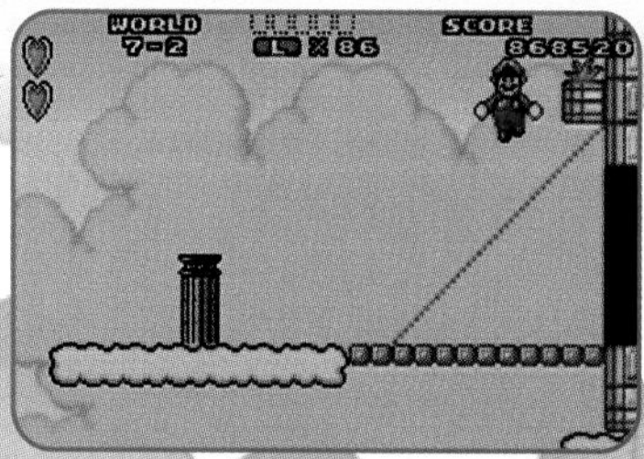

Jump down to the platform where the second Snifit used to be, then jump over to the right and pick up the third Snifit. Move all the way over to the right, Super Jump up, and throw the Snifit at the Ninji bouncing on the tiny ledge above the doorway. Jump up to the Ninji's ledge and pluck the 1UP Mushroom there.

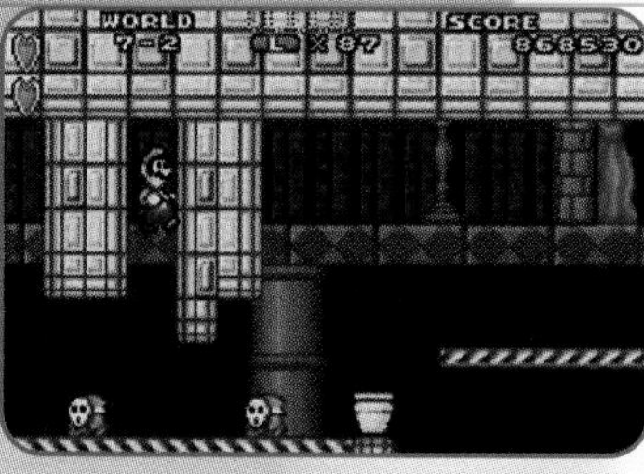

After getting the 1UP Mushroom, enter the door below to get to the next area. You appear on a conveyor belt moving right, and there's a Heart floating above. Grab the Heart if you need it, then move right. Avoid the Red Shy Guys as they pop out of the Shy Guy Generator at the right end of the conveyor belt, and jump up to the left-moving conveyor belt above and to the right.

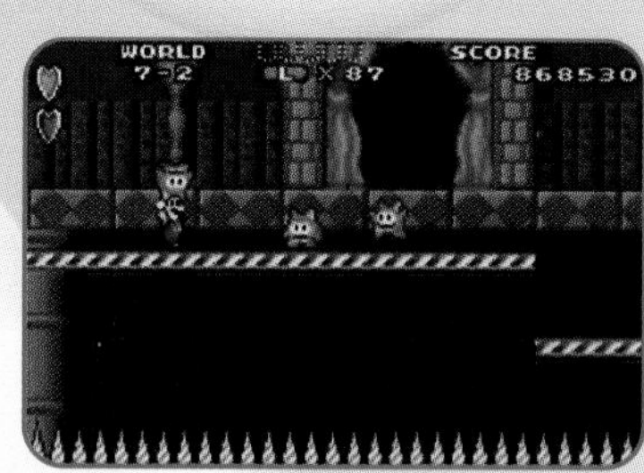

As soon as you land on the conveyor belt, press and hold ➔ to keep from falling off the left edge and into the pit below. Jump on one of the three Ninjis, pick him up, and take him with you as you move right.

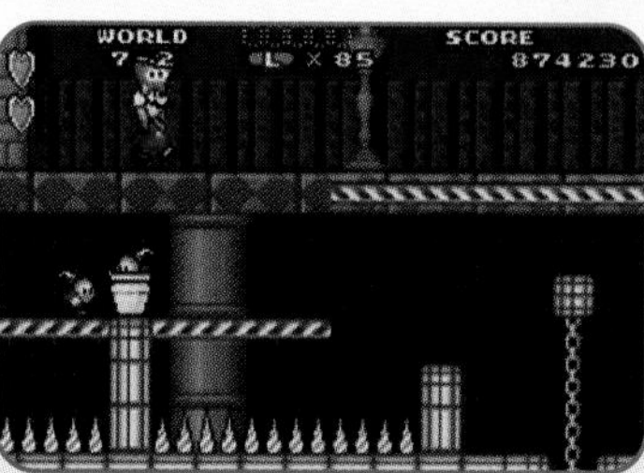

Walk off of the conveyor belt's right end onto another left-moving conveyor belt below, and continue right. Watch out for the Bob-Ombs that the Bob-Omb Generator is spawning at the conveyor belt's right end. When you reach the conveyor belt's right end, jump up onto the right-moving conveyor belt above and to the right.

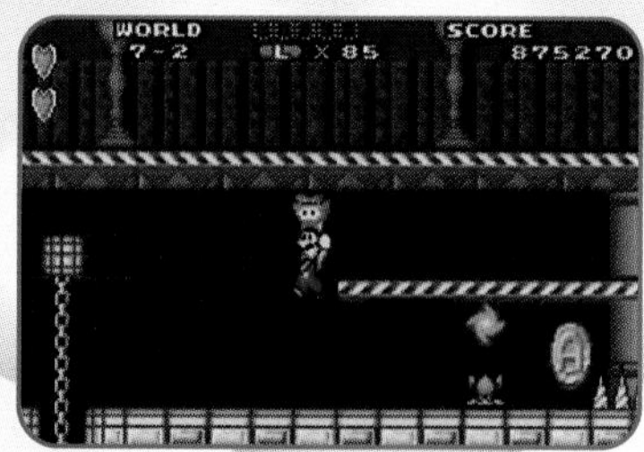

Let the conveyor belt carry you to the end and drop you down onto the left-moving conveyor belt below. Run off the left end of the left-moving conveyor belt, being careful to avoid the fireballs from the Green Panser below.

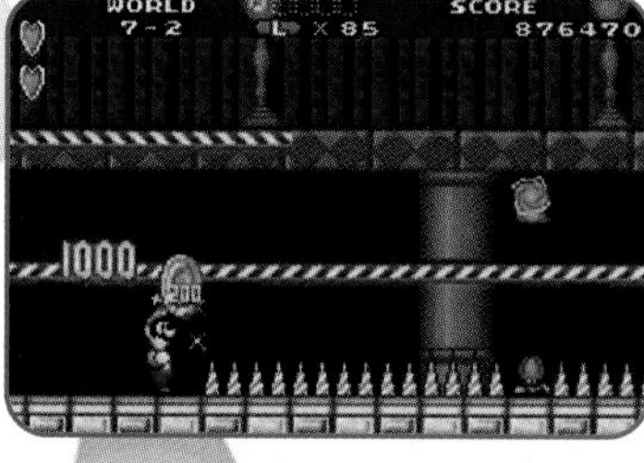

Once you're on solid, non-moving ground, walk to the right and throw the Ninji at the Panser. Walk past where the Panser used to be and collect World 7-2's first Ace Coin. Backtrack to the left and climb down the chain.

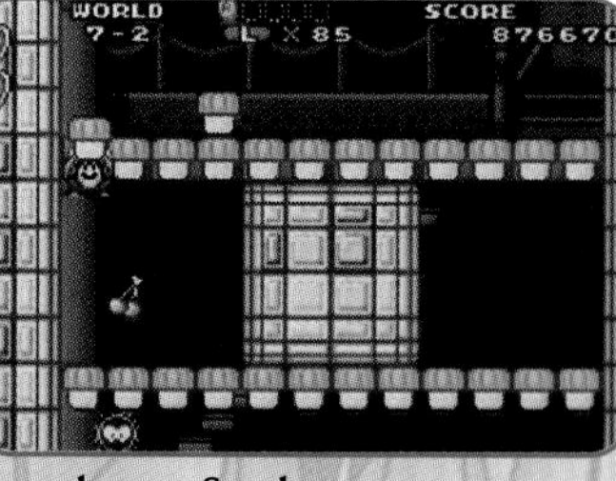

The chain takes you down to the top of a vertical cavern divided into small rooms by Mushroom Blocks. Sparks are running around most of the rooms. Pluck Mushroom Blocks from the floor to drop down into the next room; also, use the Mushroom Blocks to take out Sparks.

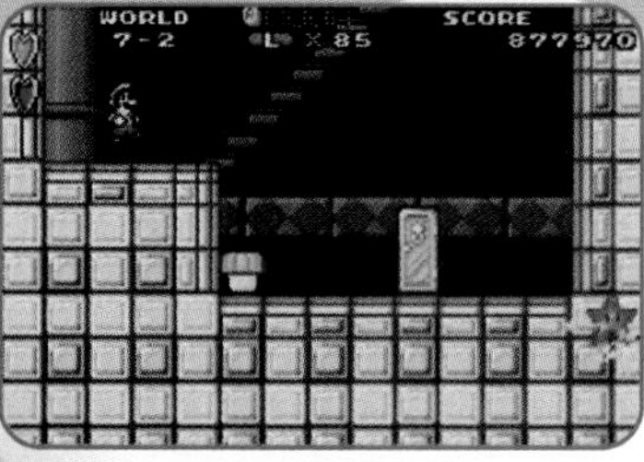

If you have a choice of rooms to fall into, always pick the one that has a Cherry in it. There are four Cherries on the way down. Follow these guidelines to get to the cavern bottom safely, where you will find the fifth Cherry. Grab it, then grab the Starman that shows up. Enter the door at the bottom of the cavern as soon as you become invincible.

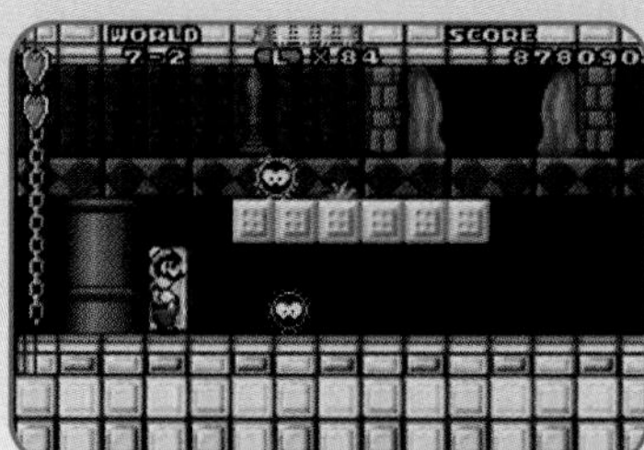

Once you pass through the door, run right across the horizontal cavern you appear in and take out as many Sparks as you can. Two Heart Radishes are on this cavern's floor. Be sure to grab them if your health is not full. There are two doors in this cavern—one around the middle of the cavern and the other at the right end. Enter the one in the middle.

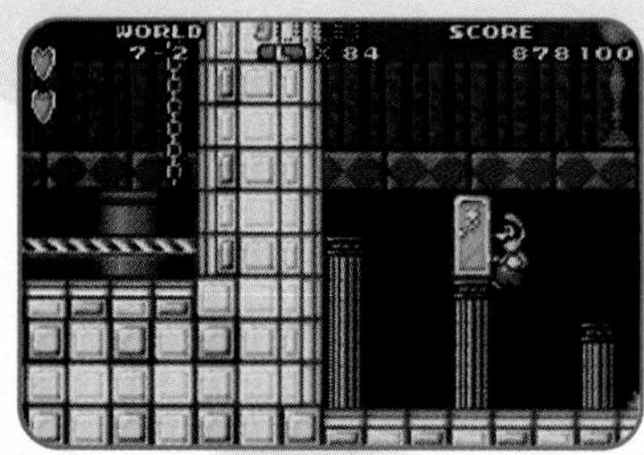

This door takes you into a small room with five pillars and two plants between them to the door's left. The plant on the right is a Bob-Omb. The plant on the left is a Magic Potion. Drop the Potion so that the leftmost pillar is visible onscreen, and enter Subspace to find a Mushroom on that pillar.

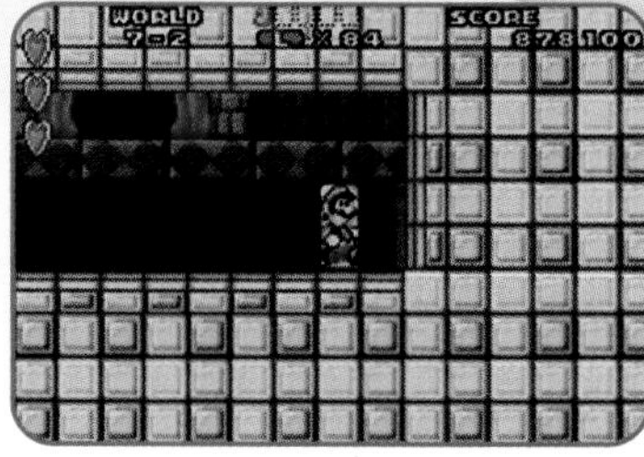

Once you get the Mushroom, go back out the door through which you entered and head right. Enter the door at the cavern's right end. You'll appear at the bottom of a vertical cavern with a chain hanging from the ceiling. Jump onto the chain and climb.

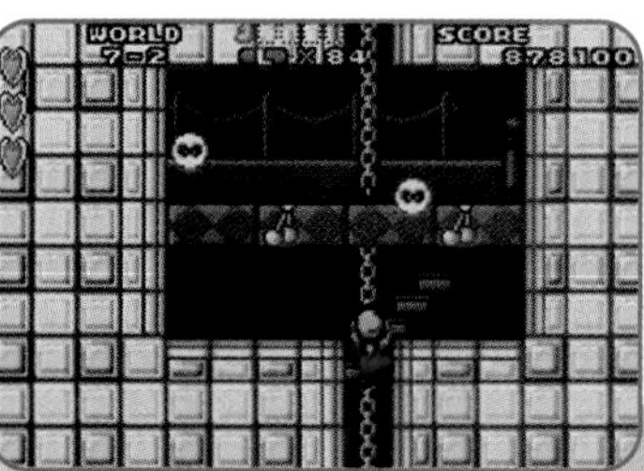

The chain leads through a series of small rooms with Sparks racing around in them. Each room also has two Cherries. The Sparks can't hit you if you are fully on the chain, so time your moves carefully and leave the chain to collect the Cherries only after the Sparks have passed by.

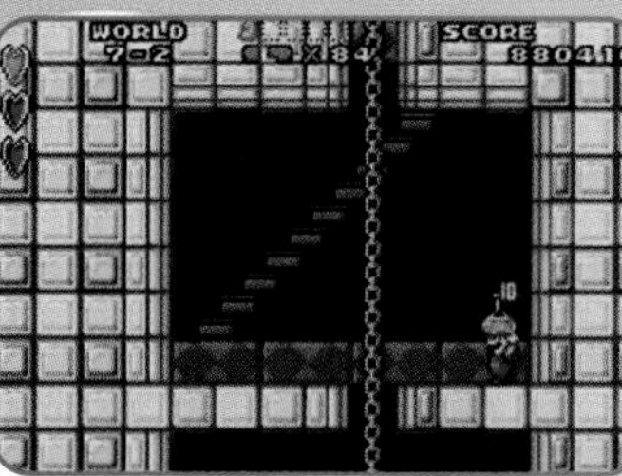

Once you reach the third room, you'll have collected enough Cherries to get a Starman. As soon as you catch the Starman and become invincible, take out the Sparks in the third room and climb up to the fourth room. Get rid of the Sparks in the fourth room and pluck the Magic Potion from the floor. Drop it anywhere in the room to get the next Mushroom.

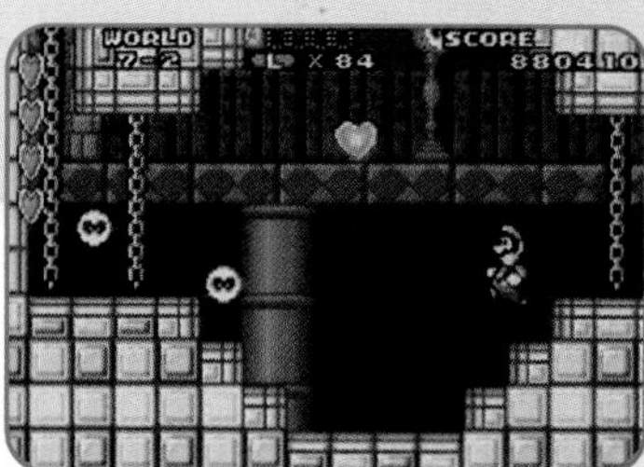

When you return from Subspace, climb up the chain to the top room and enter the door. The door leads to the right end of another horizontal cavern with chains and Sparks. Move left, collecting the Heart (if you need it). As before, time your movements carefully to avoid the Sparks.

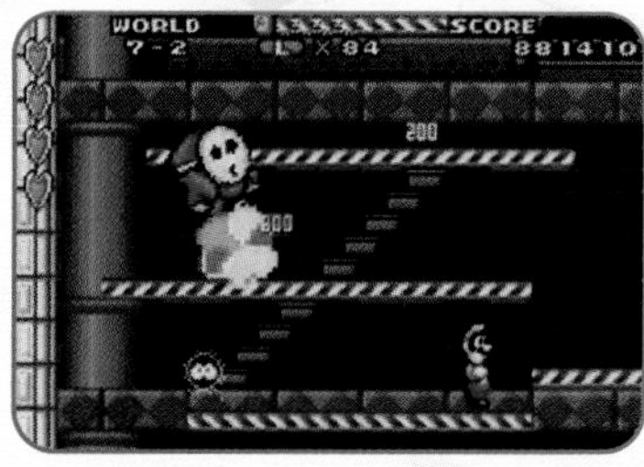

At the cavern's left end is a chain. Climb it to reach the bottom of a vertical cavern filled with conveyor belts. Along the cavern's floor are a Red Shy Guy and a Giant Blue Shy Guy. Throw the Giant Blue Shy Guy around if you need Hearts, then start jumping up the conveyor belts. Watch which direction the belts move and plan your own moves accordingly.

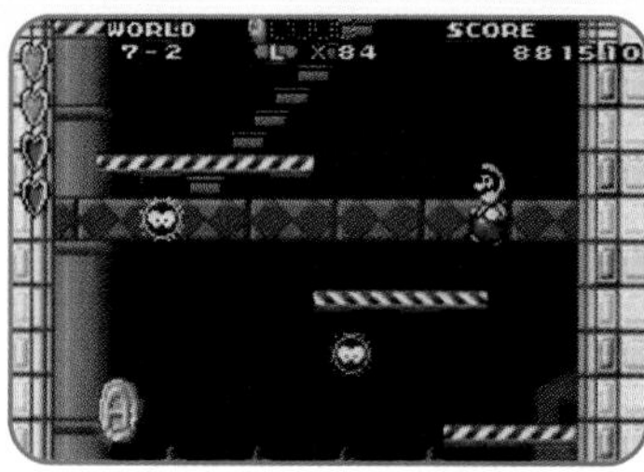

Many of the conveyor belts have Sparks running around them. Pick up any enemies you can touch without suffering damage and carry them with you to take out the Sparks. After you move up a few screens, you'll see an Ace Coin floating on the cavern's left side. Fall off the left end of the left-moving conveyor belt above the Ace Coin to get it.

Although this is the second Ace Coin you've collected, the game records it as the fourth. Don't worry. You can collect the Ace Coins in any order, and you'll have all five by the end of the level.

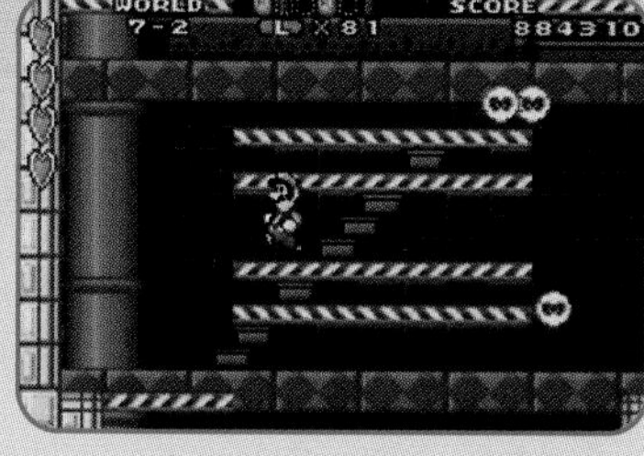

Above the second (or fourth) Ace Coin is a small, non-moving ledge. Get onto it, then carefully time your next jump onto the four conveyor belts to your upper right. Don't waste any time jumping up off of them, because the three Sparks zipping around won't waste any time trying to hit you.

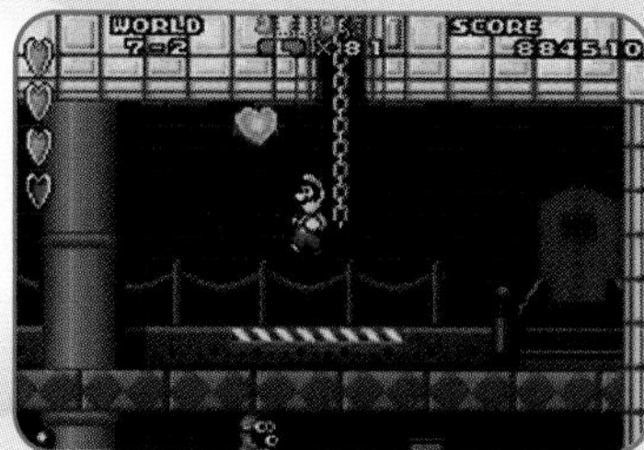

Jumping off of the four closely spaced conveyor belts takes you up to two more conveyor belts. The bottom one has two Blue Snifits, and the top one has a Blue Shy Guy. Don't waste time trying to take them out. Jump onto the top conveyor belt and onto the chain hanging from the ceiling, grabbing the Heart to the chain's left.

To the chain's upper right is a Heart. Grab it if you need it, because Birdo (the red version) is at the end of the left-moving conveyor belt to your left. Take Birdo out using the usual egg attacks and climb the chain to her left.

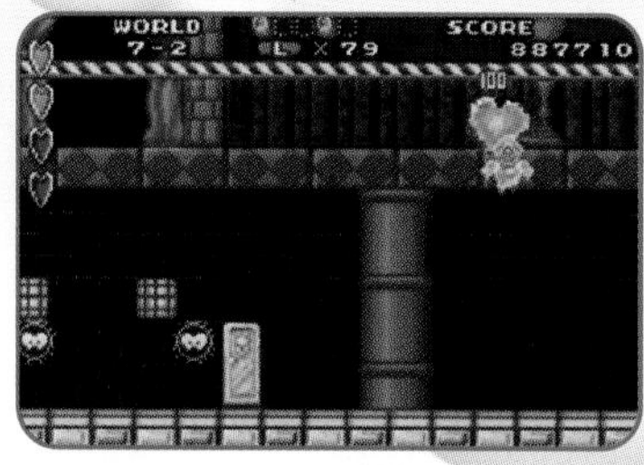

Don't let the Boss music playing in the next area alarm you; you're not going to fight Wart yet. Move right along the bottom of the horizontal cavern, carefully avoiding the Sparks, until you reach the right end. Jump up to grab the two Hearts floating there if you need them, then enter the door just to your left.

This next room has a right-moving conveyor belt for a floor and features... Birdo again! (I hope she's getting paid overtime for this.) Jump over her head and climb up the chain to her right.

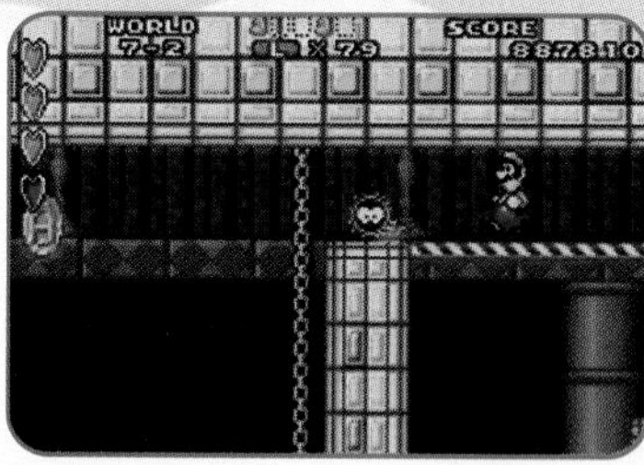

After you get to the next area, keep climbing the chain and get onto the right-moving conveyor belt at the top (this area is above the one you were just in). Run left along the conveyor belt until the end, watching out for the Spark along the way. It is almost impossible to avoid the Spark, but there is a Heart Radish at the end of the conveyor belt.

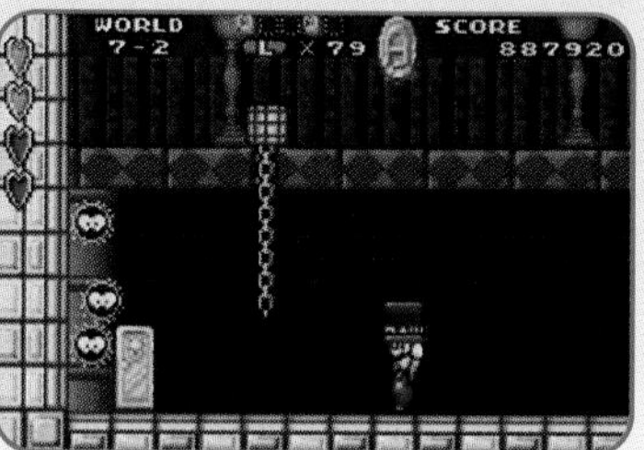

Run off the conveyor belt's left end to enter a large room with three Sparks racing along the walls, a POW Block in the middle of the floor, a door on the left side, and the third (actually, fifth) Ace Coin floating just below the ceiling. Get to the POW Block first and drop it to get rid of the Sparks. Super Jump up to grab the Ace Coin, then exit through the door.

The door takes you to the top of a vertical cavern with T-shaped columns running up and down the length of it. Drop off of the chain onto the columns, and travel down the cavern. Be careful, though: most of the columns have Sparks running around them, so look before you leap.

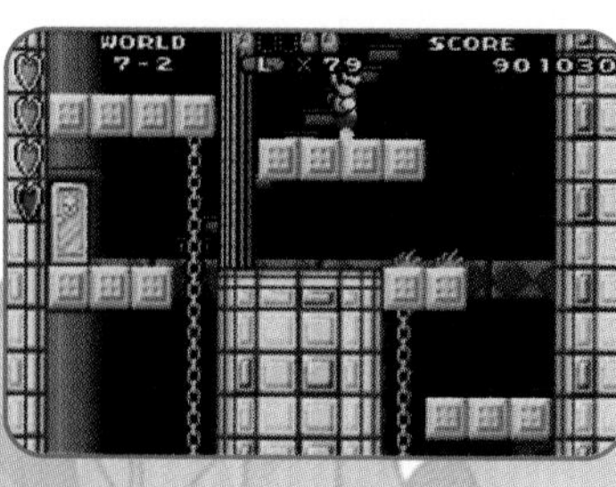

The first plant you come across is a Heart Radish on the cavern's right side. A bit farther down is a door that you can't get to and two plants that you can pluck to the right of it. The right one is a Bob-Omb, and the left one is a Heart Radish.

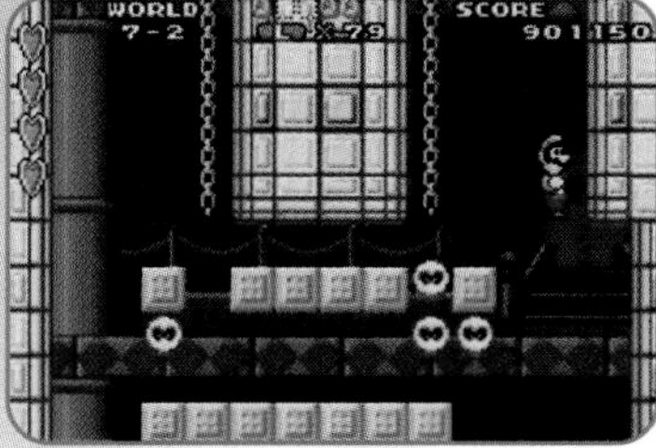

Below the two plants is a chain. Climb down it and stop just above the horizontal platform with Sparks swarming over it. Fall off of the chain to the right and hug the right wall on the way down to avoid the Sparks. When you reach the bottom, you find a chain leading down in the room's left corner. Climb down it.

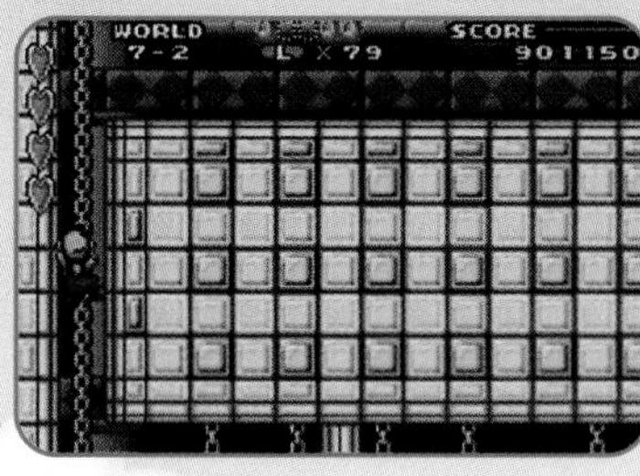

The room at the bottom of the chain is filled with vertical chains and Sparks running up and down between them. Time your move carefully and run to the room's right side. Remember: the Sparks can't hit you if you position yourself dead-center on a chain.

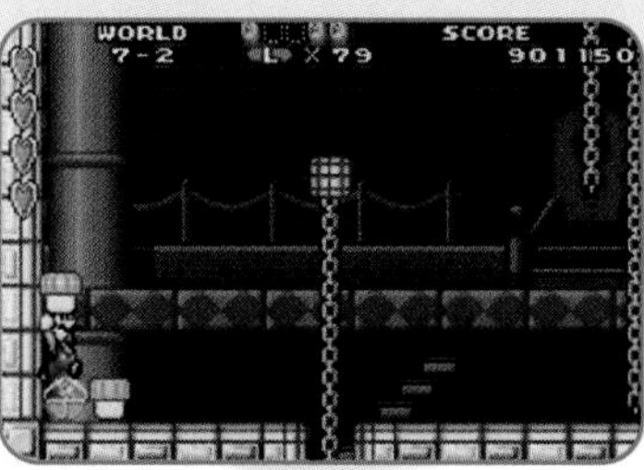

Climb down the chain on the room's right side and lift the left Mushroom Block in the corner to get a Roulette. Use the Roulette to get a Starman and quickly climb down the chain in the center of the room.

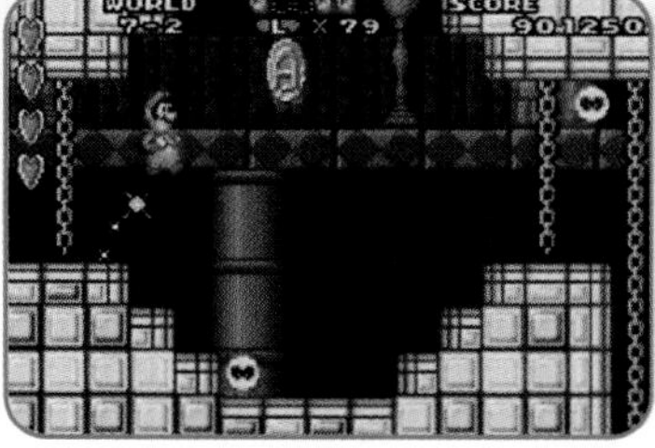

The fourth (actually, second) Ace Coin is in the next room, floating in the air to the right of the chain you climbed down. While you're still invincible, charge recklessly over there and get it (knocking out a Spark or two on the way, hopefully).

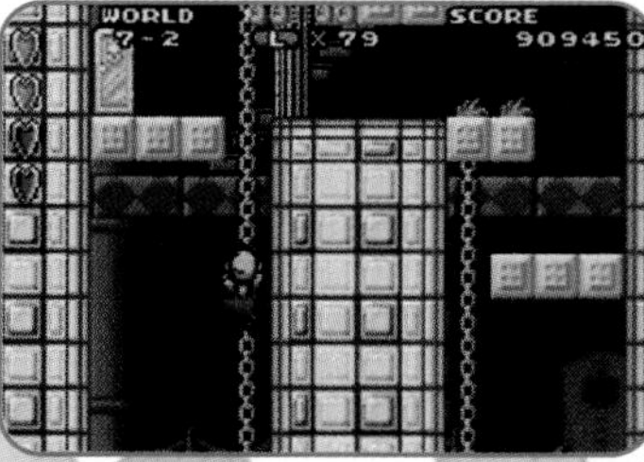

Climb back up the chain you just climbed down and keep backtracking up the chains until you come back to that horizontal platform with the four Sparks on it. Instead of continuing to backtrack and heading up the cavern's right side, take the left chain above the Sparks' platform up to the previously inaccessible door.

The door leads to a narrow ledge outside with a ladder to the left and a Heart Radish above. Grab the Heart Radish if you need it, then descend the ladder. When the ladder ends at the tiny one-block platform, move to the right onto the next ladder and continue down.

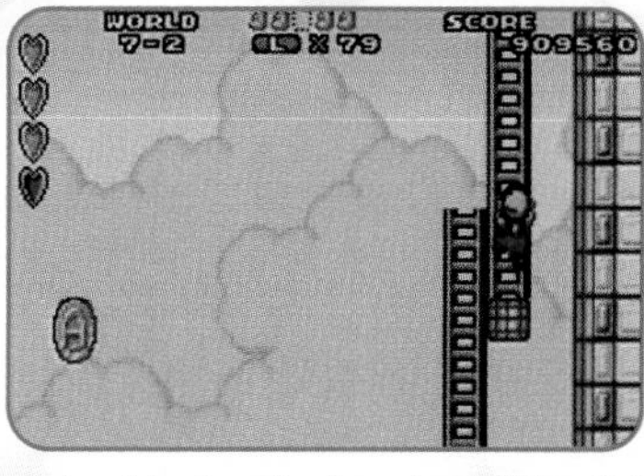

Directly across the screen from the bottom of the second ladder is the fifth (actually, third) Ace Coin. Jump off of the tiny platform at the bottom of the second ladder to get it. This is not only World 7-2's last Ace Coin, it's also the last Ace Coin of the game. Congratulations! You found all 100 Ace Coins!

After grabbing the Ace Coin, you fall to the bottom of the area, where a fire-spitting Red Panser sits on top of a pile of blocks while two Tweeters bounce around aimlessly. Grab a Tweeter, jump up the middle of the blocks (while avoiding the Panser's fire, of course), and throw the Tweeter at the Panser to knock it out.

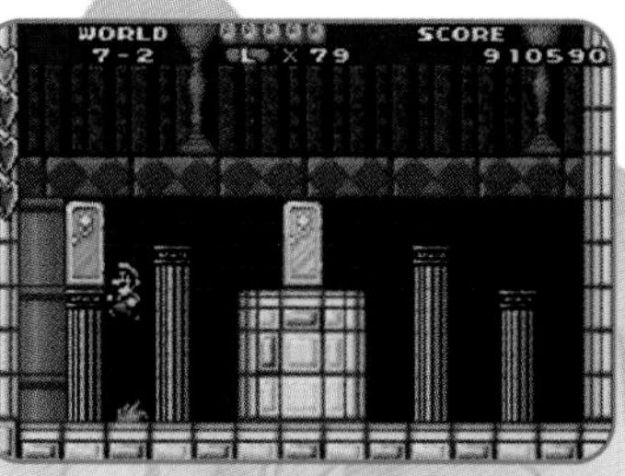

After knocking out the Panser, climb down the ladder below the blocks to reach a small room with a door. Enter the door, and you appear in a small room with four pillars and two plants between them. The right plant is a Magic Potion. Drop the Potion so that the left side of the room is visible on the screen, and enter Subspace for the third Mushroom.

Once you have the Mushroom, backtrack out the door and up the ladders. Enter the door at the top of the ladders to return to the vertical cavern above the four Sparks on the platform. Jump from the door and through the platform to avoid the Sparks.

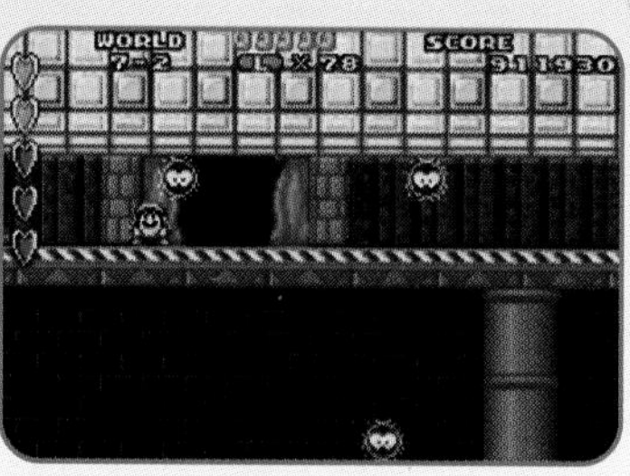

Climb up the chain along the cavern's right until you reach the T-shaped platforms. Jump up the platforms carefully to reach the chain at the top. Climb the chain to get to the ledge with the door, and enter the door to return to the room with the three Sparks and the POW Block.

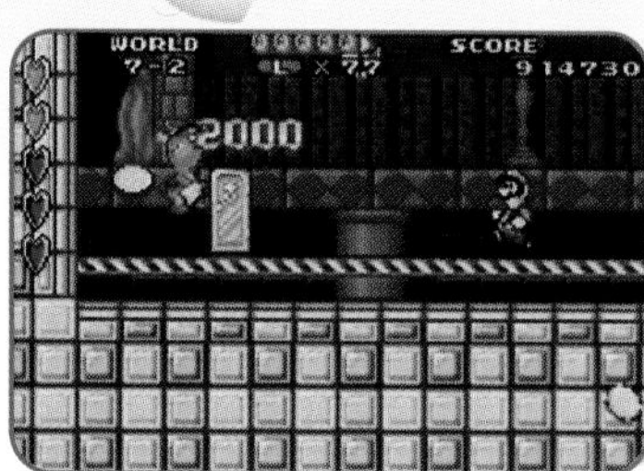

Get the POW Block as quickly as you safely can and drop it to eliminate the Sparks, then climb the chain on the room's right side to get back up to the right-moving conveyor belt. Pluck the Heart Radish before it if you need to, then get on the conveyor belt and ride it to the right while ducking to avoid the Sparks.

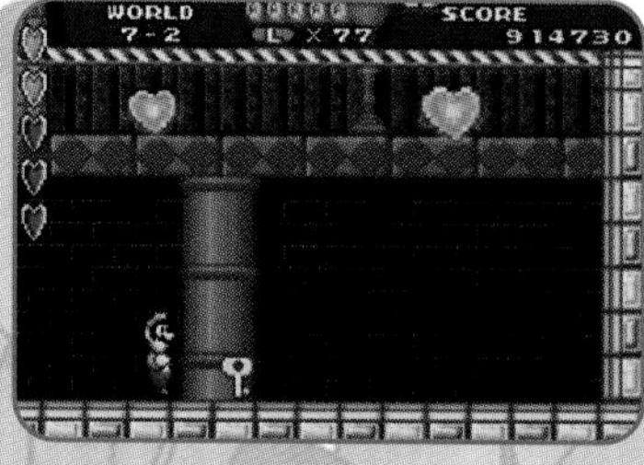

Climb down the chain at the conveyor belt's right end to return to the scrap you never finished with Birdo. Defeat her to get a Key. Pick up the Key and jump to the door at the conveyor belt's left end (if you try to walk, Phanto will get you). Enter the door.

To the right of the other side of the door are two Hearts floating in the air. Grab them if you need them, but first put the Key down on the same screen as the Hearts. That will ensure that Phanto won't attack, and you won't lose the Key, either.

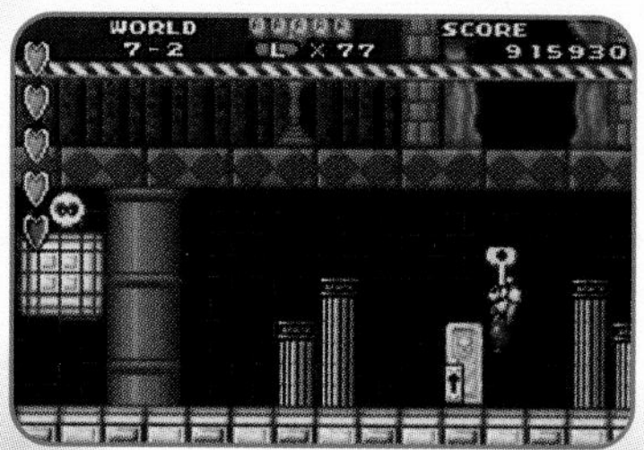

After getting the Hearts, pick up the Key again and move left. Use the Key to knock out the first two Sparks you meet. The locked door is just past them to the left. Unlock it with the Key and enter the door.

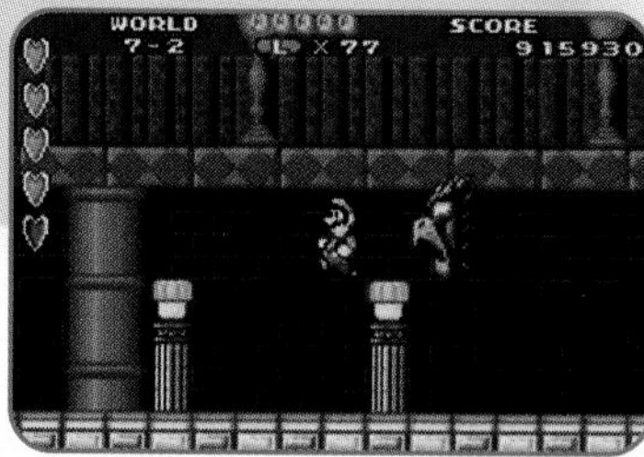

In the horizontal cavern on the other side of the door are two Mushroom Blocks, a Crystal Ball, and a gate. Seems pretty standard, huh? The only problem is, when you lift the Crystal Ball, the gate detaches from the wall and flies around trying to hit you! Hit the gate three times with the Mushroom Blocks to get it to stop, and open the pathway to Wart's lair.

Boss Fight: Wart

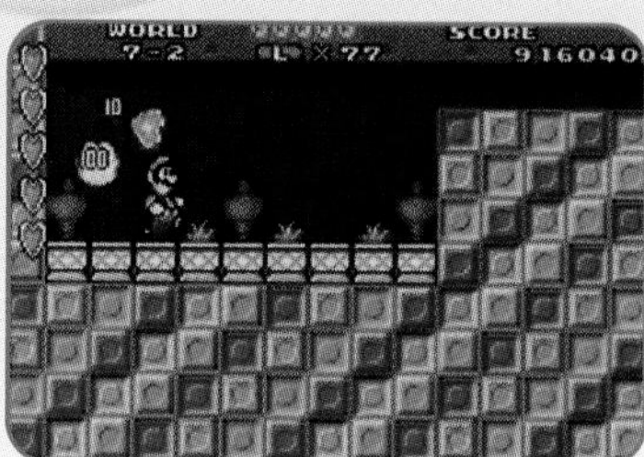

This is it, the final battle. The four plants at the start point of Wart's lair are all Hearts. Pluck them if you need them, then head right. Hop up onto the left gray platform above the weird machine in front of Wart and stand on the right edge (see screenshot below).

Once the battle begins, Wart opens his mouth, and a random Vegetable shoots out of the machine below. A split second later, Wart fires an arc of bubbles at the Vegetable and you. Dodge the bubbles, jump onto the right gray platform, and hit Wart with a Vegetable when his mouth is open, before he shoots the bubbles.

Don't try to chase down Vegetables. Stand at the right edge of the left gray platform and wait for them to come to you. If you're in the proper position, one Vegetable out of every four or five will just jump into your arms. Jump every time Wart fires his bubbles. You only need to leap over the first couple of bubbles; the others fall short of your position.

If you're having trouble getting your shot timing down, fire as soon as you see the machine spit out a Vegetable, because that's the cue for Wart to open his mouth and fire his bubbles to destroy the Vegetable. Force-feed Wart six Vegetables to end his reign of terror.

Once you've destroyed Wart, Mario and friends free the Subcons from the stoppered pipe Wart used to imprison them. The Subcons hold a parade for their saviors (and send Wart packing at the same time). They also rate which of the four characters was the Most Valuable Player, judging by how many times each defeated an end Boss.

Suddenly, the scene shifts to Mario in bed. He's dreaming of the Subcon's victory parade. Was it all just a dream, or is Mario remembering the good times he had during one of his finest adventures?

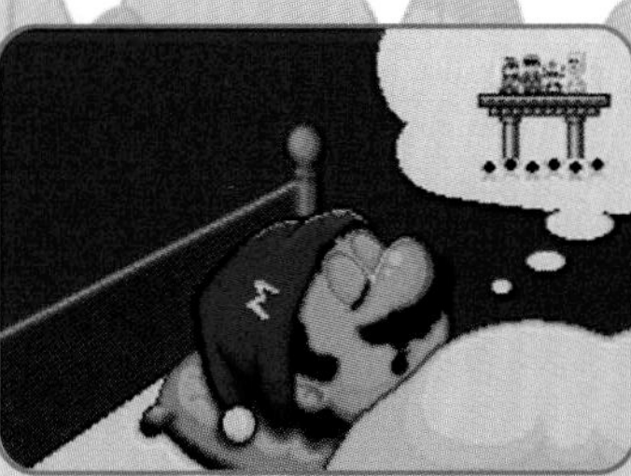

We'll never know for sure, but we do get introduced to all of *Super Mario Advance*'s cast members, friends and enemies alike, as Mario sleeps peacefully into the night.

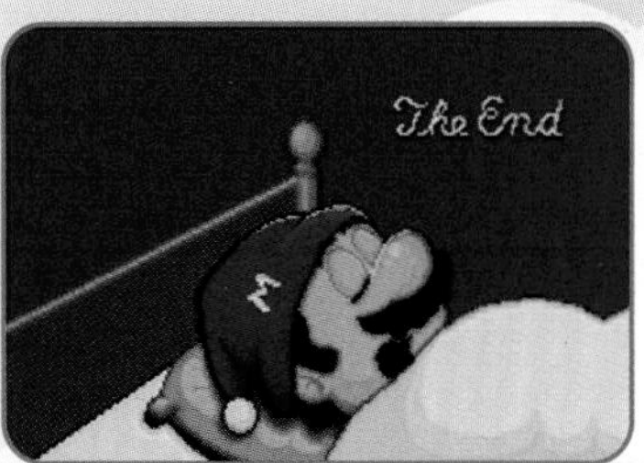

Unlocking Yoshi's Challenge

After the game is done and "PRESS START" appears, do just that. You then have the option of saving the game. Do so and you'll return to the title screen. It's got a reddish tint now, and a little Yoshi Egg wiggles in the corner. That's to signify that you beat the game and unlocked Yoshi's Challenge. See "*Super Mario Advance* Secrets" for more on Yoshi's Challenge.

Collect All 100 Ace Coins

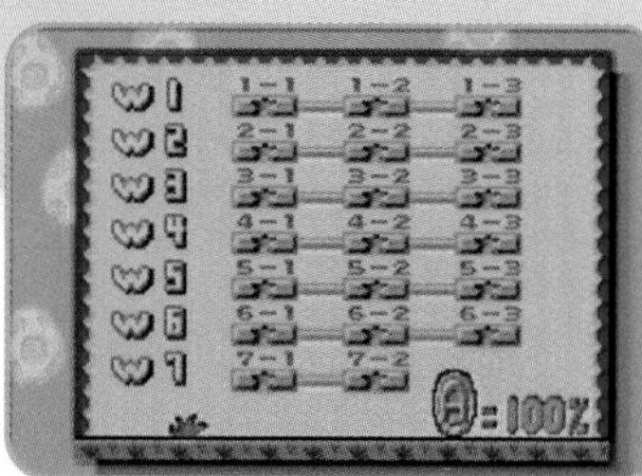

So, you've taken the time and effort to collect all 100 Ace Coins across the 20 levels, and now you're wondering what you get for your troubles. Will you settle for a sense of accomplishment? Collecting all 100 Ace Coins and beating Wart at the end of 7-2 does not unlock any secrets.

Yoshi's Challenge is available after you defeat Wart, but you do not need all of the Ace Coins to open Yoshi's Challenge. The Ace Coins are simply an added challenge.

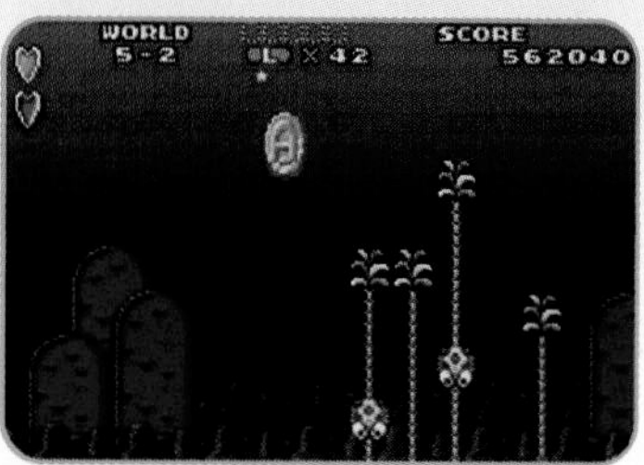

Yoshi's Challenge

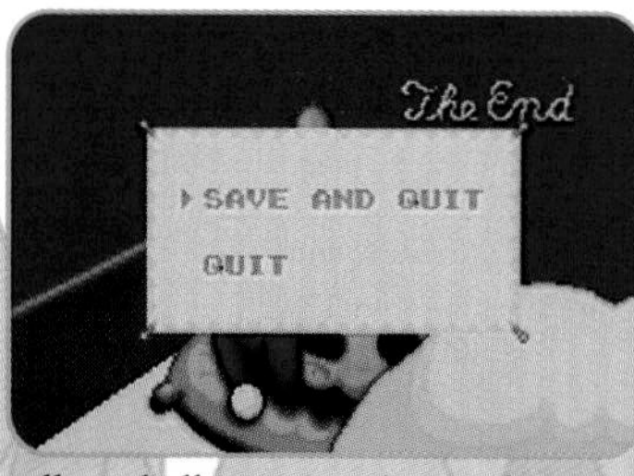

After you beat Wart at the end of 7-2, you get the option to save your game. Do so, and the game will return to the start screen, where the background has changed from blue to red, and, if you collected all 100 Ace Coins, there is now a white egg with red spots wiggling on the right side. If not all 100 Ace Coins have been collected, a white egg with green spots appears on the start screen.

That indicates that Yoshi's Challenge is now available. Select "Single Player" from the start screen and "Super Mario 2" from the next screen. Your saved game now says "Extra—0/40" instead of "World" and the last level you saved. Select your saved game to begin.

Choose your player and press Ⓐ. Instead of the familiar level grid you saw the first time through, you now get a screen that says "Yoshi's Challenge." Each world is now represented by two blank egg-shaped spaces per level. You can start on any world, but you might as well play from the beginning, because you'll have to play World 1 at some point anyway.

The idea of Yoshi's Challenge is to play through the game again and find the two Yoshi Eggs hidden in Subspace in each level, then defeat each level's end Boss to clear it. Oh, and there's one more wrinkle: if your life meter reaches zero and you lose a chance, you also lose any Yoshi Eggs you collected in that level. You must find both Yoshi Eggs and beat the level without losing a single chance. Are you up to the challenge?

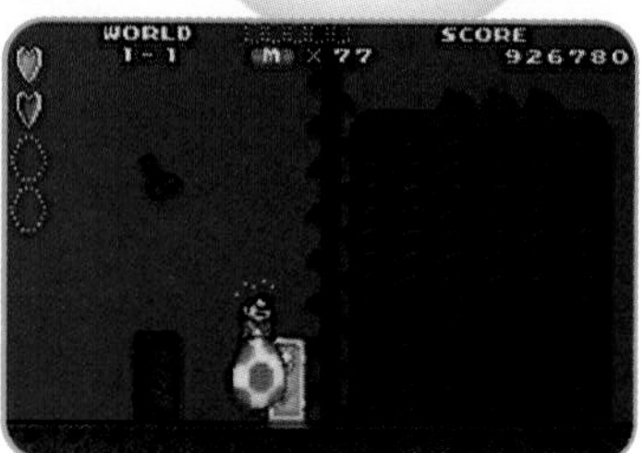

Use the walkthrough in the previous chapters and the following list of the Yoshi Egg locations to beat Yoshi's Challenge. Winning comes down to having lots of skill and patience. Good luck.

World 1-1

First Egg

Grab the Magic Potion from the platform to the left of the first vine you come to, and drop it near the base of the vine between the platform and the wooden pillar to the right.

Second Egg

Climb up into the clouds and get the Magic Potion from the first pipe you see. Carry the Magic Potion out of the pipe and drop it on the platform above and to the right of the pipe.

World 1-2

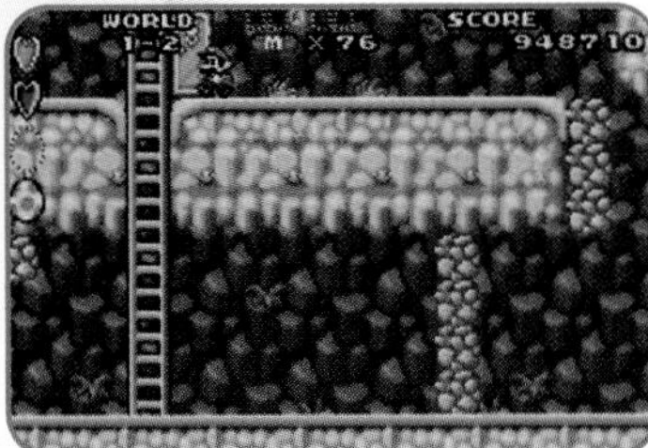

First Egg

In the cavern past the locked door, head right and blow open the wall to the Snifit's left. Grab the Magic Potion from the platform above, scroll the screen down, and drop it near the ladder. Climb down the ladder to get the Yoshi Egg.

Second Egg

After your joyride on Pidgit's carpet, pluck the Magic Potion to the pipes' left and drop it to the second vase's right. If you see both the Mushroom and the Yoshi Egg, choose the Mushroom first in order to have enough time to get both.

World 1-3

First Egg

Pluck the Magic Potion to the first wooden bridge's left and drop it on the platform below, where three jumping Ninjis are visible on the right side of the gap. The Yoshi Egg appears on their platform.

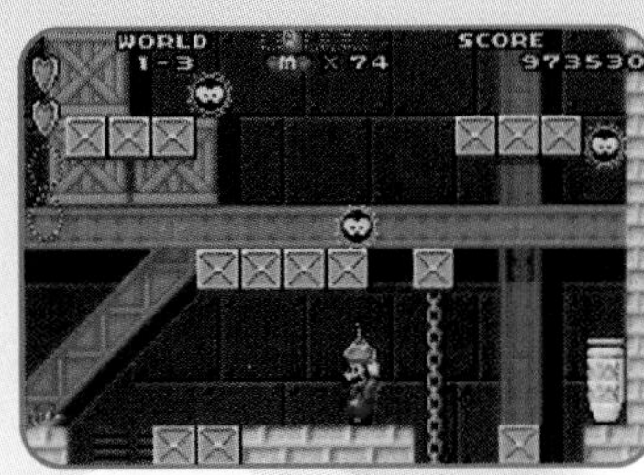

Second Egg

As you head up the vertical cavern toward Phanto's lair, duck into the pipe on the cavern's right side and get the Magic Potion inside. Drop the Magic Potion right outside the pipe; the Yoshi Egg appears on the platform next to the pipe.

World 2-1

First Egg

Run right until you come to the structure made of sandy blocks with four plants on top of it. Pluck the leftmost plant to get a Magic Potion. Make sure you can see the quicksand to the structure's right, then drop the Magic Potion. The Yoshi Egg drops into the quicksand; retrieve it before it sinks.

Second Egg

Run all the way to the right, past the door in the pyramid, and pluck the Magic Potion at the screen's far right. Bring the Magic Potion back to the left until you reach the block pyramid with the Panser on top. Drop the Magic Potion on the pyramid and get the Yoshi Egg from the top of the pyramid.

World 2-2

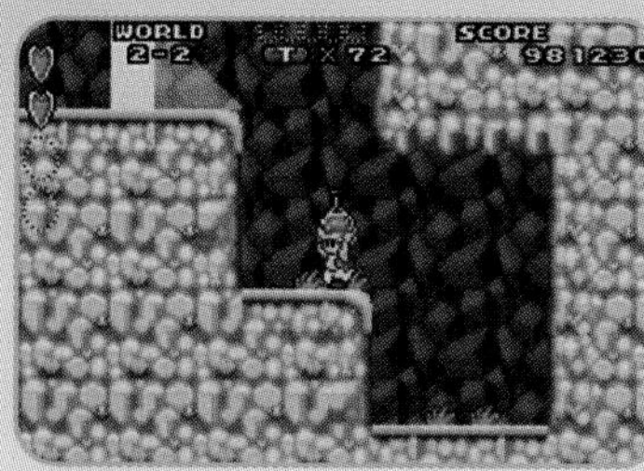

First Egg

Enter the door under the sand waterfall and blast the wall to the cavern door's left with a Bomb. Grab the Magic Potion from the top of the sandy block structure. Take the Magic Potion back to the doorway and drop it to the right of the door. The Yoshi Egg appears near where you dropped the Magic Potion.

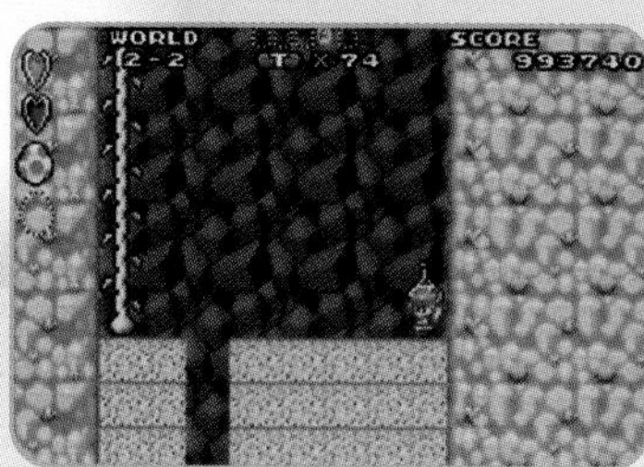

Second Egg

Dig to the bottom of the sand pit at the bottom of the vine. There you'll find a Magic Potion. Pluck it, bring it to the top of the sand pit, and drop it. The Yoshi Egg appears on top of the sand.

World 2-3

First Egg

Pluck the Magic Potion to the right of the top of the ladder at the beginning of the level, and drop it to the left on the sandy blocks. The Yoshi Egg appears there.

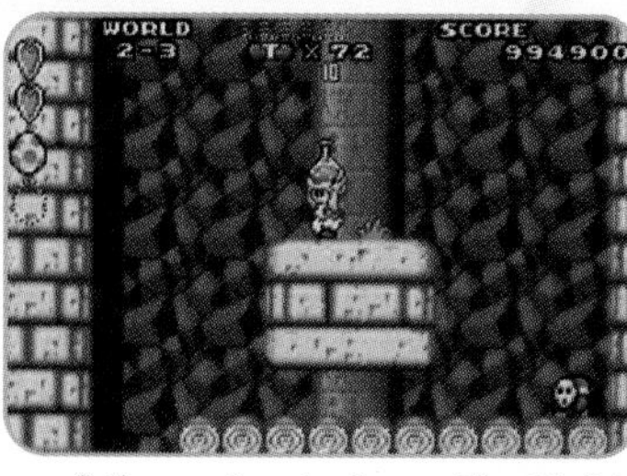

Second Egg

Once you enter the pyramid, jump down to the right and stick to the left wall on the way down. On the small platform with two plants, pluck the Magic Potion and drop it carefully on the platform. The Yoshi Egg appears on this platform.

World 3-1

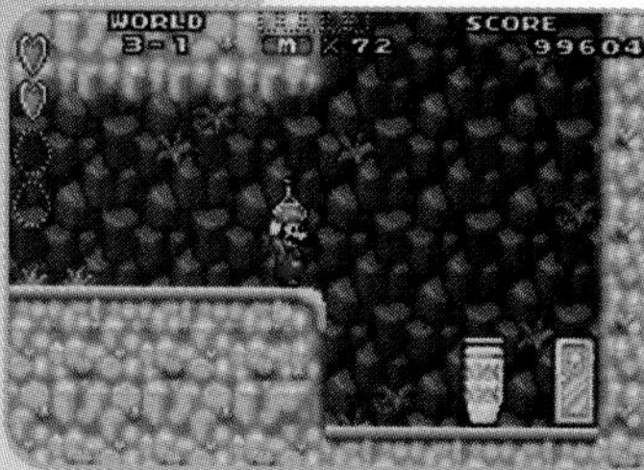

First Egg

Fall down the waterfall at the beginning of the level and stay to the center of the screen to land on the platform at the bottom. Enter the door, pluck the 10th plant from the left to get a Magic Potion, and drop the Magic Potion next to the pipe at the tunnel's right end to get the Yoshi Egg.

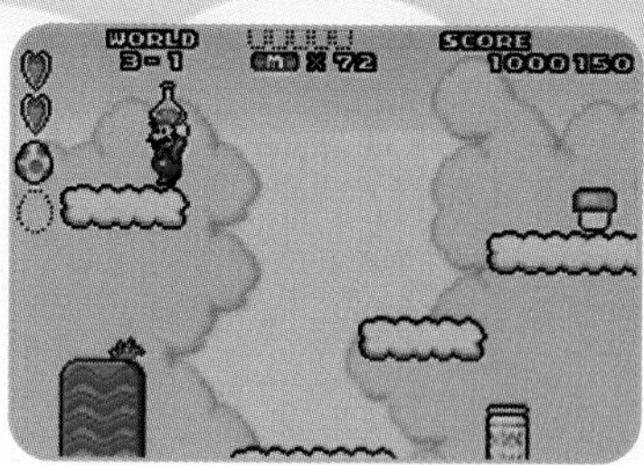

Second Egg

Run right, past the Giant Shy Guy in the clouds, to the green platform to the Panser's right. Pluck the left plant on the platform and drop it on the cloud platform above. The Yoshi Egg appears on the cloud platform.

World 3-2

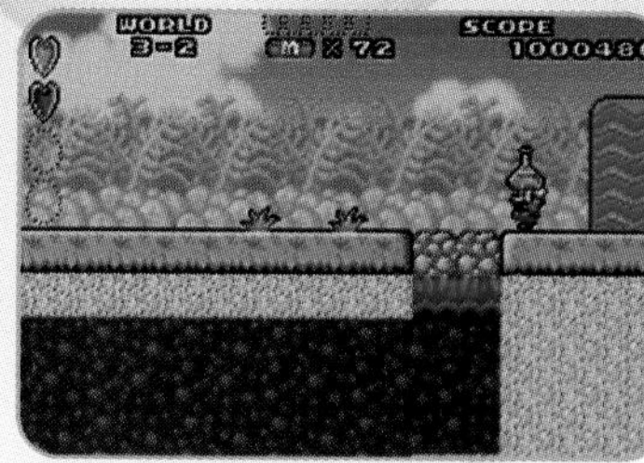

First Egg

From the start, run all the way to the right and pluck the left plant on the last grassy platform to the right to get a Magic Potion. Drop the Magic Potion on the destructible blocks to the platform's left to get the Yoshi Egg.

Second Egg

At the subterranean cavern's left end, head through the stone wall, which you have to bomb open by dropping the Bombs so that they explode in midair. In the room with the two cells of Porcupos, bomb open the roof of the left pit and pluck the Magic Potion to its right. The Yoshi Egg appears in the left pit.

World 3-3

First Egg

The fourth plant to the right of the third pillar from the beginning of the level is a Magic Potion. Drop the Magic Potion near the pillar next to the POW Block, and get the Yoshi Egg from the top of the third pillar.

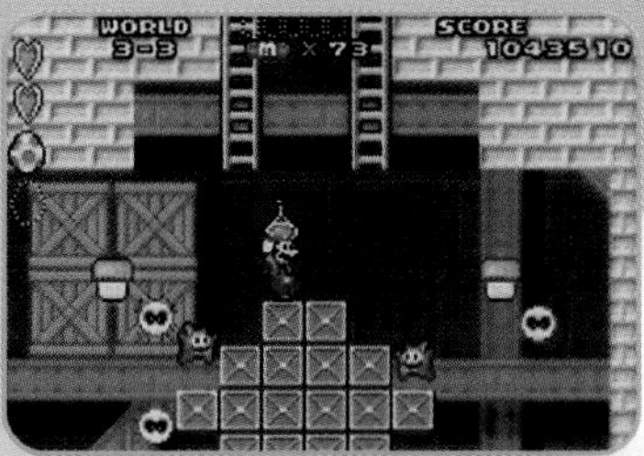

Second Egg

Enter the locked door later in the level and move up the vertical cavern until you reach the horizontal blue box platform with the Sparks and Ninjis on it. Climb the right ladder above the platform and pluck the right plant. Go back down and drop the Magic Potion on the blue platform to get the Yoshi Egg.

World 4-1

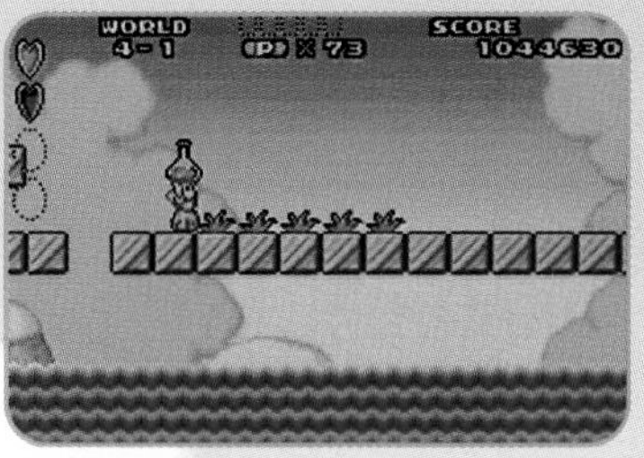

First Egg

Head right until you come to the two parallel platforms with the Heart floating over the top one and a plant on the bottom one. Pluck the plant to get a Magic Potion, and drop it next to the row of five plants to the right. The Yoshi Egg appears to the plants' right.

Second Egg

At the right end of the first part of the level, pluck the plant on the snowy platform to get a Magic Potion. Drop the Magic Potion on the platform. The Yoshi Egg appears in the little alcove to the right, where you find the Rocket Ship plant.

World 4-2

First Egg

Move through the level until you enter the door to the area with the spouting whales. Head left and pluck a Magic Potion from the leftmost whale and drop it on the next whale to the right to get the Yoshi Egg.

Second Egg

Continue right until you reach the three ascending platforms containing three plants each. Pluck the rightmost plant on the rightmost pillar to get a Magic Potion, and drop the Magic Potion on the icy stairs to the platform's right to get the Yoshi Egg.

World 4-3

First Egg

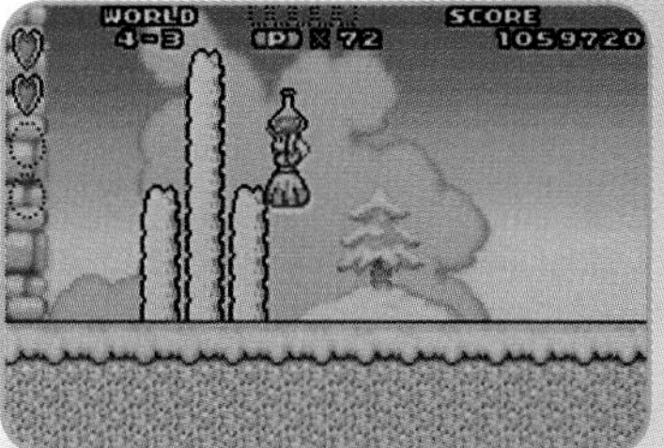

At the beginning of the level, pluck the plant to the entrance's left to get a Magic Potion. Take the Magic Potion to the left and drop it near the three snowy pillars. The Yoshi Egg appears on the tall middle platform.

Second Egg

Once you reach the outside of the castle with the cloud platforms to the left, pluck the first plant to the right to get a Magic Potion, and carry it up the clouds. Drop the Magic Potion on the first parapet to the highest cloud platform's right to get the Yoshi Egg.

World 5-1

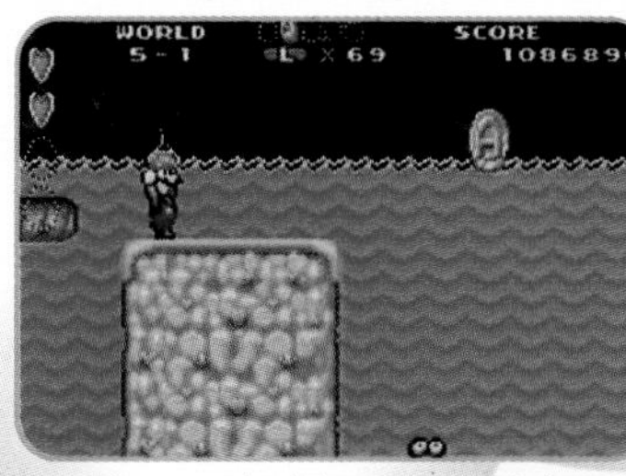

First Egg

In the large cavern with the waterfalls, head right and pluck the second plant from the left to get a Magic Potion. Carry the Magic Potion past the waterfall you cross by jumping on the Trouters, and drop it on the second platform to the right to get the Yoshi Egg.

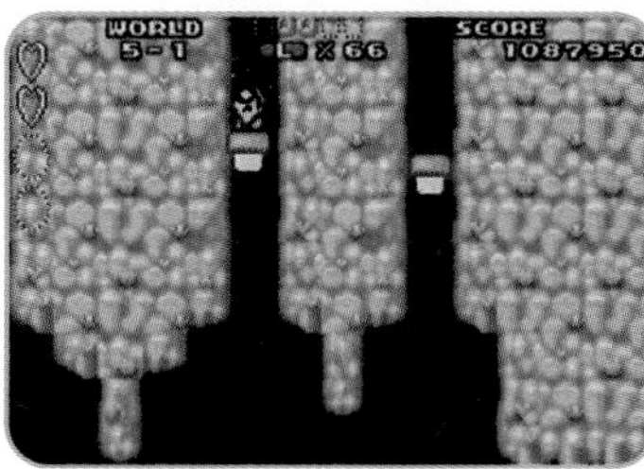

Second Egg

At the waterfall cavern's right end, leap up to land on the rock wall above the top of the screen, and move right to fall down the first of two tunnels blocked by Mushroom Blocks. Pluck the Mushroom Block to fall to the floor, then pluck the leftmost plant on the floor to get a Magic Potion. Drop the Magic Potion underneath the gap you just opened, and the Yoshi Egg will fall down the gap and onto the ground.

World 5-2

First Egg

Enter the first pipe you come to and pluck the right plant at the bottom to get a Magic Potion. To get the Yoshi Egg, bring the Magic Potion with you out of the pipe and drop it when you reach the four narrow platforms or use the Magic Potion under the Panser.

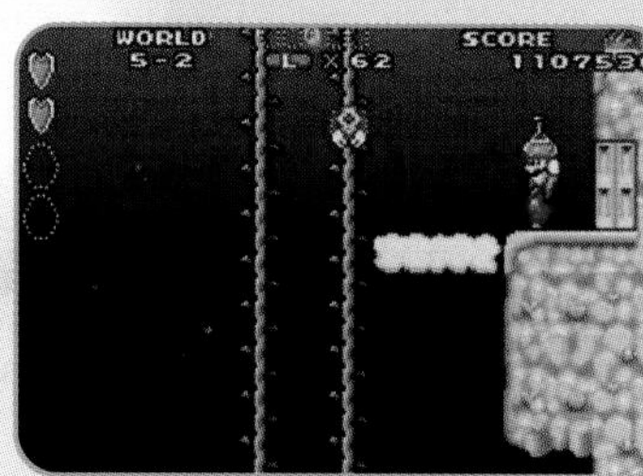

Second Egg

Once you climb into the clouds, head up until you see the two Snifits on either side of the screen. Pluck the plant underneath the right Snifit to get a Magic Potion, and ride a Hoopster all the way to the top of the clouds. The Yoshi Egg appears when you drop the Magic Potion on the cloud platform with the door.

World 5-3

First Egg

After climbing the ladder from the start point, pluck the plant on the immediate right of the top of the ladder, and head right past the Albatosses and Bob-Ombs until you reach the first T-shaped log platform. Drop the Magic Potion to the platform's right to get the Yoshi Egg.

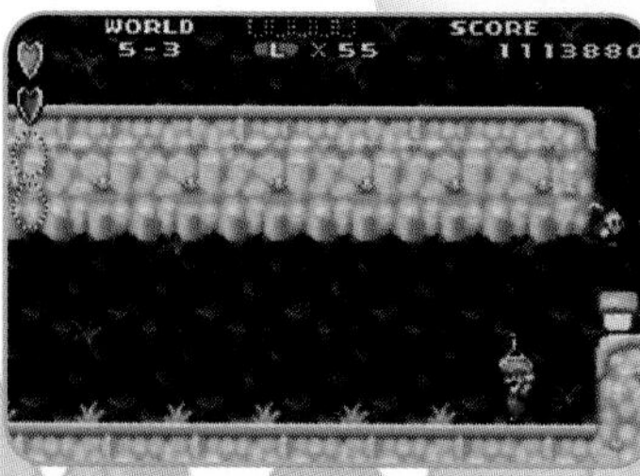

Second Egg

In the subterranean cavern, lift the Mushroom Block off of the Bob-Omb Generator and lead the Bob-Ombs to the stone wall near the ladder to blow it up. Jump down to the lower platform and pluck the first plant to get a Magic Potion. Then, to get the Yoshi Egg, drop the Magic Potion on the small grassy platform of the lower level.

World 6-1

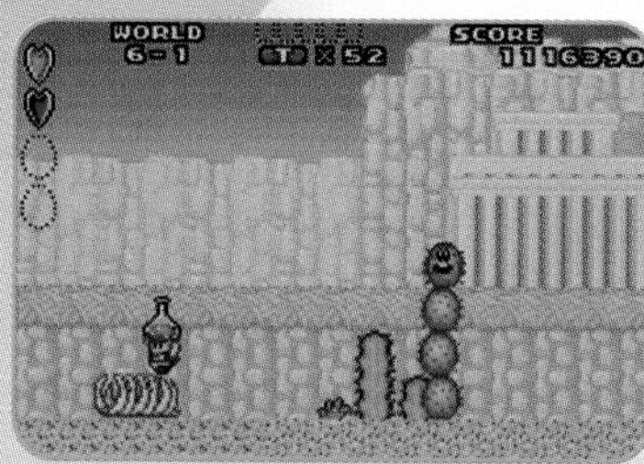

First Egg

Enter the first pipe you come to and pluck a Magic Potion at the bottom. Carry the Magic Potion out of the pipe and drop it onto the bone platform to the pipe's right. The Yoshi Egg drops into the quicksand next to the platform. Jump over to it and grab it before it's totally submerged.

Second Egg

In the cavern with the 21 pipes, head all the way to the right. Pluck the second plant from the left above the locked door to get a Magic Potion. Bring the Magic Potion to the left and drop it in the middle of the row of pipes to get the Yoshi Egg.

World 6-2

First Egg

Ride the Albatosses until you reach the tall, narrow pillar with the plant growing out of the top. Pluck the plant to get a Magic Potion and drop it where you found it to get the Yoshi Egg.

Second Egg

You can either return to the beginning of the level, exit and re-enter it to reset all of the plants, and grab the same Magic Potion you just got, or you can eliminate the Panser and pluck the Magic Potion from its platform. Either way, ride an Albatoss all the way to the right and drop the Magic Potion on the platform just to the left of the door at the right end of the level. The Yoshi Egg appears on this platform.

World 6-3

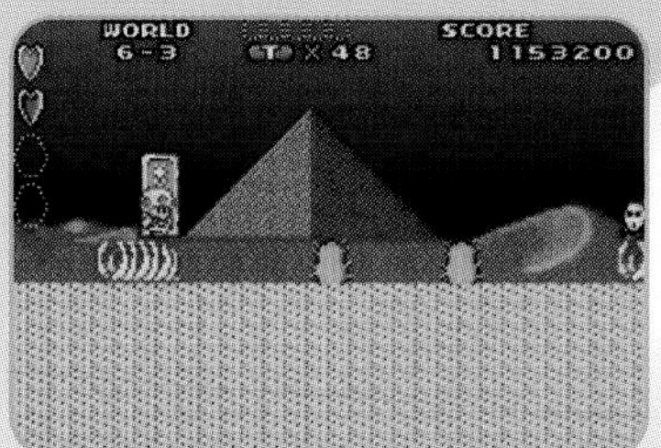

First Egg

From the top of the ladder leading up from the start point, grab the first plant you come to and drop it on the second bone platform to the right. The Yoshi Egg drops from the sky between the two stubby cacti and quickly sinks. Grab it before it sinks completely.

Second Egg

Once you reach the area with all of the cloud platforms and vines, climb up and enter the first pipe you come to. Pluck a Magic Potion from the bottom of the pipe, bring it with you as you leave the pipe, and drop it on the cloud platform to the pipe's left to get the Yoshi Egg.

World 7-1

First Egg

Move all the way to the right in the first main area until you reach a column with a plant at the top and a Shy Guy Generator farther to the right. Pluck the plant from the top of the pillar to get a Magic Potion, and drop the Magic Potion to the left on the destructible stone platform's right edge. The Yoshi Egg appears on this platform.

Second Egg

Near the top of the vertical area farther on in the level, below the door at the top, are two cloud platforms. There's a Snifit on the left one and a plant on the right one. Get rid of the Snifit, pluck the plant to get a Magic Potion, and then drop the Magic Potion onto the Snifit's platform to get the Yoshi Egg.

World 7-2

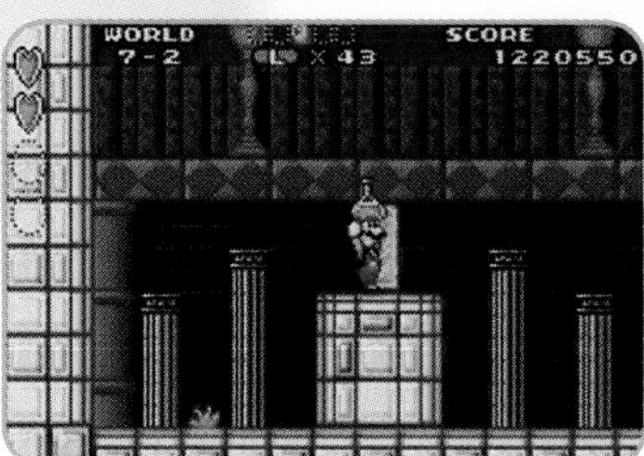

First Egg

Once you reach the outside doorway on the extremely narrow platform, drop all the way down and enter the door at the bottom to reach the room with two plants and four pillars. Pluck the right plant to get a Magic Potion, and drop the Magic Potion near the tall pillar on the right. The Yoshi Egg appears on top of the pillar.

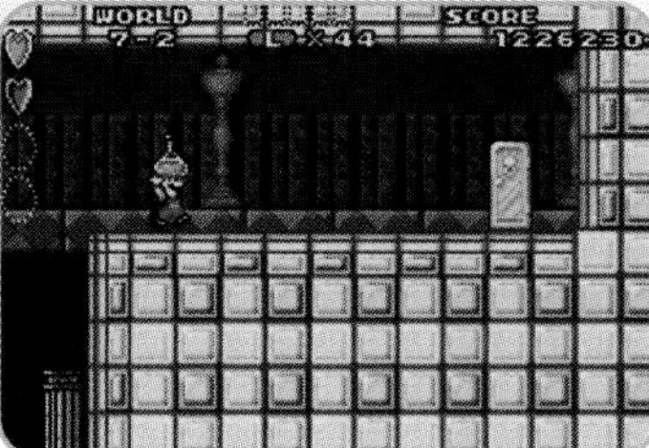

Second Egg

In the other pillars-and-plants room—the one with five pillars—pluck the last plant you come to and bring it back to the ledge near the door through which you entered to get the final Yoshi Egg. Beat Wart without losing any chances to complete Yoshi's Challenge.

What Do I Get Then?

After all of that hard work, the payoff might seem a little slim. You get a nicely illustrated "Perfect!" bouncing around the screen, and the wiggling Yoshi Egg on the title screen hatches into a waving Yoshi. Of course, just completing the challenge is quite an accomplishment. Congratulations!

Mario Bros.

Unique to *Super Mario Advance*, *Mario Bros.* is an updated version of Mario's first classic solo arcade adventure. If you played the original arcade game, you'll have no trouble mastering the new version. If you've never played it before, prepare for some good old-fashioned arcade fun. *Mario Bros.* has three modes of play: the single-player Classic version, the cooperative multiplayer Classic version (for two to four players), and the head-to-head multiplayer Battle version.

Classic

Single-Player

What You Need: One Game Boy Advance and one *Super Mario Advance* Game Pak

From the *Super Mario Advance* title screen, select "Single Player," then select "*Mario Bros.*" from the next screen. The *Mario Bros.* title screen appears. Press START to begin.

The objective of *Mario Bros.* is straightforward: survive as long as you can and try to beat your previous high score. You score points by defeating enemies as they pop out of the pipes at the top of the screen. Stand on the platform underneath the enemies, press Ⓐ to jump up and flip them onto their backs, then jump up to their level and run toward them to kick them off the screen while they're flipped over. When you eliminate an enemy, a Coin pops out of one of the pipes at the top of the screen. Collect it for more points.

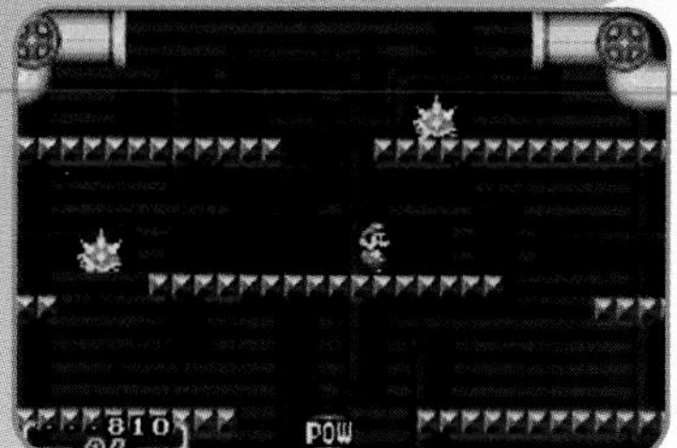

Two POW Blocks are also onscreen—one at the top and one at the bottom. When you jump up and bump a POW Block, all the enemies act as if you just bumped them once from below. Those requiring one bump to flip them over wind up on their backs, and those requiring two bumps need one more to flip them over.

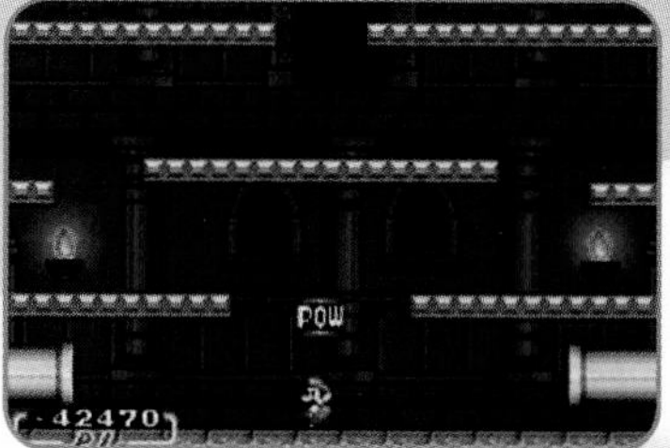

Enemies appear from the two pipes to the right and left of the top of the screen and move in one direction down the screen, "wrapping" from the right edge to the left (and vice versa). If an enemy leaves the left side of the screen, it reappears on the right side and continues its descent. When it reaches the pipes at the bottom, it disappears and reappears from one of the pipes at the top. Fireballs of different colors also appear on the sides and top of the screen and move across it. You can only eliminate the fireballs by bumping them from below when they're touching a platform. If one hits you, you lose a chance.

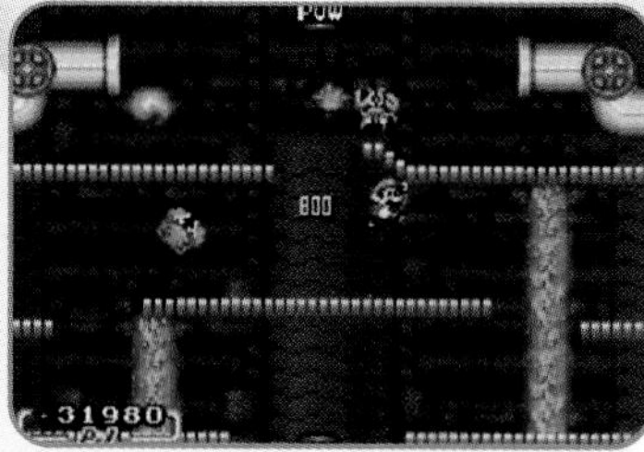

An enemy that you bump from directly below bounces straight up. If you bump an enemy just ahead of the direction in which it's traveling, it bounces slightly backward, and if you bump behind it, it bounces forward. If two enemies heading in opposite directions meet, they both change direction.

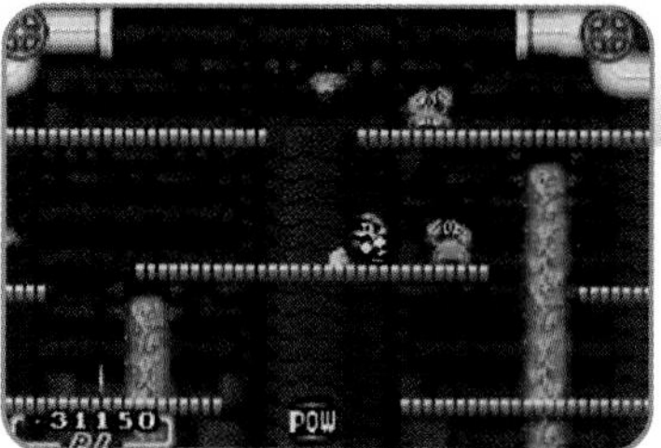

If you run into an enemy that is not flipped over, you lose a chance and disappear from the screen, only to reappear on a small temporary platform above the pipes. You can remain on this platform until it disappears in a few seconds, or you can jump off of it to resume playing. You begin the game with three chances and can acquire more by getting perfect scores in the Bonus Stages or by kicking five enemies in a row. This combo is difficult because you must kick the next enemy before the previous one is off the screen.

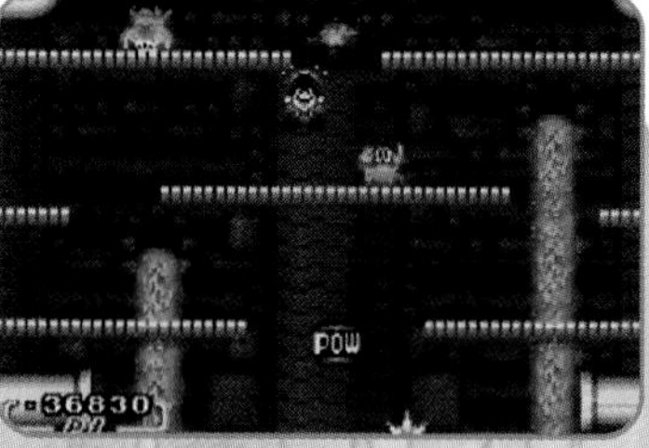

Eliminate all of a stage's enemies to clear that stage and proceed to the next. The last enemy always appears in a different color and is faster and more aggressive than other enemies of its kind. Watch out for these; it's easy to misjudge their movements.

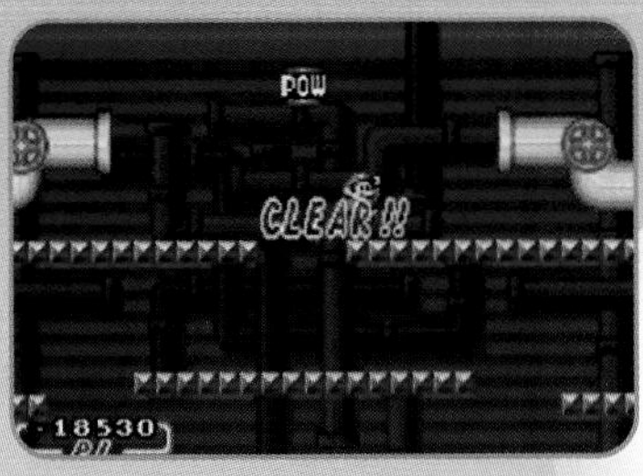

After every few stages, you get a chance to play Bonus Stages. There are no enemies in Bonus Stages, only a bunch of Coins scattered around the stage. Collect the Coins for bonus points, and collect all of the Coins for a Perfect rating and a 1UP. Any POW Blocks used before a Bonus Stage are refreshed and ready to use again on the stage following the Bonus Stage.

Tips for Classic Single-Player *Mario Bros.*

- *Stay as close to the middle of the screen as possible. It's easy to be surprised and knocked out by an enemy "wrapping" around from the other side of the screen.*
- *Momentum is important. Keep moving, because it takes a second or two to get up to speed. You can also dash by holding Ⓑ.*
- *Try to bump enemies down onto the level you are on. This keeps you from wasting time jumping up onto their platform to eliminate them.*
- *You can eliminate flipped enemies while they're flying through the air right after your bump, so don't wait for them to land if you don't have to.*
- *If you flip an enemy, eliminate it quickly; otherwise, it'll flip back over and move even faster than before.*
- *If you need to use a POW Block and have the luxury of choosing which one, always go with the top one. It's harder to reach and getting to it isn't always an option when many enemies are onscreen.*
- *If you quickly knock out several enemies in a row, you score more points. Plus, for each one after four, you receive a 1UP.*

Multiplayer

What You Need: One Game Boy Advance for each player, one *Super Mario Advance* Game Pak for each player, and one fewer Game Boy Advance Game Link® cable than there are players (one cable for two players, two for three payers, and three for four players).

The multiplayer version of *Mario Bros.* Classic is identical to the single-player version, with each player controlling a Mario and cooperating to clear each stage (refer to the single-player instructions and tips above). We're not talking about a big love fest here, however; the player with the most points is the game's winner.

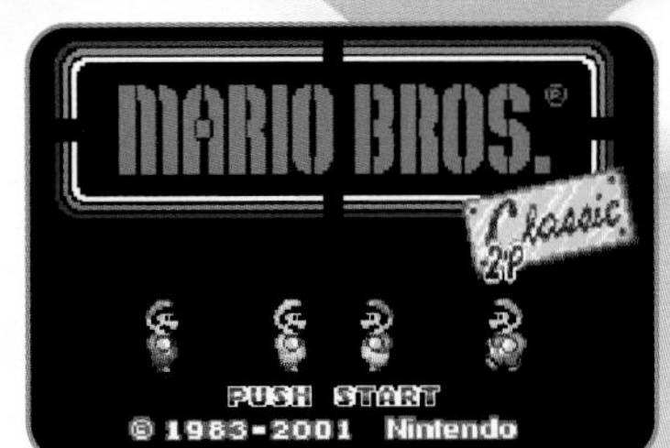

Before turning on the Game Boy Advance, make sure you have the Game Link cables connected properly. Refer to *Super Mario Advance* instruction manual pages 7-10 to connect the Game Link cables. Once the Game Boy Advance systems are linked correctly, each player should turn on the power, select "Multiplayer" from the title screen, and choose "Classic" from the *Mario Bros.* title screen.

Tips for Classic Multiplayer *Mario Bros.*

- *Don't get in each other's way. Make sure you each stake out half of the screen so that you don't both get swarmed by enemies. Of course, if you're playing for keeps, ignore this tip.*
- *When another player eliminates an enemy, get to the top of the screen and grab the Coin that bounces from the pipe.*
- *If another player bumps an enemy and flips it over, get to the enemy first and knock it off for the points.*

Battle

Three- and Four-Player Version

What You Need: One Game Boy Advance for each player, one *Super Mario Advance* Game Pak (in Player 1's Game Boy Advance), and one fewer Game Link cable than there are players (two cables for three players and three for four players).

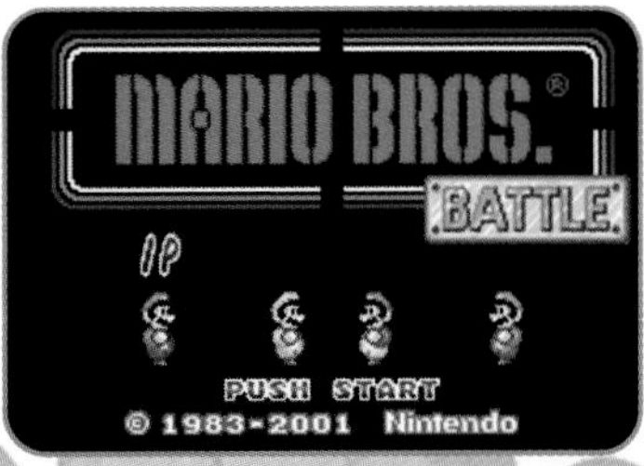

Mario Bros.' Battle Mode is a multiplayer-only mode exclusive to *Super Mario Advance*, and you only need one Game Pak to play! If each player has a Game Pak, you can skip the initial load time during game setup. Refer to *Super Mario Advance* instruction manual pages 7-10 to connect the Game Link cables. Once the Game Boy Advance systems are linked correctly, each player should turn on the power, select "Multiplayer" from the title screen, and choose "Battle" from the *Mario Bros.* title screen.

After that, Player 1 should select the Game Level, Fireball, and Handicap options from the following screen. Use ↑ and ↓ to select an option and ← and → to change the option. When finished, press Ⓐ to load the game information to every player without a Game Pak. If all players have Game Paks, the loading process is skipped.

While Player 1's Game Boy Advance checks the Game Link cable connections, any players without Game Paks will see the Game Boy logo on their screens. After Player 1 presses START, a flashing Nintendo logo appears on the screens. Mario will move from left to right across the screens as the data loads; the Mario is the same color as the one the player will control in the game. If you get an error message, turn off all of the power switches, recheck the connections, and start again.

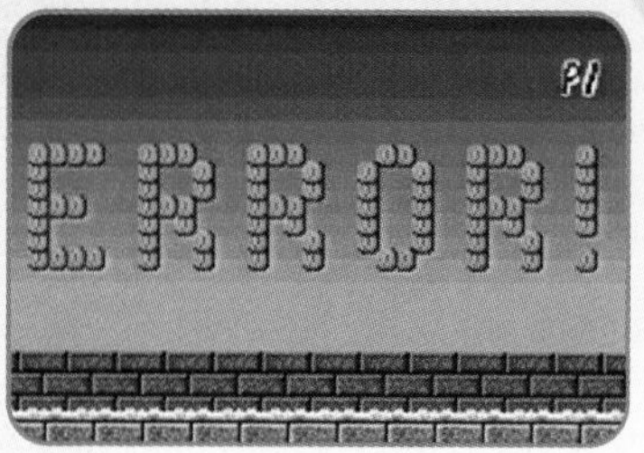

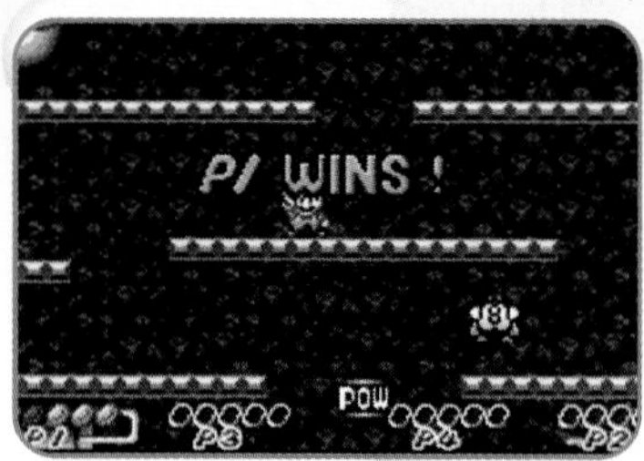

Once the Battle game begins, play it as you would the Classic version. The main difference between the two versions is that the first player to collect five of the Coins that appear when enemies are defeated, or the last player left after everyone else is knocked out, is the winner. If a player begins the game with a handicap, that player must collect that many fewer Coins to win. Mario's eternal enemy Bowser also shows up occasionally to cause trouble. Players begin as Super Mario. If they are hit once, they become a normal-sized Mario, and if they are hit again, they are out of the game.

Tips for Three- and Four-Player *Mario Bros.* Battle

- *Bump your rivals from underneath to stun them for a few seconds. Do it just before an enemy reaches them to take them out.*
- *If someone stuns you, press Ⓐ repeatedly to shake it off.*
- *Jump on top of your rivals and press Ⓑ to pick them up. Press Ⓑ again to throw them.*
- *If someone picks you up, press ← and → repeatedly to escape.*
- *Jump and hit the POW Block to stun your rivals and the onscreen enemies.*
- *Jump on top of the POW Block and press Ⓑ to lift it. Press Ⓑ again to drop it and stun everyone.*
- *Remember: the winner is the player who collects five Coins first. Let other players take care of eliminating enemies; stay toward the top of the screen and get the Coins as they appear.*
- *You don't need to collect Coins if you can eliminate the other players before any of them gets five Coins. Make good use of the POW Blocks to stun rivals, or pick them up and toss them into an enemy's path.*

Two-Player Version

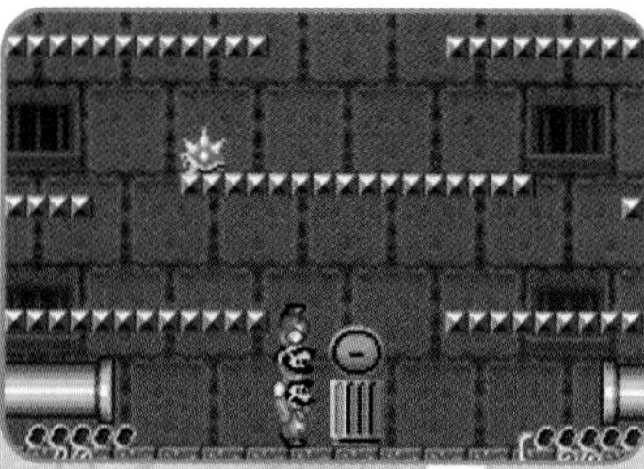

The only difference between the two-player version of Battle and the three- and four-player version is the Garbage Can addition at the bottom of the screen. Pick up your rival by pressing Ⓑ, carry him or her to the Garbage Can, and press Bagain to throw your rival in when the lid opens. When a player is inside the Garbage Can, that player is out of action for a few seconds until the lid opens again. Press ←, →, and /or Ⓐ to jump out of the Garbage Can and receive a special item (see the "Enemies and Items" section).

Tips for Two-Player *Mario Bros.* Battle

- *If your opponent stands on the Garbage Can and prevents the lid from opening, Super Jump to knock him or her off and escape.*
- *When your opponent is in the Garbage Can, use the opportunity to collect Coins.*
- *If you start getting behind in the Coin race, remember that you can get your rival knocked out and still win, even if your rival has more Coins than you.*

Enemies and Items

Enemies

Spiny

Spinys are *Mario Bros.*' weakest enemies. Bump 'em to flip 'em, and kick 'em off the screen.

Crab

Not only are Crabs faster than Spinys, but flipping them requires two bumps, and they move faster after the first bump. Try to bump them backward on the first bump and forward down to your platform on the second bump.

Fighter Fly

Fighter Flies move slowly, but they hop across platforms rather than walk. You can only bump them when they are on the ground.

Freezy

You don't need to flip Freezy over to knock him out—just bump him to shatter him. If you don't get him quickly, though, he'll freeze a platform, making it slick and hard to move on.

Fireball

As with Freezy, knocking out Fireballs only takes one bump, but you have to time it carefully and bump them when they're touching the platform above you. They appear from the sides and top of the screen, and can be red or green.

Items

Koopa Shell

Press Ⓑ to throw a Koopa Shell and send it zooming across the platforms. It damages any enemy or character it hits.

POW Block

Drop or hit a POW Block from beneath to bump every enemy onscreen once and stun any rival player who's touching a platform.

Fish Skeleton

Fish Skeletons are useless and smelly. Throw them away.

Egg

Sometimes you get an Egg when you leave the Garbage Can. Drop it to break it open and get a Coin, Heart, or Starman.

Coin

Collect Coins from the top pipes after enemies are defeated, or break open an Egg to get one. In Battle mode, the character to get five Coins first wins. In Classic mode, Coins are worth extra points.

Heart

Break open an Egg to get a Heart. If you are normal-sized Mario, a Heart will turn you into Super Mario.

Starman

Starmen are found in some Eggs and make a character temporarily invincible. While invincible, run after enemies and rival players to defeat them.

Super Mario Advance Quick Reference

This chapter is a quick reference guide for *Super Mario Advance* gamers who want the challenge of playing through the game without a walkthrough but need a little help finding all of the Ace Coins, Mushrooms, and Yoshi Eggs. Each of the following screenshots shows the area in which you can find the hidden items in each level, but it's up to you to discover exactly where they are. If you need more assistance, refer to the walkthrough for the area you're in. Happy hunting!

World 1

World 1-1

Ace Coins

Mushrooms

Yoshi Eggs

World 1-2

Ace Coins

Mushrooms

Mushrooms

Yoshi Eggs

Yoshi Eggs

World 1-3

Ace Coins

World 2

World 2-1

Ace Coins

Mushrooms

Yoshi Eggs

World 2-2

Ace Coins

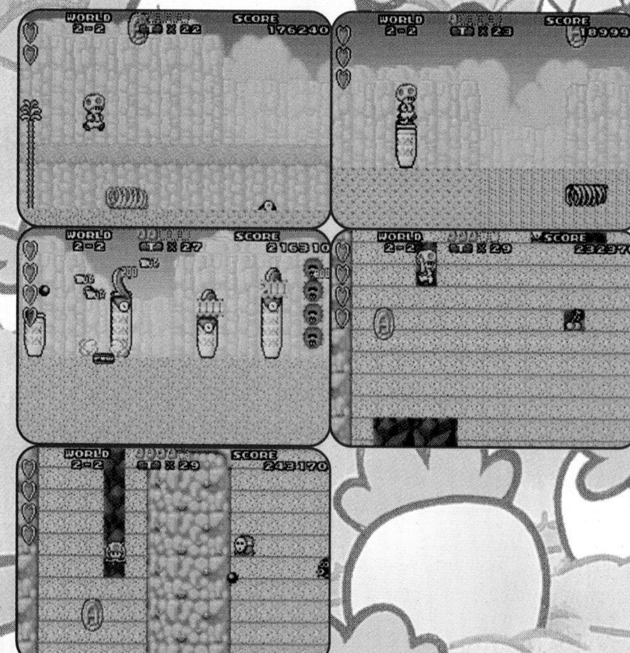

Mushrooms

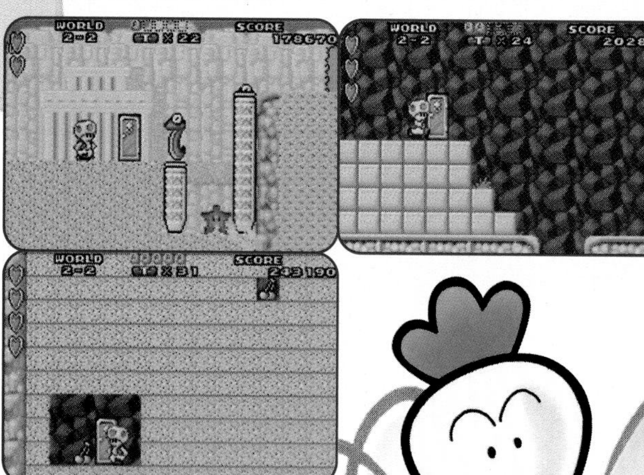

Yoshi Eggs

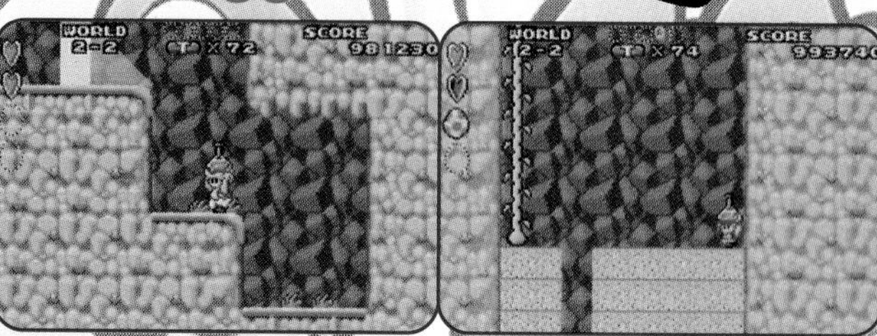

World 2-3

Ace Coins

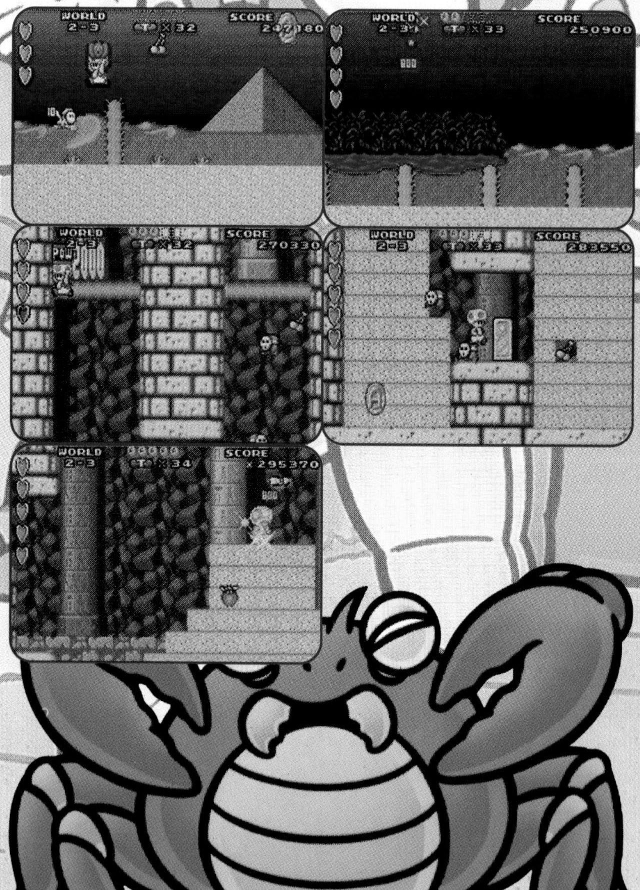

Mushrooms

Yoshi Eggs

World 3

World 3-1

Ace Coins

Mushrooms

Yoshi Eggs

World 3-2

Ace Coins

Mushrooms

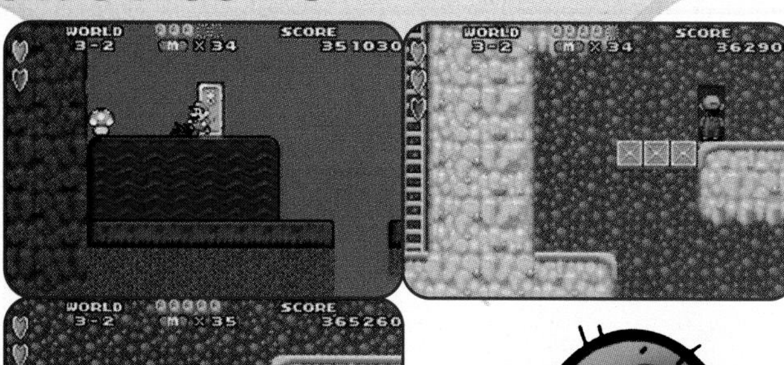

Yoshi Eggs

World 3-3

Ace Coins

Mushrooms

Yoshi Eggs

World 4

World 4-1

Ace Coins

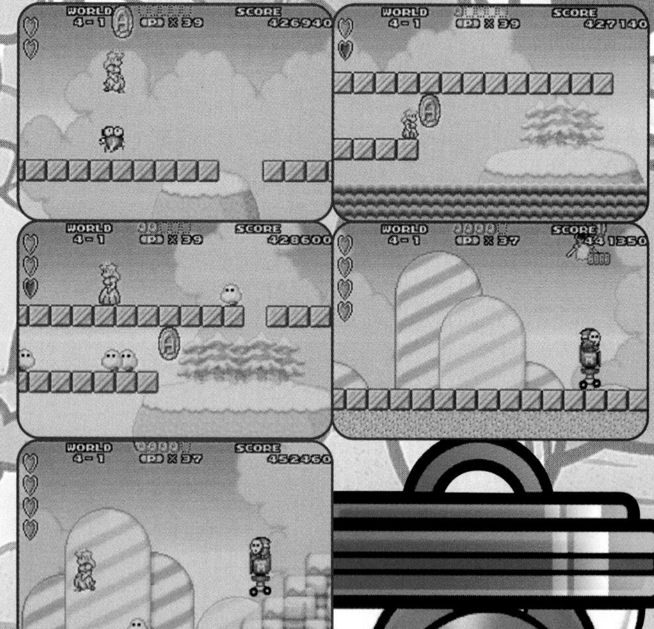

Mushrooms

Yoshi Eggs

World 4-2

Ace Coins

Mushrooms

Yoshi Eggs

World 4-3

Ace Coins

SUPER MARIO ADVANCE

Mushrooms

Yoshi Eggs

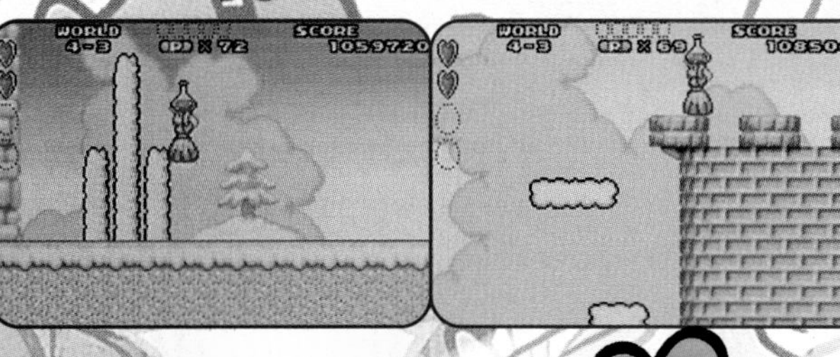

World 5

World 5-1

Ace Coins

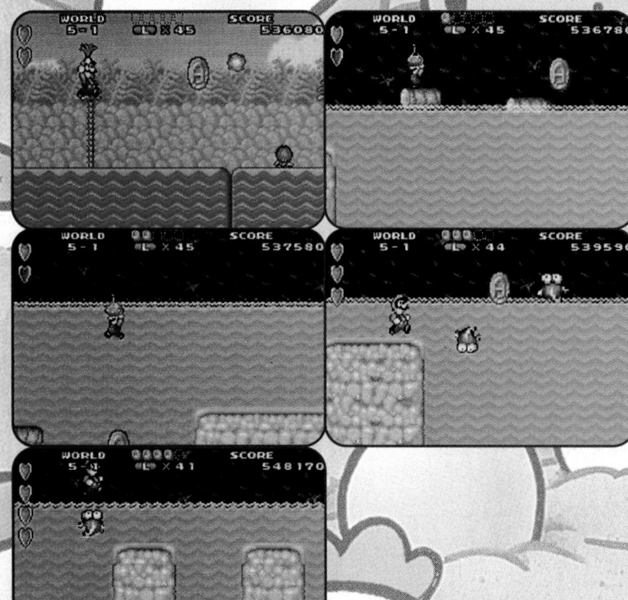

Mushrooms

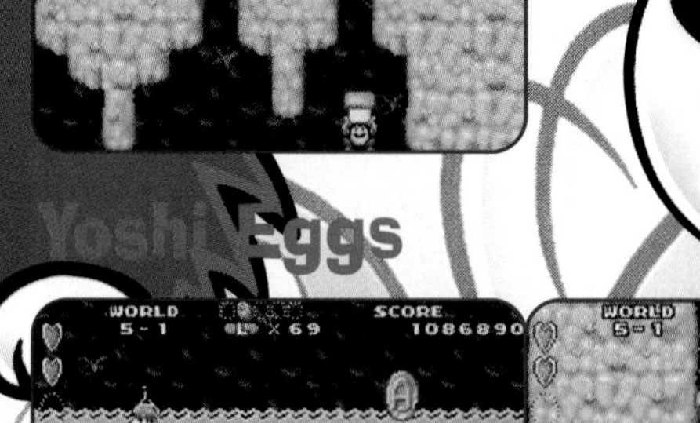

Yoshi Eggs

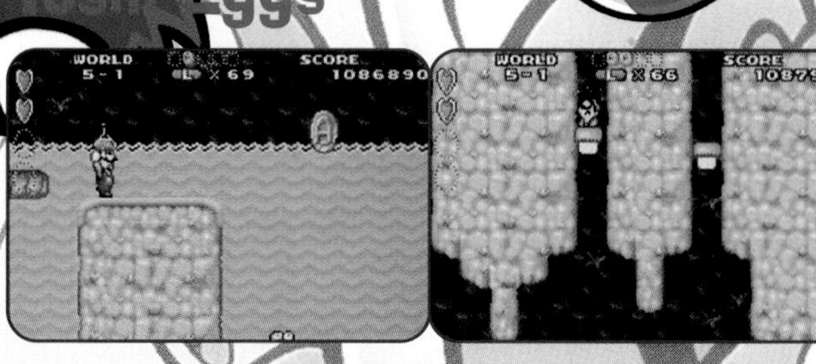

World 5-2

Ace Coins

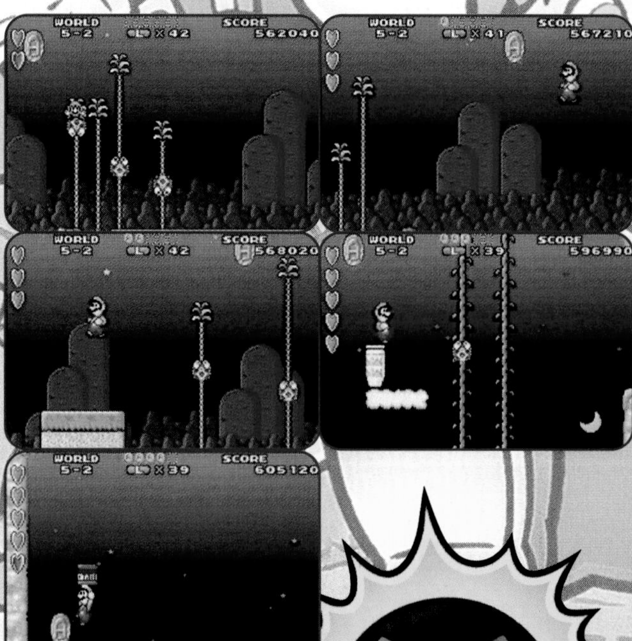

Mushrooms

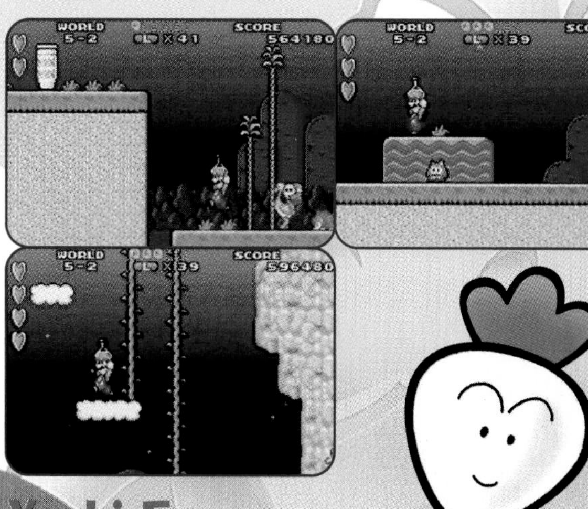

Mushrooms

Yoshi Eggs

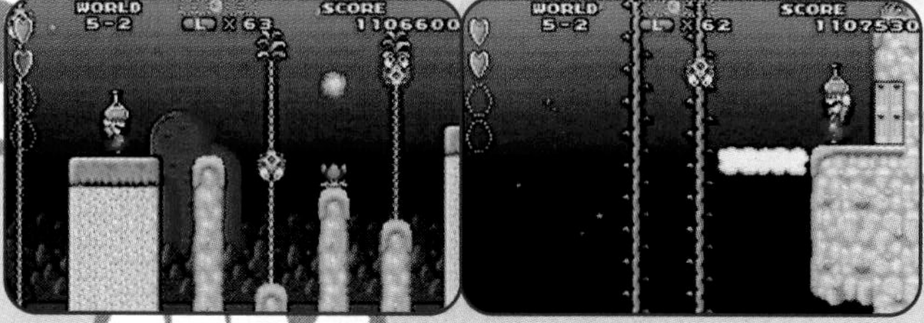

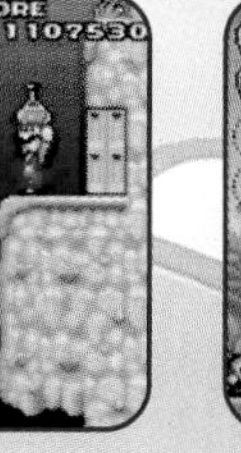

Yoshi Eggs

World 5-3

Ace Coins

World 6

World 6-1

Ace Coins

SUPER MARIO ADVANCE

Mushrooms

Yoshi Eggs

World 6-2

Ace Coins

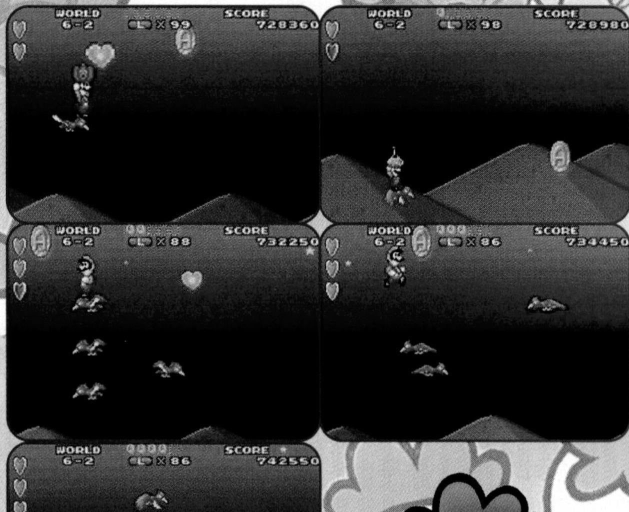

Mushroom

Yoshi Eggs

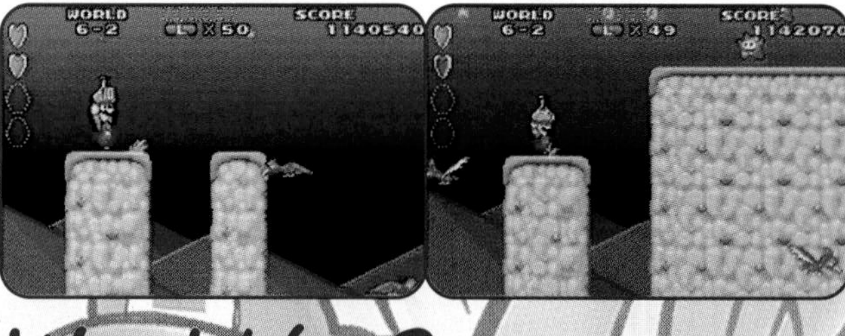

World 6-3

Ace Coins

Mushrooms

Yoshi Eggs

World 7

World 7-1

Ace Coins

Mushrooms

Yoshi Eggs

World 7-2

Ace Coins

Mushrooms

Yoshi Eggs